The Theatre of Tom Stoppard

The Theatre of Tom Stoppard

Anthony Jenkins

University of Victoria, British Columbia

Second edition

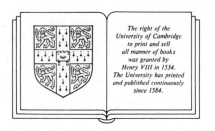

The right of the
University of Cambridge
to print and sell
all manner of books
was granted by
Henry VIII in 1534.
The University has printed
and published continuously
since 1584.

Cambridge University Press

Cambridge
New York   Port Chester
Melbourne   Sydney

Published by the Press Syndicate of the University of Cambridge
The Pitt Building, Trumpington Street, Cambridge CB2 1RP
40 West 20th Street, New York, NY 10011, USA
10 Stamford Road, Oakleigh, Melbourne 3166, Australia

First published 1987
Reprinted 1988
Second edition 1989
Reprinted 1990

Printed in Great Britain at the
University Press, Cambridge

British Library cataloguing in publication data

Jenkins, Anthony
The theatre of Tom Stoppard – 2nd ed.
1. Stoppard, Tom – Criticism and
interpretation
I. Title
822′.914   PR6069.T6Z/

Library of Congress cataloguing in publication data

Jenkins, Anthony, 1936–
The theatre of Tom Stoppard.
Bibliography.
1. Stoppard, Tom – Criticism and interpretations.
I. Title.
PR6069.T6Z7   1987   822′.914   86–21572

ISBN 0 521 37391 4 hard covers
ISBN 0 521 37974 1 paperback

FP

For MARION,
BRONWYN and MEGAN

Knowing, being known . . .
Having that is being rich.

Contents

Fore words

Had *Lord Malquist and Mr Moon* become a best-seller in the autumn of 1966 and had *Rosencrantz and Guildenstern Are Dead* vanished – as Ros and Guil do – after that year's Fringe Festival at Edinburgh, the modern theatre could have lost its most adroit manipulator of stage pictures. I mention this not just as an interesting might-have-been but as a way of isolating Tom Stoppard's particular brand of theatricality. *Malquist* gives us the punster and word magician who skips from one chimera to the next with the same playfulness that animates his radio and stage scripts. The novel obviously comes from the centre of Stoppard's imagination. Its distorting mirrors and cartoon characters are fundamental to the way Stoppard perceives life, and must have an important place in any discussion of his theatre. Yet despite the theatricality of the novel's dialogue and illusory pictures, ultimately a relationship between reader, narrator and story cannot be likened to one which involves audience, performers and 'happening'. It is this idiomatic difference which Stoppard seizes upon to make things work on stage or in the sound studio.

In Stoppard's theatre, the stage is, first and foremost, a stage, just as the radio is a box of sounds. Two attendant lords tossing a coin on a bare stage create an immediacy which does not translate into a *description* of two coin-tossing attendants. The picture itself is an event and depends on the various rhythms at each spin of the coin, the actors' facial and bodily gestures, the speaking silences between them. More particularly, this image embodies the *play* which will follow and transport us into a chancy, bewildering, ominous world, at the same time that it stresses the fact that we watch two performers using all their skill as two bungling players. *Rosencrantz* explores the boundary between seductive reality and overt bravura. Its opening sequence also makes capital out of our subconscious feeling that, at any moment, something can go wrong with a performance. Stoppard flaunts that risk-taking in the first scene of *Jumpers* where things do go wrong with Dotty, the chanteuse, and might do so, in an unplanned way, for the actors who jump in from the wings, stumble about with a tray of glasses, or swing to and fro in an aerial striptease. Both episodes provide us with a means of looking at the rest of the evening's play, just as the elaborate sound picture which begins *Artist Descending a Staircase* affects our interpretation of every other episode. Should a scene seem realistic, Stoppard encourages us to forget we are in a theatre or listening to the radio and then subverts that convincing illusion with images which are equally convincing and disruptively contradictory.

This fascination with the way words and images convey meaning, connecting thought to speech or title to picture, shows Stoppard's temperamental affinity with Wittgenstein and Magritte. But it also has something to do with the fact that though he is supremely at home with the English language he does not take it for granted. He was eighteen months old when his family left Czechoslovakia. His father, Dr Eugene Straussler, worked as a medical officer for the Bata shoe company. Just before the Nazi invasion, the Strausslers were transferred from Zlin to Singapore, and in 1942, as the Japanese moved against Malaya, Mrs Straussler and her two sons were evacuated to India. Dr Straussler stayed behind and was killed some time after the Japanese occupation. In Darjeeling, Tom's mother met Kenneth Stoppard, a major with the British Army in India. They were married in 1946, and the boys took their stepfather's name. Soon after that, the Stoppards moved to England and, round about 1950, settled in Bristol. Surrounded by English in Singapore, Stoppard did not 'live' it until he went to his first school in India so that, like Wilde or Shaw, he came to the language not as a foreigner but as someone who was fractionally 'other', and so saw more clearly that words are signs. Samuel Beckett, born beyond the pale, cultivated that awareness by writing *Godot* in French and then translating it back into English; for Stoppard, that invigorating estrangement, however subliminal, remains an accident of history.

In *The Real Thing*, Henry says to Annie, "I don't think writers are sacred, but words are". To demonstrate that, Stoppard has him pick up a cricket bat and explain how pieces of wood have been put together with intricate simplicity. The analogy between writer and batsman could not be more English; it also combines elegance and play to serious intent. That same combination of stylish play worries some of Stoppard's critics. The most vociferous tend to be American, perhaps because they take less delight in elegant glances to silly mid-on and prefer words to be smacked into the stands by a no-nonsense baseball bat. Walter Kerr's *New York Times* review of *Dirty Linen* (1977) offers the most famous critique of Stoppard's games: "Intellectually restless as a hummingbird, and just as incapable of lighting anywhere, the playwright has a gift for making the randomness of his flights funny . . . Busy as Mr Stoppard's mind is, it is also lazy; he will settle for the first thing that pops into his head."

His detractors, at home and away, find him heartlessly intellectual, cold, obsessed with patterns. To them he seems an essentially frivolous dazzler who has little or nothing of substance to say. However, since *Every Good Boy Deserves Favour* (1977) ushered in a line of more obviously 'political' plays, that picture of him has changed. John Russell Taylor in his retrospective article, "From *Rosencrantz* to *The Real Thing*", for *Plays and Players* (1984) has fixed him with a neat, amusing pin: "Enfant Terrible shapes up as Grand Old Man, intellectual joker finds sense of responsibility, Tin Man welds heart to sleeve. It is neat, tidy, and dramatically satisfying as a progression." But Poor Tom is still a-cold, for Taylor adds that "one may be left with a sneaking feeling that one preferred the rake unreformed, the joker unsobered".

Stoppard's career seems to me to be all of a piece. Though his style has become more reticent and his statements more direct, he continues to exploit the play in plays. *Squaring the Circle* (1984) is as jokey about ways of looking and saying as *Rosencrantz* was. He has always been completely serious about frivolity and stylishness as ways to make ideas fly. And though his beliefs are surprisingly uncomplicated, they come from a benevolent, if sceptical mind. His assurance that, beneath their confusion and cruelties, human beings *are* worthwhile and that the proof of this lies in man's ongoing search for a just community may sound unfashionably optimistic but it generates the play in all his major works. There is no despair in Stoppard, yet to call *Rosencrantz* "Beckett without tears" (Robert Brustein: *New Republic*, 1967) ignores the very human bewilderment and terror that eventually overtake the jolly pair. It is this humanity which interests me in Stoppard, and it appears much earlier than most commentators allow.

The radio plays contain the essence of those qualities. Each achieves a delicate balance between form and content, play and pain. The medium's intimacy allows us to concentrate while words slither or somersault; without the distraction of visual pictures, we move steadily closer to the littleness behind his characters' desperate or jaunty loquacity. Yet the verbal ebullience never works loose from the supporting structure. Each of these plays, from *The Dissolution of Dominic Boot* to *The Dog It Was That Died*, is a miniature marvel. That balance is much harder to attain in the theatre because everything, including the central idea, has to be bigger, but it is by that union of form, idea, and human passion that the plays either stand, wobble or fall. *Jumpers* achieves a brilliant unity and, on a lesser scale as a sort of staged radio play, so does *Every Good Boy*, while *Rosencrantz* (a mite too 'talky') and *The Real Thing* (problems with focus in the last two scenes) have a flawed splendour. It took Stoppard longer to translate his particular kind of theatricality into the vocabulary of the television cameras: his early farce, *Teeth*, is a one-shot triumph and *Professional Foul* and *Squaring the Circle* show him continuing to test himself and the medium.

Despite these verdicts, I do not intend to rank the plays into leagues and divisions, like one of Stoppard's Dogg football results: "Tube Clock dock, Handbag dock; Haddock Clock quite, Haddock Foglamp trog". My main purpose is to show how and where they work or don't as performances and strategies, since play scripts, like music scores, are difficult to realize from the printed page. Because I also want to show their interconnection, I approach them chronologically, as steps on a journey to the 'real' Tom Stoppard – or to as much of him as they allow us to see. For that reason, I ignore his adaptations from other writers, though those plays also have moments of ingenious staging. In focusing on the texts as theatrical games, I have avoided nods of approval or gestures of rage to this or that particular critic; instead, the essential names appear in the notes. Naturally my ideas have been shaped by a host of conflicting opinions, to which David Bratt's *Tom Stoppard: A Reference Guide* (Boston, 1982) gave useful directions. But I would like to acknowledge those which have been especially influential. Stoppard's own interviews, notably in Ronald Hayman's *Tom Stoppard* (1974 and 1976), *Theatre Quarterly* (1974), and *Gambit* (1981), have been my sheet-anchor, while Kenneth Tynan's profile in *Show People* (1979), Jim Hunter's *Tom Stoppard's Plays* (1982), and Tim Brassell's *Tom Stoppard* (1985) gave me ideas to ponder and reckon with. Except for *Dogg's Our Pet* (Inter-Action Inprint), all quotation from Stoppard's work comes, as noted, from the standard British or American editions of Faber & Faber or Grove Press.

I am most indebted to Colleen Donnelly, who typed and retyped with unflagging energy, accuracy and dedication, and to Doreen Thompson, whose own work on Stoppard over the years has challenged and stimulated mine. In addition, she generously provided me with the materials she had gathered for her MA thesis, *Soya Beans and Cricket Bats*. The staff of the University Library in Victoria and the National Sound Archive in Kensington were always helpful. I am also grateful to the University of Victoria's English Department, to my colleagues, Joan Coldwell, David Thatcher, Bill Benzie, and to my wife, Marion, for support, advice and encouragement along the way.

Chapter 1

A free man

As Tom Stoppard tells it, he was lazing in the water off Capri when suddenly he realized he was twenty-three, unpublished, unheard-of, and unlikely to be otherwise.[1] At the end of that vacation, he turned his cards in at Bristol's *Evening World*, where he had worked for two years as feature writer and second-string arts critic, and, armed with their contract for a twice-weekly column,[2] headed metaphorically for deeper waters. The image is teasingly appropriate. His early work, before the success of *Rosencrantz and Guildenstern Are Dead*, shows him testing his energies, looking for a distinctive style that would allow him, like George Riley, the determined fantasist of his first play, "a walk on the water".

So Stoppard did not burst upon the world like Athene from the head of Zeus; he might not even have become a playwright. Although he has said that young writers in the early sixties thought of the stage as the route to success after John Osborne's *Look Back in Anger* (1956) and the "new" drama that followed,[3] Stoppard in those years also tried his hand at radio and television scripts, theatre criticism, short stories, and a novel. If his experience as a journalist, reviewing plays at the Bristol Old Vic, had given him a taste for "showbiz", as a freelance writer he was prepared to slog away at such assignments as a season's worth of weekly episodes for *A Student's Diary* on the BBC Overseas Service; these were to depict the day-to-day life of an Arab student in London (though he did not actually know any such student at the time).[4] Those scripts have disappeared, as have the five episodes he wrote for the BBC's long-running daytime radio serial, *Mrs Dale's Diary*. One wonders how Stoppard managed to attune himself to that programme's middle-class respectability without sliding into the parody that the good lady's diary entries invite: "I'm rather worried about Jim [her husband] ... yesterday, Mother gave us all such a shock." For, in the early work that does survive in print, it is a gift for parody that already stamps large segments as *echt*-Stoppard.

A Walk on the Water, the play he wrote in 1960, which he has described somewhat derisively as *The Flowering Death of a Salesman*,[5] may originally have been a pallid reflection of Robert Bolt's *Flowering Cherry* (1958), which itself pays more than passing obeisance to Arthur Miller's *Death of a Salesman* (1949). However, by the time Stoppard's play reached the West End stage as *Enter a Free Man* (1968), the text had been largely rewritten in a way that moves the piece from those quasi-realist origins. Its first Act, in particular, now stands as a sustained burst of manic energy that holds its own with the later plays.

By comparison, Bolt's play has dated rather badly. What seemed so effective and moving at the time, especially through the performances of Ralph Richardson and Celia Johnson, adds up to little more than a well-made theatricality which pays lip-service to the new realism of the late 1950s. The set of *Flowering Cherry*, for instance, supports the rhythms of everyday living with its kitchen sink, fridge, stove, and dining-table and, at the final moments, the back wall becomes transparent, in a Millerish way, in order to reveal Jim Cherry's vision of row after row of blossoming fruit trees. But the action itself is simply a conventional middle-class family drama and is shaped to the sentimental demands of effective curtain lines. At the end of the first Act, Isobel Cherry, unable to bear her husband's lying fantasies, runs into the garden where she leans "*against the gate, throws her head back,* [and] *cries exhaustedly*: Oh, let me, let me, let me leave him!"[6] At the same time, in ironic counterpoint, Jim is at the kitchen table showing off to his daughter's friend in front of his son by reciting the "muse of fire" speech from *Henry V*. Cherry's invocation to "the brightest heaven of invention" neatly underscores his incapacity to distinguish truth from dreams, but psychological realism gives way to theatrical tidiness when his memory fails at the words "But pardon, gentles all . . ." and the curtain falls on the juxtaposition of this repeated phrase and Isobel's reiterated "let me leave him".

The tidiness of *Enter a Free Man* is of a different order since, in Act 1 at least, we are not required to enter the characters' lives or feelings. What may read like two-dimensional realism on the page becomes, on the stage, a series of zany, rapid-fire set pieces which owe more to *The Goon Show* or *Hancock's Half Hour* on BBC radio than to anything in Bolt's play. *Free Man* opens on a mood of bright heartlessness, the essence of this type of comedy in which one character scores off another with a string of destructively witty one-liners. Linda "is eighteen, self-assured, at least on the surface, and can be as cruel or warm as she feels like being".[7] When she sums up her father, George Riley, as "the man who's on his way . . . to the pub on the corner" (10), the lights come up slowly on the suburban bar which shares the stage with the Rileys' living-room (and hallway) where Linda talks to her mother, Persephone. The comic deflation works, as it were, *in absentia*, as Riley bursts through the pub door with a self-dramatizing flourish, "Enter a free man!", and Linda, from the other side of the stage, dismisses him as "Poor old Dad". The buoyancy that is necessary to keep us at a distance from the comic malice is established by this cheeky wit and by the efficiency and speed of this initial overlap between home and pub. In addition, before any of this action, as the houselights dim, a tinkling version of "Rule Britannia" initiates the bouncy irreverence.

Such overt artifice allows us to sit back and watch George jump through a number of contradictory hoops, and those leaps come so fast upon each other that we have no time either to question their credibility or to feel for George in his trials, other than to offer a smile of recognition as he moves through one frustrating confrontation to the next. Stoppard's technique here is very like the radio comedy of the 1950s, though that influence may not be a directly conscious one. He envisions George as "a smallish untidy figure in a crumpled suit . . . a soiled fifty with a certain education somewhere in the past: it gives him a tattered dignity now" (9). Stoppard has explained that he allowed for that vaguely distant education so that George might voice his bewildered hopes articulately;[8] that remark probably reflects an original, realist notion of George, but, as rewritten, Riley needs no such motivation. He is funny because like Tony Hancock, for example, he is the paradigm of rumpled self-importance,[9] small in stature but enormous in his own dreams, who reacts to those around him with a predictability which, to us, seems hilariously mechanical but which, to him, seems novel and incomprehensible. He remains undefeated because he never learns from past experience. As Stoppard describes him, he is "unsinkable, despite the slow leak".

This self-confident inadequacy is constantly tested through collision with someone who is either unintelligent and naive (Bill Kerr to Tony Hancock) or cagey and worldly-wise (Sid James). After Riley's jaunty entry (undercut by Linda from the sidelines and by an "it's him again" from the bar), he blithely accosts Brown, an anonymous-looking stranger, in the hope of cadging a drink. Unperturbed by failure, he turns to Able, a dim-witted but admiring sailor, to whom he can display his own superiority until the point of explosion where he is unable to countenance such gormlessness any longer:

RILEY: A man is born free and everywhere he is in chains. Who said that?
ABLE: Houdini?
RILEY (*turning*): Who?
ABLE: —dini.
RILEY: Houdini. No.
ABLE: Give up. (13)

On the other hand, with Harry, "flashy, sharp, well dressed", he is himself the naive butt. For when Riley explains his latest invention, a supposedly reusable envelope with "gum on both sides of the flap",

3

Harry leads him on into ever-increasing fantasy by pretending to take his self-image seriously and so feeding his vanities. By the end of this sequence, Riley is convinced that, with his brains and Harry's capital, his fortune is made: "A partnership – my goodness – did you hear that? I'm walking now, I'm on my way, committed – I'm walking and I'm not going to stop" (23).

At home, Riley's life follows a similar pattern, with his wife as dogged victim and his daughter as the superior sniper, though the fact that they are relatives and female adds a variation. Persephone's absorbed dusting and vacuuming make her an unsatisfactory audience and encourage her husband's my-wife-doesn't-understand-me attitude. Faced with his daughter's barbs, Riley envisions himself as the misunderstood parent, slaving for his family yet lacking respect. The fact that Linda is the sole bread-winner and gives her father weekly pocket money, since, as an "inventor", he does not consider himself a candidate for unemployment benefits, does nothing to deflate Riley's martyred dramatics.

Yet though these clashes of character depend for their effect on a transparent exaggeration of stock situations, Act 1 is no mere formula. The conflicts explode at high speed and are punctuated by extended arias in which Riley gives voice to the injustice of an unappreciative world. That tempo is sustained by flights of rapid, tangled cross-talk reminiscent of *The Goon Show*. Other *Goon* effects are the continuing catch-phrase (Riley's frequent hints that he wants a cigarette or a drink from Able) and the sort of sequence which builds on a cliché from popular fiction. Picking up Harry's suggestion that the innocuous Brown may be an industrial spy, Riley launches into an elaborate parody of a cunning, smooth-talking interrogator:

You can trust me. I'm just an ordinary man like yourself. I know you're only doing your job – it's a dirty business, but when it's all over we're still people, aren't we? The world goes on. I expect you're sick of it all – life on the run – always looking over your shoulder, waiting for the knock on the door, the unguarded word, the endless lies, loss of identity – it's no life at all. (25)

To hold these diverse materials together, Stoppard has organized a tight, economic structure. The pub episode ends with one of Riley's arias, during which he leans against a table, centre stage. The lights slowly go down within the bar, leaving him alone in spotlight until the other half of the set is gradually illuminated and, still talking, he is back in his living-room an hour or so *before* he decided to leave home for ever (as he often does on Saturdays). By backtracking, Stoppard allows us to view Riley's complaints about his family's lack of appreciation with prior knowledge that he will be equally frustrated and inadequate in the outside world. The reversed time-loop also adds comic point to Riley's delusions. We measure his annoyance over Persephone's placidity against the romantic fiction he weaves around Florence, the girl in the bar who truly does not understand him. Similarly, the fact that we know he will be swept into that romantic fantasy and into his illusory partnership with Harry subverts Riley's criticism of Linda's dream knight-in-armour and her "living in a fool's paradise". The Act ends at the point where it began. "Rule Britannia" tinkles away, but we now realize it issues from one of Riley's latest inventions, a patriotic clock which plays that tune at noon and midnight (inconveniently). Riley has freed himself from his ungrateful family, and when the words repeat themselves as he enters the pub, "a free man", we understand what Linda means by "Poor old Dad".

The second Act, however, does not have the same panache. Partly this is because there are few surprises. The play's energy flags because Riley can only journey downwards; we know there can be no substance behind his dream of success with Harry and Florence. Nor is this predictability offset by any inventiveness in the way the pair effect Riley's awakening. Florence, as was apparent from the start, has not the slightest notion what she means to him, and Harry, tired of yesterday's joke, simply rips open one of Riley's envelopes to show the uselessness of its double-gummed flap. Stoppard makes the pair undisguisedly brusque in order to wring the pathos from Riley's plummeting expectations. Even Able laughs at him, and he leaves the bar, "hurt to anguish". The degree of that hurt signals the major problem with Act 2, for at points like this we are urged to feel for Riley as an individual; he is no longer the farcical automaton. Yet as motivated individuals, rather than cartoon figures who move through a series of stock situations, the characters of *Free Man* wobble disconcertingly.

This change of focus, which pulls the play apart, is detectable from the moment Riley tells his family that he is "going into industry" (61). Linda, no longer the sniper, gently begs him to unpack his bags. If he will "stay and be like other people", they can go together to the Labour Exchange, where he can register and draw benefits until he finds a job that suits him. The cartoon Riley would have reacted to this with blustering pride, but Stoppard requires him to speak "to her with equal gentleness and the same air of explaining to a small child". The mood is sentimental, the tone a quiet yearning, and the rhythms those of Miller's Willy Loman:[10]

LINDA: Dad, you don't have to – dad, you're making it up – you *know* you are – you don't have to –
RILEY (*almost jubilant, but still quiet*): I'm not! It's all *true*!

LINDA (*nearly crying*): Dad, you *dreamed* it.

RILEY: No-o-o! You'll see – I'm not *alone* this time – Oh Lindy, I'll come
back in a Rolls Royce and then you'll believe me again and it'll be happy
again. (63)

This passage rings false not simply because it is derivative but
because it asks us to ponder family relationships, whereas the earlier,
unsinkable Riley was not the sort of figure to invite speculation about
his domestic happiness or unhappiness. Similarly, after he leaves,
Persephone, whom we have seen two-dimensionally, is suddenly
given a brain and a heart as she appeals to Linda's sympathy:[11]

It costs him – every time he comes back he loses a little face and he's lost a lot
of face – to you he's lost all of it. You treat him like a crank lodger we've got
living upstairs who reads fairy tales and probably wishes he lived in one, but
he's ours and we're his, and don't you ever talk about him like that again.
(*Spent.*) You can call him the family joke, but it's our family. (*Pause.*) We're
still a family. (67–8)

If we are to take this seriously as a revelation of true feeling beneath
the cardboard cut-out housewife, we must wonder how she can
accept her daughter's escapade with her latest motorcycling knight
or, for that matter, how Linda, who has a sharp sense of self-irony,
could fall to a succession of hard-riding smoothies.

Fortunately, by the end of the play, the characters are back in a
cartoon world, and we no longer have to worry over motivation. We
hear the sounds of rain, a clap of thunder, and water begins to pour
from a tangle of pipes on the living-room walls. It seems that one of
Riley's inventions has actually worked, until it is discovered that there
is no way of turning off this indoor-rain-machine for houseplants. As
Linda rushes around with buckets and saucepans, Riley appears to
admit defeat, only "the trouble is, I think I was *meant* to be an
inventor" (84). The final moment is nicely ambiguous. Though Riley
agrees to go down to the Labour Exchange "and inquire", Linda is
prepared to wait and see how he feels in the morning and offers him
an extra five shillings, since his week's pocket money went at the pub.
Riley accepts it, "just to tide me over", and enters the sum in his
notebook, as he has done every week for the past three years. He may
yet be free from the dole and once again afloat.

Flawed though it is, *Free Man* is not as weak as Stoppard himself
has said. To some extent it is "a play written about other people's
characters"[12] but, revised over the years, it shows a talent for verbal
fireworks and a sensitivity to the possibilities of stage space, even if
dialogue, action, and content are not yet interlocked or distinctively
Stoppardian. As *A Walk on the Water* it was performed on commercial
television in 1963, but to little notice during the aftershock of Ken-

nedy's assassination, and staged in Hamburg the following year, where *Old Riley geht über'n Ozean* was booed by an audience who expected kitchen-sink naturalism. The play was broadcast on BBC radio (1965) and, in its final form, presented after the acclaim given *Rosencrantz*, it suffered by comparison and was dubbed "disappointingly arch and obvious".[13] *Free Man* opened in March 1968 and closed two months later.

A second play from the early sixties, *The Gamblers*, never did receive a professional performance, though it was produced at the University of Bristol in 1965. Stoppard has jokingly referred to it as "Waiting for Godot in the Condemned Cell", yet he also describes it as "my 'first' play – that is the first play I regard as *mine*, after I'd cleared the decks with *A Walk on the Water*".[14] The text has not been published, but the passages that have appeared in print[15] do offer a foretaste of Stoppard's themes, style, and fascination with the arbitrary nature of the human condition. In particular, the play's two characters seem initially to be on opposing sides of a political revolution but are in fact two halves of the same coin. The Prisoner, who used to be the jailer before joining the insurgents, awaits execution simply because the revolt failed; had it not done so, the man who is now his jailer would be in prison since he is the regime's chief executioner. The Prisoner gambled and lost, though, by the play's end, the wheel of chance has revolved again and the Jailer, having decided the Prisoner is not the stuff of martyrs, changes places. The expectant crowd will not realize the difference: the Jailer wears the Prisoner's hood; the Prisoner dons the executioner's mask; they are indistinguishable, as they always have been. So, too, are the opposed forces in the larger scheme of things:

They're two parts of the same wheel, and the wheel spins. Do you know what I mean? . . . The life cycle of government, from the popular to the unpopular. The wheel goes slowly round till you get back to the starting point, and it's time for another revolution.

Yet however the wheel spins, from revolution to revolution, the Prisoner would always remain anonymous and unheroic.

He is entirely aware of his own littleness and of the ironies of his situation; a cog in the wheel, and a weak one at that, he has only become important because the victorious party needed a victim of some consequence and so promoted him into a captive 'leader'. That self-consciousness towards the ironies of one's own eternal inadequacy was to become one of the hallmarks of Stoppard's work. It distinguishes the Prisoner from a figure like George Riley, who has no such sense of inevitable failure. That knowing fatalism belongs to Beckett's Vladimir, and *Godot* has also provided Stoppard with a way of dramatizing human littleness through music-hall slapstick. In an attempt to reach God, since He will not come down and burst the prison open, the Prisoner clambers up a pile of furniture and on to the Jailer's back. When that achieves nothing, he urges the Jailer to stand on him. This sequence also exemplifies the Beckett joke which Stoppard admiringly defines as "a constant process of elaborate structure and sudden – and total – dismantlement".[16] It is particularly funny when a speaker boobytraps himself:

JAILER: You are the sun on the horizon. (*Consciously theatrical*) . . . The sun
   of hope and truth about to flood a golden land of equality and fraternity
   – and – and –
PRISONER: Liberty.
JAILER: Liberty! Yes! A golden land where liberty is – *compulsory*!

Although Stoppard will never share Beckett's view of life's empty absurdity, that influence does lead him to toy with metaphysics and away from the routines of situation comedy. He has his own version of "nothing is certain", and those perceptions begin to inform the argument of *The Gamblers*. Its plot, on the other hand, owes something to Nabokov, whom Stoppard also admires. Yet the exchange of prisoner for jailer is a contrived one; the play's shaping does not convey the necessity which the characters purport to be trapped by.

Form and content support each other perfectly, however, in the three radio scripts Stoppard wrote between 1964 and 1966. His inventiveness seems to burgeon in response to the discipline and challenge of creating pictures and action in sound only. Released from the pressure of a large-scale narrative, he can concentrate entirely on pattern as a means of saying and looking at an idea through his own idiosyncratic fancy. The tight spiral of the first script, *The Dissolution of Dominic Boot*, re-creates both the hero's ascending distress and the imprisoning circumstances he tries to break from. In *'M' Is for Moon among Other Things*, Stoppard prods below the patterns and begins to *explore* the pathos of imprisoned littleness. Here, he finds a distinctive way for his characters to voice their bewilderment towards themselves and life around them, and this develops into the playful metaphysics of *If You're Glad I'll Be Frank*. In all three plays he draws the listener into that world and into his characters' unease by condensing plot, dialogue, and sounds, so forcing us to deduce much of what is happening, to participate, to share in those little lives. As he gains assurance, Stoppard begins, through sound and dialogue, to "ambush" his audiences. In these scripts, he finds his own voice and his own vision of life's puzzling uncertainty.

The Dissolution of Dominic Boot, broadcast by the BBC in early 1964, is a candyfloss confection upon the moving-wheel theme, stripped of all metaphorical suggestion. The idea is as simple as it is entertaining: "The peg for *Dominic Boot* – a man riding around in a taxi trying to raise the money he needs to catch up with the meter – is the only self-propelled idea-for-a-play I ever had and I think I wrote it in a day."[7] Stoppard extends one dramatic image (in the vein of Riley's spy-interrogation) into fifteen minutes of action-packed panic. Sound effects, dialogue, and particularly deft cross-cutting between scenes create a sort of short-hand language which the listener must interpret in order to keep up.

No sound is wasted, and many serve a double function by furthering the action and weaving secondary threads that tie the episodes closely together. The opening moments illustrate this economic multiplicity:

Fade in street – traffic.
VIVIAN: Well, thanks for the lunch – oh golly, it's raining.
DOMINIC: Better run for it.
VIVIAN: Don't be silly . . . . (*Up*) Hey, taxi!
DOMINIC: I say, Viv . . .
VIVIAN: Come on, you can drop me off. (*To driver*) Just round the corner, Derby Street Library.
(*They get in – taxi drives.*)
DOMINIC: Look, Vivian, I haven't got . . .
VIVIAN: Dash it – that's taken about ten shillings out of my two-guinea hairdo – honestly, I'm furious. Don't you ever have an umbrella?
DOMINIC: Not when it's raining. (49)

Vivian is instantly characterized as a demanding, self-centred shrew who gives Dominic no chance to confess to his lack of cash. In fact, one of the major jokes is that we never do hear him actually explain his predicament to anyone. The hairdo and missing umbrella, besides instigating the taxi-ride and Vivian's grumbles, are two of the connecting threads. A few scenes later, Dominic's mother, who is equally critical and self-absorbed (no wonder she "likes that girl"), joins him in the taxi to talk about her hair and his never having an umbrella. This then occasions the next sequence, a few words from the cabbie about who used to cut his own mum's hair, and that snatch of family history enables Stoppard to mask a crucial piece of information when later, amidst continued chat about who cuts whose hair, Dominic learns that the driver owns a shop: "clothes, furniture, stuff, second-hand" (56). By the final sequence, Dominic – still umbrella-less and soaking wet – has sold everything he owns, except for a pair of pyjamas, to the driver in exchange for the fare.

By building repeated patterns of dialogue and by cutting rapidly from scene to scene, Stoppard is able to dispense with large sections of the plot. This technique draws the listener more intimately into the action since it forces him to piece things together for himself. After Vivian has left the taxi, we hear Dominic's inner thoughts and the chink of coins as he tries to meet the fare. Against the noise of the idling engine, the driver, silent up till then, asks (a shade sarcastically) if he is waiting for the rain to stop: "No, um, the Metropolitan Bank, Blackfriars, please." We instantly cut to the bank as a cashier asks Dominic to step to the end of the counter. Whereupon, through a brief interview and a tangle of muddled names, we deduce that Dominic is overdrawn and that the bank has already refused two cheques from the restaurant he lunched at with Vivian. The action then moves swiftly to a second bank where the repeating pattern suggests Dominic's troubles in two brief lines. We can guess the rest for ourselves.

Whole playlets about the characters' lives are also implied by the dialogue. The changing relationship between Dominic and the driver is particularly well-managed. The latter is introduced as a silent presence at the receiving end of Vivian's orders, and when he does speak, his slight sarcasm immediately conjures up the cliché of a world-weary cabbie, though he is moved to some wonderment when Dominic asks to be taken to a third bank. As the ride grows longer, the driver regales his passenger with a family detail or two, but never beyond a certain point: business is business. Such hard-nosed camaraderie then motivates the parody scene in which he bargains for Dominic's belongings, dismissing them as junk which, for a friend (his erstwhile passenger is now "Dom"), he agrees to cart away for ten bob. Dominic does not find his actual friends much more forthcoming. Stoppard has him borrow fourpence from the driver and ring up Charles. Tone of voice creates levels of meaning, especially on radio, and this solo phone-call allows the actor wide scope to manipulate stress and pause to suggest how distant a friend Charles is and how disgusted he feels at being asked to repay a loan by someone who can afford to travel around by cab.

Stoppard's ongoing preoccupation with characters who are called either Boot or Moon seems to have begun about this time. Having moved to London, he was writing theatre reviews and miscellaneous snippets for *Scene* magazine and would often sign them "William Boot", the name of a journalist in Evelyn Waugh's *Scoop*. In Stoppard's imagination, anyone called Boot shows a certain aggressiveness in trying to shape his life, whereas a Moon is more kicked against than kicking.[18] In some ways, Dominic may seem like a Moon until one considers his previous self-assurance. His mother and fiancée may both be bossy, but he is no doormat. He survives by airy promises and dud cheques (robbing banks "in a modest way") and has kept his job at the office, despite his extended lunch-hours, by adopting a mask of charming roguery. The play shows us his dissolution from Boot to Moon.

As the taxi-meter ticks onwards and his panic mounts – the names of the three banks, for instance, are made increasingly absurd – he struggles valiantly to remain in control. He tries to borrow from the firm's petty cash, but Miss Bligh has just spent it all on postage stamps; he breaks into his gas meter, but the take falls short; it costs him more to go to Croydon than the two pounds he recovers from Charles. When his parents fail him, his last recourse is to Vivian, who pushed him into his plight in the first place. But she is locked in her librarian's world and cross with him for taking taxis when he is supposed to be saving for their marriage. So Dominic cracks at last: "OH, YOU STUPID COW, SHUT UP AND GIVE ME TEN POUNDS FOR THE LOVE OF GOD!" (57). From that climactic outcry on, Dominic is a drowning man – in more ways than one. Fleeced by the taxi-driver, sacked by his boss, he stands weeping in his sodden pyjamas, and the waters close over his dazed head as he is bundled into another taxi:

MISS BLIGH: . . . Don't cry, Mr Boot. Your pyjamas are getting awfully wet . . . I should do up your front, Mr Boot, you'll catch cold . . . Pull your socks up, Mr Boot. (*Up*) Taxi! . . . come on, Mr Boot. Come on, you can drop me off . . .   (58)

Throughout its fifteen minutes, the comedy is kept aloft by the breezy energy of Stoppard's narrative, and to find weighty significance in the fact that Dominic is defeated by machines (the two meters) or commerce (the banks, the junk shop, paper-work at the office) would overload things. The play stretches a single, ridiculous idea to the ultimate or, in Stoppardese, it is about a man who is always being urged to pull his socks up and who can usually manage to pull the wool over people's eyes until he is bereft of footwear.

A second short play, broadcast a few weeks later in the same series, shows that Stoppard can indeed explore human relationships. For the first time, he builds a schema out of his *own* particular vision of life's absurdity. Neither of the two characters in '*M*' *Is for Moon among Other Things*[19] is called Moon, although both are Moonishly passive and confused (lunatic?): two self-absorbed individuals who occasionally collide, harmoniously or disconcertingly, as they plod on through the logic of their own blinkered lives. Each of the characters in *Dominic Boot* and *The Gamblers* is also enclosed in his little box, but this play presents the comic irony of such loneliness directly. The theme goes back to *Free Man*. Riley, in particular, creates a complete world of his own which is more real to him than actuality, so that his wife, whose real name is Constance, has become Persephone, probably because he sees her as provider and destroyer, like the Greek goddess. The wife in *'M' Is for Moon* is also called Constance and though, in outline, she is just as much a cliché as her predecessor, Stoppard now takes us behind that façade in a convincing and ultimately rather tender way.

Most of the play's dialogue is interior monologue and creates an autumnal picture of a middle-aged, middle-class, childless couple whose thoughts are somewhat richer than their humdrum lives. Accordingly, the pace of this play is generally languid. Nevertheless, Stoppard conveys the pair's boring existence in a far from boring way. He begins with something of a sound puzzle which immediately provokes the listener's interest, although this tricksy ambush is neither as provocative nor as meaningful as it is to become in the later plays. At first there is a silence, then a masculine grunt and a rattle of paper. A silent second or so later, we hear an odd "flip", a sigh, and a woman's voice whose manner and quality should persuade us that the words are interior thoughts even if their meaning is not instantly apparent. By the time we recognize the flips as the sound of turning pages, the voice is followed by a further grunt and a man's spoken thoughts. We now have our bearings: she is mulling over an encyclopaedia of some sort, and he is absorbed in a titillating news story. But when Constance starts counting off months in her head, the connection "tonight", "my pills", "February the fifth, March the fifth . . ." may mislead some listeners, even if the couple do not sound (to 1964 ears) sufficiently *advanced*. When we later discover that Constance's worries about the date and the pills are not contraceptive – at half-past ten she will be exactly "Forty-two-and-a-half, and all I've got is a headache" – the deception has served to underline the fact that sex is something Alfred only reads about in papers.

It is characteristic of Stoppard that he should make one detail perform several functions like this – he considers the habit a matter of temperament rather than something he consciously works at[20] – and the musings of Constance and Alfred (one can hardly call them conversations) create a series of related layers, one on top of each other, just as the scenes in *Dominic Boot* overlap. Constance's desultory flips through the *M to N* volume convey the loneliness of her empty life, and even when she voices her feelings to Alfred, he is not there to listen. Her queries about the date also exemplify the way she and her husband talk past each other. The effect is partly musical as these two disembodied voices develop their separate motifs which occasionally run together in unharmonious chords, but the repetitions and crossed lines also impress upon the listener the importance of the date, "August the fifth, nineteen sixty-two". For when Alfred decides to turn on the television, coming in on the last minutes of *Dial M for Murder* (a wry touch that), the first item on the news is the announcement that "Marilyn Monroe, the actress, was found dead in her Los Angeles home today . . ." (63).

Placed at almost the exact centre of the script, this is the point to which the seemingly aimless dialogue leads and upon which its concluding layers of irony depend. Constance herself sees none of these connections. Quite literally, Marilyn does not appear among the entries in her encyclopaedia. She shows no interest in the fact that the actress died alone after an overdose of pills, since, for her, Marilyn is all that she herself is not. She allows herself a passing curiosity about Marilyn's age and whom she was trying to phone when she died, but as Constance settles into bed, she too reaches for her sleeping-pills – "I think I'll take an extra one tonight" – to take her mind off the evening when the Gilberts came to dinner, a fiasco of which her husband had previously reminded her:

ALFRED: . . . D is for Débâcle – that which occurs when Mrs Gilbert is offered meat by her husband's chief accountant's wife on a Friday!
CONSTANCE: (*Crying*) Well, I wouldn't have forgotten if you hadn't been so awful on the phone – (65)

Perhaps she should not have phoned Alfred at the office, but as the clock strikes half-past ten, 5 August 1962 has only one significance: she is forty-two-and-a-half, and by the end of the month she will have reached *O to P*.

The entire script plays with the meaning of meaning. Having first led his listeners to question the meaning of the opening sounds and misled them as to other meanings, Stoppard allows them into Constance's thoughts about whether her life has any meaning. Had she some choice, she would at least have something by which to measure her present existence. At seventeen, she had made a choice of sorts; up till then she had always been known as Millie, her middle name, "then I went over to Constance, it sounded more grown-up" (63). But she regrets the loss of a less confusing time, when she did not need to measure or judge and when the letters in her first ABC stood for one object only: A is for apple, M is for moon. Though she now realizes that M can stand for Moon among other things, she does not consider the multiple meanings each of those M-words can have. Depending on one's perspective, 'Moon' suggests different things to different people, as does 'Millie' – or 'Marilyn'.

So Constance finds no meaning in the actress' suicide, and the listener perceives an ironic one, while Alfred invests the news with his own sexual fantasies. For him, that death is symptomatic of a hard, selfish world in which no one took the trouble to listen to "the poor girl" or to recognize her need and loneliness. But he, too, cannot measure that against his domestic circumstances. He ignores his wife's sleeping-pills and forgets his anger with her on the phone. As he turns out the bedroom light and Constance flips through more Ms in her lonely drift towards N, O and P, Alfred is aground on his one particular M, imagining Marilyn's phoning him (presumably *not* at the office) and his own caring reply:

> ... Do you feel better already? – Well, it's nice to have someone you know you can count on any time, isn't it? ... Don't cry, don't cry any more ... I'll make it all right ... (*Up – sigh*) Poor old thing ...
> CONSTANCE: Oh, you mustn't worry about me, Alfred, I'll be all right ... (*Thinks*) Marshmallow ... Mickey Mouse ... Marriage ... Moravia ... Mule ... Market ... Mumps ...   (67)

With this final moment, as Constance misinterprets her husband's solicitude and thinks he intends it for her, the delicate comedy turns the play back on itself, and we recall the constant misunderstandings between the pair because of their separate perspectives and the multiple meaning of words.

In 'M' Is for Moon, Stoppard's structure and style carry, and are intrinsic to, his theme. The interior threnodies of Constance and Alfred supply separate perspectives which dictate the way the pair react to Marilyn's suicide. By allowing the listener to participate in both those worlds, and to measure them more objectively against the details surrounding the actress' death, Stoppard creates a third perspective so that we experience for ourselves the fact that meaning depends upon point of view. Compressed into fifteen fleeting minutes, this multi-layered structure may not be completely apprehensible, and it is not surprising that the idea originated as a short story. Yet, as a listening experience, the play offers more than a gentle comedy of manners. From the outset, Stoppard forces us to cast about for our bearings. Whether we are totally aware of it or not, we search for a frame of reference, a way of measuring events and investing them with meaning. And something in Stoppard's own way of looking at things seems to have found a clear focus within the limiting and limited format of this brief radio play.

With his next script, If You're Glad I'll Be Frank,[21] broadcast two years later in 1966, Stoppard has mastered the genre and arrived at a personal vision, as evidenced by his playful delight in the possibilities of the medium and by the unconstrained way he welds farce to philosophy. Commissioned for the BBC's *Strange Occupations*, a never-to-materialize series of half-hour plays about ridiculous jobs, real or imagined, *If You're Glad* is sparked off by supposing that the voice of TIM, Britain's speaking clock, is not in fact a recording but belongs to a lady doomed endlessly to announce the passing seconds.

When Frank Jenkins dials the number, he is surprised to recognize the speaker as Gladys, his long-lost wife. Convinced she is being held against her will, Frank rushes to the rescue, but he too is a slave to time. As the driver of a London bus, he is bound to his timetable. If he drives fast enough to get ahead of schedule, he can snatch those few seconds to ring Gladys or fight through to "the top man in speaking clocks" in order to demand her release. But ever at his back comes the voice of Ivy, his tragedy-queen conductress, to remind him he is falling behind or that his passengers are becoming increasingly restive. The growing frenzy of these scenes is reminiscent of *Dominic Boot*, as Frank tries to reach Gladys but is beaten back by the clock or by the Post Office bureaucracy. But as an innocent-against-the-system, Frank is not allowed much personality. He is as open and honest as his name, likes a laugh or two, and is a stickler where time is concerned. The script's comic bubble rises instead from the minor characters and from the games Stoppard plays with sound as he creates their regulated world.

He orchestrates the clockwork precision of their daily arrival at the office by playing tricks with the well-worn sound effect of Big Ben. The scene is established by loud sounds of traffic and the Westminster chimes as the great clock "begins its nine a.m. routine" (46). Suddenly traffic noise vanishes; the continuing chimes sound muted now, and we are in the vestibule as the hall-porter murmurs, "Nine o'clock. Here we go." Precisely on the first stroke of nine, the lowest-ranking employee enters the hallway, letting in the sounds of traffic and an amplified Big Ben; these fade again on the second stroke as the street door closes, and the pattern is repeated as the staff enter at every odd-numbered stroke. Each person is greeted by the porter and replies in a way that reveals his place in the hierarchy and provides a lightning self-portrait. Myrtle, the secretary, responds with a gay "Hello, Tommy", and so on up to the entrance of the First Lord and his orotund "Morning, Tommy". We then follow Lord Coot through a second door, through which all the other voices have passed, and then through more doors and past the ranks until he arrives at his inner sanctum (47). Myrtle's greeting, "Good morning, your Lordship", shows the unctuous respect of a family retainer, and the Lord's reply suggests he sees her as a sort of housekeeper (though to the others she is more of an upstairs maid).

If a new secretary gives the Lord some pause, in such an orderly world where everyone has his appropriate niche, her arrival at precisely 1.53 a.m. allows Stoppard to twist an old slogan, "The Post Office never sleeps", and to prepare us for Gladys, who also can never sleep as she signals each passing ten seconds. That new recruit also occasions an explanation as to the workings of the Lord's empire: other voices are at work around the clock, like UMP (cricket scores), POP (music), EAT (recipes), and the secretary's job is to keep them under continual surveillance. Cooty is Lord of all he surveys and has his spies; since people are not machines, "the strain is appalling, and the staffing problems monumental" (48). So Stoppard plants the suggestion that the hall-porter is another of the Lord's informers. Their morning greeting had been followed by the Lord's "(*Conspiratorial.*) Anything to report?" and we later hear that they lunch together, "like brothers". But neither of them seems to notice the sexual hanky-panky between Myrtle and (at least) two of the staff, liaisons which dramatize the way this bastion of efficiency rests upon human frailties of which the chief exemplum is Gladys herself.

Gladys is on the verge of breakdown, and to depict her predicament Stoppard creates an inner and outer voice. Principally we hear the free association of her thoughts under which runs the continuous soundtrack of her impersonal, automated phonespeak, although those announcements can interject across her personal anguish or they can fade out altogether. However, this tension between her private feelings and her automaton's role as TIM is not the major reason for her approaching disintegration. Her strange occupation has given Gladys a disturbing vision of what Time means, and it is this which threatens her peace of mind. Formerly she had sought to find peace in simplicity. She would have liked to be a nun but was unable to "believe *enough*" to pass muster with Mother Superior. The promise of serenity attracted her to Frank with his sunny laugh and simple joke ("if you're Glad I'll be Frank") when they first met at a dance; reliable as clockwork, he would drive past her window twice a day "with a toot and a wave . . . everything the same" (57). TIM offered even greater sameness until, through that unending repetition, she experienced a portion of eternity as the seconds stretched ahead and behind her to infinity.

In Gladys' monologues, Stoppard solves the problem of how to transmit complex ideas to a listener who cannot set his own pace down a printed page or turn back for a second try. Here, he creates a style that "fall[s] into something halfway between prose and verse" (45). The effect is akin to modern verse-drama: a barely perceptible

rhythmic beat, a syntax that is more formal and organized than that of
everyday speech, and a spare, undecorated vocabulary release the
listener from the confusions of naturalistic speech-patterns and
enable him to concentrate more closely on what is being said. Many
of Gladys' lines have a tang of T. S. Eliot, though they are usually less
cerebral and more irrationally disconnected:

> I can hear them all
> though they do not know enough to
> speak to me.
> I can hear them breathe,
> pause, listen,
> sometimes the frogsong of clockwindings
> and the muttered repetition to the
> nearest minute . . .
> but never a question of a question, . . .   (61)

Towards the end, as Gladys nears collapse, her speeches echo the
rhythms of Lucky's long monologue in *Godot*: "yes, yes, . . . it's asking
too much, / for one person to be in the know / of so much, for so
many . . ." (65). Either way, the rhythmic and verbal patterning is
formalized enough to support ideas which guide us to a final understanding of why all clocks and our regard for them are so absurd.

Gladys has seen that nine today is not the same as nine tomorrow.
Time flows on endlessly and reduces man to a miniscule part of that
flow. Yet from a human perspective, time is divisible into ticks and
tocks which give our lives importance. Through Gladys, Stoppard
makes us see that Frank's slavish obedience to his timetable is not
simply a funny joke but absurdly sad as he drives around in circles,
and the satire on departmental bureaucracy widens and deepens
when we are made to recognize Lord Coot's ludicrous concern for
efficiency as a magnification of every man's belief that he is time's
master.

But what makes Gladys crack is neither the physical effort of her
job nor her feeling that it is pointless to divide time into units of ten
seconds. Her position has become absurd because she feels compelled to keep on, despite her knowledge. Part of her dares not answer
Frank's pleas over the phone because were she only to cough or
sneeze she would bring the Post Office's whole elaborate system
tumbling down. Another part of her knows that the disruption would
make no difference; time would go on without her, so she yearns to
blow the system to pieces. She has seen the void, and "if you can't
look away / you go mad" (51).

The struggle against madness stands as the common denominator
between the two centres of the play's action. Stoppard marries farce

to the play of ideas by making both Frank and Gladys the puppets of circumstance. Under the conventions of farce, an ordinary, respectable, outwardly conformist character suddenly becomes vulnerable, either through misunderstanding or coincidence, and is catapulted into a number of increasingly extravagant misadventures which reduce him to a helpless automaton, no matter how he tries to assert himself. In that tradition, Frank's phone-call to TIM precipitates him into situations over which he has less and less control. Each time he arrives at the Post Office in his fight to reach Gladys, he gets a little farther, and we hear his running feet and gasps for breath as he charges into the building. But the harder he tries, the greater are the forces that pull him back. Finally, the rush-hour traffic-jams give him four spare minutes and he bursts into a Board meeting to the clamour of porter, clock, horns, Ivy, the bureaucrats, and the "noise of rioting passengers" at his heels. Then Frank is brought to a stunned halt, not by the crescendo of protests behind him but by a blank wall of smiling reasonableness as the First Lord explains, "My dear fellow – there's no Gladys – we wouldn't trust your wife with the *time* – it's a machine, I thought everyone knew that" (68). To general laughter, Frank tumbles back to his everyday self.

Though farce usually explodes into frenzied physical action like this, Gladys also suffers the dizzy panic of a farce figure. Completely motionless, she is like someone on a precarious height ("serenity" in her case) who is pulled at by an increasing vertigo whenever she looks down, yet she cannot stop herself from doing so. In her case, too, the First Lord's reasoning restores her, though to the automaton state she so desires. In the concluding scene we no longer hear her in close-up but as a voice through the phone, just as she was in the first scene. Yet while she subsides into mindless repetition, her final thought about Lord Coot, "He thinks he's God", suggests that the frenzy could start all over again. As it could with Frank, for when Ivy leads him away she tells him "you'll have to go on looking", for Gladys. In this way, Stoppard unites the play's two seemingly disparate styles, farce and philosophy, and the pleasure we derive from that union is also a sort of vertigo. After the slight disorientation of the script's opening words, when Frank gasps "It can't be!" in reply to TIM's "At the third stroke it will be . . .", we are whirled up by the escalating action and made dizzy by Stoppard's ideas in the manner of a ferris-wheel ride.

In all three of these radio plays, Stoppard experiments with ways of making episodes overlap or interlock so that a script's full meaning derives almost solely from its patterned structure: the medium is the message. Although he claims "that a lot of one's work is the result of lucky accident. . . . What's wrong with bad art is that the artist knows exactly what he's doing",[22] these plays exhibit an astute interplay between action and dialogue. His other early writings do not possess that architectonic economy and density. This is partly due to the fact that on radio "actions" are sounds, so that the materials with which he builds share a homogeneity, whereas on stage or particularly on television the pictured action does not lend itself so readily to such intricate dovetailing.

His television script, *A Separate Peace*, is an exact contemporary of *If You're Glad*, yet despite a number of ideas they have in common, the teleplay is comparatively loose and uncharacteristic. Action and dialogue run side by side; they do not intertwine into a structure which in itself provides meaning. Nor has Stoppard organized the pictured action in ways that are peculiar to television; *A Separate Peace* could be presented in any medium. There are only two sets, the office and a private ward in the Beechwood Nursing Home, and the action alternates consistently between them simply to further the plot.

The cameras come in on the night nurse seated at the office's reception counter. John Brown enters through the main door, looks around him, and proclaims everything "very nice".[23] It transpires that he wants to be admitted as an emergency case even though there is nothing wrong with him. The hospital is a private one, and "it's the privacy I'm after – that and the clean linen" (168). The only incident that is specifically visual in this sequence occurs when Brown makes to unzip one of his cases to show that he has the wherewithal to pay for a room and catches his finger in the zipper; as he sucks his wound, a doctor arrives, looking somewhat tousled after being awakened in the small hours of the morning. When asked "what seems to be the trouble?", Brown extends his finger so that the doctor wonders why he came all the way for that. After some argument, it is agreed that Brown be admitted for "observation", even though, as he himself repeats when the Nurse starts to pick up his bags, "No, no, don't you . . . There's nothing the matter with me" (169). Like Gladys, Brown wants serenity and orderliness; consequently, after he has followed the nurse into his private room, he pronounces himself satisfied with its atmosphere and with the promise of a daily routine: "Like clock-work. Lovely" (170).

But hospital life does not develop into a metaphor of clockwork existence as Glad's TIM job does, since we see little of that routine in action. Instead the script's interests are purely narrative as we follow the doctor's efforts to find out why Brown should want to be a patient and where he comes from. His chief aid in this is Maggie, an attractive young nurse, whose role is to engage Brown in friendly bedside chats which might yield clues as to his identity. Whenever we return to the office, the doctor is either on the phone to the local police or is discussing Brown's case with Matron; these scenes mark the staff's assessment of what Maggie has gleaned, and they plot the next step in their investigations. Since the ward scenes are the more extended, Stoppard avoids complete stasis by having Brown agree to occupational therapy: we see him putting the finishing touches to a comically misshapen basket, and later he has left his bed and is at work painting a rural landscape on his walls.

The dialogue also furthers plot but needs no visual action to support it. Brown's early conversations with the staff manage a slightly jokey quality due to the way he interprets almost everything they say in the light of his own determined plan:

MATRON: Now, what's your problem, Mr Brown?
BROWN: I have no problems.
MATRON: Your complaint.
BROWN: I have no complaints either. Full marks.
MATRON: Most people who come here have something the *matter* with them.
BROWN: That must give you a lot of extra work. (172)

The chats with Maggie are more conversational, since she is trying to lower his defences; they are saved from utter flatness by the way Brown blocks her every attempt. Although their banter when affectionate sounds a trifle insipid, the catalogue of the staff's latest theories about Brown and the latter's explanations of his own motives inject energy into the piece. The ideas are, in fact, more lively than their expression, though on occasion Brown can sound like Oscar Wilde: "To stay in bed for tea is almost impossible in decent society, and not to get up at all would probably bring in the authorities" (171).

Television at its most conventional is singularly passive; its audience sits back and watches a story unravel in pictures to which the dialogue is generally subordinate. *A Separate Peace* makes few demands on the viewer. The dialogue and the cutting from scene to scene neither jolts our expectations nor forces us to participate by experiencing a character's dilemma in ourselves. We are not disorientated, as we are by the radio scripts and later stage plays, although the circumstances which dictated the original transmission may have caused mild puzzlement, since *A Separate Peace* was designed to illustrate a short documentary (about chess players) which immediately preceded it: "The play . . . does not in fact illuminate what I think about chess players, in whom aggression is probably more important than the desire to escape, but I persuaded myself that this, the only idea I had at the time for a play, fitted well enough."[24]

Brown's plan to separate himself from the world starts things off provocatively, and his nostalgia for his years as a prisoner of war (as a Private who has found private peace) has a quirky ring to it: "It was like winning, being captured. The war was still going on but I wasn't going to it any more" (180). For the rest, Stoppard unrolls the story in a single line.

There were more complicated and inventive twists and turns to *Neutral Ground*,[25] transmitted by Granada Television in December 1968, though written three years before – earlier, that is, than *A Separate Peace*. Where Brown looks for a permanent refuge in a no-man's-land, *Neutral Ground* concerns an individual who has been abandoned there. Stoppard was commissioned to write it for a series based on myths and legends, which never got off the ground, and he now claims to have felt somewhat dismayed when the play was eventually presented as a separate entity. The plot adapts the Philoctetes legend to the world of John Le Carré in a rather ingenious and ambitious way.

In Sophocles' play, Odysseus and Neoptolemus, son of Achilles, have travelled to the deserted island of Lemnos in order to bring back Philoctetes to Troy, for he possesses the bow and arrows of Hercules which, according to prophecy, can bring victory to the Greeks. It was Odysseus who had caused Philoctetes to be marooned there at the beginning of the war because the latter's sufferings from a noxious snake-bite made him too burdensome a passenger. So he sends Neoptolemus and several of his followers on up to the exile's cave in order to win his trust and deceive him into boarding ship. Eventually, however, Neoptolemus confesses to his true role, but Odysseus arrives to urge him to leave Philoctetes to his fate since the wounded man hates them too much to go with them to Troy. But on his way to the ships, Neoptolemus' conscience again troubles him and he returns the bow to its rightful owner. Prepared now to stand against Odysseus and the anger of the whole Greek army by taking Philoctetes homeward as he had first promised, Neoptolemus is prevented only by the divine intervention of Hercules himself, whose shade commands them all to Troy.

Sophocles' play raises political issues: whether an individual should be prepared to act dishonestly for the sake of the common good; the clash between one who is physically weak but morally stubborn and one who commands force but is morally slippery. Yet, though Stoppard applies this plot to the agents and counter-agents of modern politics, his play convinces least when he attempts to deal with purely political ideas. What speaks to him in Sophocles is the game of false appearances and the fact that much can be said for and against both sides in the struggle so that a comparatively straightforward and commercial script contains within it a characteristic interplay between truth and illusion plus a certain amount of intellectual leap-frogging from case to counter-case.

Stoppard's inventiveness shows most in the way he has transposed major details from Sophocles. The island becomes a tiny inland country south-east of Trieste. For two years, Mr Marin (code-name Philo) has been trapped there between East and West. Before the title credits come up on the screen, in what turns out to be a flashback, we watch his arrival by train at the Austrian border where a fellow passenger to whom Philo had given his fur hat is gunned down. Later flashbacks show how Otis (the Odysseus character) abandons him because that accidental shooting "makes you look too clean for words, it's like a diploma" (136). Convinced that the Russians knew Philo was a Western agent and had been feeding him false information for months, Otis cannot be sure that his escape from Moscow has not been engineered. Like his namesake, Philo is a poisonous burden and like him he is needed again later. Otis finds out that the information he once thought false "could make a lot of important sense and we need Marin to read it" (155), so he sends Acherson (Achilles' son) and Carol (Chorus) to pose as a salesman and his wife on a working holiday in Montebianca.

This deception is made more complicated by the fact that the viewer does not know the two are anything other than they seem to be when they first appear, and because we have already seen two obvious agents. Derived from a rival Trojan embassy in Euripides' lost play, this anonymous pair, dubbed Laurel and Hardy in the script because of their contrasting size, accord with the traditions of wise-cracking hit men. Their part in the plot sends them chasing one chimera after another: bursting into an attractive widow's bedroom, missing Philo by minutes and, on taking Acherson for his last ride, falling to what they thought was a toy gun. In contrast, the deceptions practised by Otis' agents involve the emotions of the players. Acherson comes to pity Philo, and it takes a none-too-pleasant conference with Otis to persuade him to "just get him on that train".

The interchange between past and present and the cross-cutting between both sets of agents work smoothly, yet the dialogue often feels flat and is, Stoppard confesses, overwritten in places. Admittedly, most scenes involve characters who are foreign to each other. The script derives occasional fun from a stilted idiom, as when Carol reads out from the guidebook, "the views are unexampled by the largest traveller", a sentence Laurel gleefully applies to his fat friend. However, the freely emotional sections also ring hollow. And nobody who had suffered from the political realities of Europe would indulge in the highflown sentiment that clothes Philo's reasons for returning:

My memories are good ones now. I don't think about the commissars, the fear, the system, all the things that changed when the Russians came . . . I particularly remember the peppers lying around the edges of the square – red, orange, yellow, green, and all shades in between, all sunset and forest colours, . . . on a summer evening after the market. (*Pause.*) That's what you are giving back to me.   (159)

Yet there are many subtleties of characterization which lift the script above cloak-and-dagger melodrama. Taking a hint from Edmund Wilson's *The Wound and the Bow*, Stoppard has seen that personal sympathies, not political loyalties, are the crux of the Philoctetes legend.

At this point in his career, Stoppard was probably content to make his script craftsmanly and marketable. An earlier play, *This Way Out with Samuel Boot*, from 1964, had been rejected and, in synopsis, appears to have been much more adventurous.[26] Samuel Boot, another of Stoppard's stubborn individualists, wants nothing to do with money. His younger brother, Jonathan, is compulsively acquisitive: "There's no out. You're in it, so you might as well fit. It's the way it is. Economics." Undeterred, Samuel decides to steal his brother's hoard of trading-stamps and give them away; as he does so, a scrambling mob of housewives tramples him to death: "He was a silly old man, and being dead doesn't change that. But for a minute . . . his daft old crusade, like he said, it had a kind of dignity." After that script had been turned down, Stoppard's agent, Kenneth Ewing, advised him to "stick to theatre. Your work can't be contained on television."[27]

Chapter 2

Now you see him

Undaunted by his setbacks with television, Stoppard had other irons in the fire. Three short stories appeared in 1964, the year *Samuel Boot* was rejected, as part of Faber and Faber's *Introduction 2: Stories by New Writers*. These short pieces are like nothing else in Stoppard's repertoire, though certain ideas will reoccur later. Stoppard has always been a self-cannibalizer, adapting and refining his thoughts. A hopeless, raw pain caused by an unyielding woman, moral questions about the responsibility of journalists, these themes will crop up in *The Real Thing, Dirty Linen*, and *Night and Day*. The second story even reflects the dejected ambition of a twenty-seven-year-old, unpublished, little known, and unlikely to be otherwise. Years later, in reply to a query about his habit of steering away from personal feeling, Stoppard replied smoothly (but feelingly?), "Well, I don't see any special virtue in making my private emotions the quarry for the statue I'm carving. I can do that kind of writing, but it tends to go off, like fruit. I don't like it very much even when it works . . . Let me put the best possible light on my inhibitions and say that I'm waiting until I can do it well."[1] Early in his career, in stories which could not expect a wide readership, Stoppard here lets his guard down.

The most haunting of the three stories, "Reunion", is a mood piece in which an unnamed man and woman recover a moment's empathy, only to go separate ways. Its precise notation of external detail and the way one of the characters searches to express an inner confusion owe something to Hemingway, particularly to stories like "Cat in the Rain". The rise and fall of emotion between Stoppard's antagonists provides an objective framework for a similar rise and fall within the male character, whose strivings we are invited to share.

Having loved and lost, the man experiences a grief, an ache, a panic ("it") which threatens to unbalance him: "It kept coming like the sea, never falling back as far as it came" (121). To break the silence between himself and the woman, he tries for a careless jocularity; "He watched and there was nothing, and paused." He tries again; "He watched and there was nothing." Upon his third attempt at idle chitchat, "He watched."[2] The woman finally reminds him that he came there uninvited. Her comment had been meant as a rebuff, but he clings to those words as some sort of opening. She has said something, so he attempts to establish their reunion on an "old friends" basis. Her empty, agreeable, stone-walling remarks and the way the man precisely notes the kitchen in which they sit and "the new thickness of her ankles, thighs and body" (presumably she is pregnant and so belongs undeniably to her husband) act as a counter-weight to his self-pity, so that the man's sentimental agony builds under continual outside pressure like a coiled spring. This tension is extremely effective.

While he tries to keep the jokiness going, she cuts through to basics: "He'll be back soon" (122). He considers smashing the milk bottle that stands inconsequentially upon the table. Such violence would be like screaming "the word" in the silence of a public library, "and he would be all right". Back on the surface, he pushes beyond pleasantry, asking if things are better than when the two of them were together.

"You're sorry for yourself", says she. He agrees, and when he reaches out to touch her she stands away. In defence, he launches his ideas about the word "which if shouted at the right pitch and in a silence worthy of it, would nudge the universe into gear" (123). The idea grows as he contemplates violating the silence of the reading-room at the British Museum. She reacts to that with vague amuse-ment. His pain, "it", falls back farther than before, and he is encour-aged to elaborate: you cannot shout "Love" in a crowded room, "What do you suggest?" Entering the game, she posits "Fire!" so that, feeling their togetherness, he laughs and marches round the kitchen building idea upon idea. Perhaps the word would not be an English one. So out comes a stream of nonce words until, unable to check himself, he plunges back to the real purpose of his visit: "I do love you . . ."

Touching her, trying to push back the pain, he veers desperately into a fiction about the way artistic types like her husband beat their wives and starve their children, and on into how he misses her doing the things he remembers her doing, but especially "you in bed" (124). Instinctively, she glances towards the window for her hus-band's return, even though she only looks out onto rooftops. "We could be very good. . . . We nearly were", he urges (125). She recommends "a marvellous affair" with some girl. In one last throw, he tells her "[her husband] isn't coming back . . . ever . . . I'm not going away, ever", to which she politely agrees until, finally, she tells him to "shut up". The tide of feeling wells up; his body disconnects; to count numbers or yell out "the word" would no longer help him: "only murder would stop it now, and it took a long time, stairs and streets later, before he got a hold on it again, without, as always, having murdered anybody".

The simplicity of this situation has puzzled those commentators who look twice before accepting their Stoppard "straight" or who misread the jokes that the man erects to cover up his feelings. Trying to make the woman behave as "old friends" do, the man succeeds in reaching a moment of shared laughter, only to ruin things by confessing how he really feels towards her. Stoppard may have learnt from his American mentor how to construct a mimetic prose whose structure follows the emotional ebb and flow between his two characters, but the realism points to the genuine pain of a young man on being turned down for someone else, and he handles that truth cleverly by allowing us to emote with the man while exposing his self-indulgent attitudinizing. "Reunion" is essentially dramatic, presenting a situation and its subtext. It also introduces the first in a procession of bewildered, lovelorn males and, more quirkily, of unreachable females, that stretches from here to *Jumpers* and on into the last Act of *The Real Thing*.

The other two stories derive from Stoppard's life as a journalist. "Life, Times: Fragments" projects Stoppard's own feelings (in 1963) on being twenty-six/seven and going nowhere as a writer. Earlier he had transposed Bolt's Jim Cherry, who balked at rejecting a safe job in exchange for his dream, into George Riley, who *has* taken the plunge but has not found a route to success. Here, in one of a series of fragmented scenes, the "I" lolls on a Spanish beach: "I was sitting up to my navel in sea when I remembered I was not twenty-six any more, and whatever it was I'd been waiting for slipped by then, between waves, as quickly as that. I was twenty-six and biding my time and when the next wave came I was twenty-seven and losing" (127).

The fragments alternate between an "I" and a "he" narrator to convey the sort of fantasy an unrecognized young writer might very well indulge in: rejection slip after rejection slip – just wait till I'm dead, then some critic will discover me and make his reputation. Arrogantly dismissing all the modern world's great writers – "the models are no good any more, we've had all that, we're on our own now" (128) – he leans towards his lady, who takes somewhat longer to remove the day's make-up than he does to destroy the literary canon. He whispers, " '*I am – I feel – seminal!*' and she, getting up, faceless for the dark, said, 'No, do you mind if we don't tonight. I've run out of the stuff.' " This scene plunges into bathos with a Stoppardian extravagance, and the piece ends with a comically vengeful hit at unappreciative publishers and critics.

At fifty, the persona, "the oldest sub in London", remembers how his lady left him almost thirteen years before and, Ros-and-Guil-like, he embarks on a parodied Lord's Prayer: "Lead us into sensation and deliver us from libel . . ." (129). Then in self-parody he adds, "You should see me. I am drowning with the panache of someone walking on the water. That's not bad. I could slip it in somewhere. When people ask me what I do, I say I'm a writer." But without public acceptance no one can call himself a writer. Wishing he had found a publisher and unsure about God, "for a long time he compromised by praying at his typewriter". However, after the umpteenth rejection slip, he falls on his knees: "And the Lord heard him and He sent an angel to the writer as he knelt, and the angel said, 'The Lord thanks you for your contribution but regrets that it is not quite suitable for the Kingdom of Heaven.'" In the concluding fragment, someone finally reads his work and "could not put it down" (130). A famous critic is the first to find the writer's suicide note: "'I have discovered the body', he added, swiftly ransacking the furniture, 'of his work.'" As a consequence, both he and the dead writer acquire fame.

Where these fragments turn the frustrations of a free, but so-far-unsuccessful man into a comic, liberating fable, "The Story" considers a theme which Stoppard will return to more than once: the responsibility of the press.[3] This piece, the most conventionally structured of the three, creates an ironic contrast between a reporter's single-minded concern over the day-to-day workings of his job and its cost, in human terms, to the person whose story he reports.

Jack, the narrator, describes one of his weekly visits to a neighbouring court of law. His Runyonesque insider's jargon, as he details the relationship between the *Sun*, the paper he works for, and the wire services to whom "we phone over anything good that breaks", is shaped into an off-hand, matter-of-fact prose in the manner of Truman Capote.[4] In the course of the morning, a man comes before the judge for interfering with a little girl while teaching her to swim. Jack starts to jot down the particulars, then dismisses the whole incident: "you can't do much with an indecency, at least not in the *Sun*, and a two-par filler on someone outside the circulation area is neither here nor there because you can't mention the kid's name or anything" (132). He almost changes his mind when he learns that the accused, James Blake, is a master at a famous school, "but I couldn't be bothered" (133).

Back in the city, Jack bumps into Diver, the local Press Services man, and chances to mention the indecency case and the school Blake taught at. Diver suggests he puts out a couple of paragraphs, which was nice of him since that meant Jack would "get paid what was going" (134). So he phones a filler through to Press Services, pops a variation of it into the *Sun*'s overnight basket, "to cover myself", and sends a third version to International-Express. By early evening, his wire-service story "had reached the local daily in Blake's area", and they phone Jack for more details, as do several of "the boys" from the national tabloids. The next day, Blake's case was in most of the newspapers, and a week later he was in them again, having killed himself by jumping in front of a London tube train. About a month later, a few small cheques arrived in payment for the story: "I don't know what I spent [them] on" (136). These events happened two years ago, and though Blake's suicide preyed on Jack's mind for some weeks, "finally I got rid of it" (131). But Jack is not rid of it, and seeing Diver standing on the same street corner brings it all back. His story comes out from those guilt feelings, even if, as a reporter, he would not admit that. So each reader has to decide for himself about the moral issues in the incident.

The anecdotal nature of this last piece would translate readily into film. Stoppard sold a script to ITV, and *A Paragraph for Mr Blake* was screened in October 1965. The publication of these three quasi-autobiographical stories, together with his radio and television plays, were gaining him a modicum of public acceptance. A publisher's note, outlining the success of the writers who had been included in Faber and Faber's first anthology, predicted similar success for the five authors selected for *Introduction 2*. They had "a very reasonable chance of establishing themselves among the more interesting novel-ists of the future" (9).

Stoppard then secured a contract for a novel from a second publishing house; the book was published in 1966, the year of *If You're Glad, A Separate Peace*, and the original version of *Rosencrantz and Guildenstern*. As he awaited the latter's student première, "I was very light-hearted about the whole thing... there was no doubt in my mind whatsoever that the novel would make my reputation, and the play would be of little consequence."[5]

Lord Malquist and Mr Moon[6] is Stoppard's most ambitious work prior to *Jumpers* (1972), so it is not surprising that he should have felt his future would lie in the success of that novel, especially since no professional company seemed interested in *Rosencrantz and Guil-denstern* at the time. Stylistically, the novel represents the culmination of six years' exploration and experiment; thematically, it contains all the ideas from the previous plays and short stories. Stoppard had wildly shaken up the kaleidoscope of his personality to present his most intricate and characteristic design to date, and how we view that pattern depends on the book's many reflecting mirrors. What we see from one angle looks entirely different from another. The novel builds out of, and ultimately offers a commentary upon, ways of looking at life. In the manner of the radio plays, structure and style combine to force us to experience those shifting perspectives in ourselves, and the book proves all the more disconcerting because in its two hundred or so pages we can never rely for long on any one perspective.

The novel's opening section, "Dramatis Personae and Other Coincidences", as that title suggests, thrusts towards the reader a diverse cast of characters who seem to have no logical relationship to each other. Stoppard goes out of his way to make them as unlikely a combination as possible and emphasizes that disparity by describing them in a pastiche of styles, each element of which stands in glaring contrast to its neighbours. We come upon them *in medias res*, as the self-regarding, dandified Lord Malquist dismisses the human race with a mere flick of an aphorism: "'When the battle becomes a farce the only position of dignity is above it', said the ninth earl (the battle raging farcically beneath him)" (8). Moon, his amanuensis, unable to extricate himself so carelessly, has difficulty in concentrating. He scribbles down garbled fragments of Malquist's polished phrases as they ride along Whitehall in a coach-and-pair. Already we have two perspectives: Malquist's egotistical pronouncements and Moon's inept account of that sermonette, distracted as he is by an inner voice which keeps on questioning him. The two also react differently to the people who press against the coach: Moon adopts an expression he thinks suitable to a respectful populace; Malquist stares at them blankly until a fat woman emerges from the crowd, hurls "a tight roll of paper, loose end flying", and falls beneath the carriage wheels.

This all seems like a comic rerun of St Evremonde's coach ride in Dickens' *A Tale of Two Cities*. We are back in the eighteenth century, as Malquist arrogantly throws a handful of shining gold pieces into the street and his frightened horses bolt towards St James's Street. The fat lady lies supine in their rear: "Breeding . . . a lady does not move." Then we are jarred into a new focus by Malquist's studied theatricality; fondling one of the coins "and stripping off the gold tinsel, he popped the resultant chocolate into his mouth" (12). Still more unsettling is the undisguised transition to the next sequence where two cowboys, bristling with narrow-eyed antagonism, ride towards each other in a broad parody of second-class Westerns that flounders into bathos when "L.J. [for Long John]" Slaughter cannot control his ambling mare whom he keeps on calling "boy". Only a dedicated *aficionado* could be expected to trace the oblique connection between the cowboys and Mr Moon. "Slaughter was a left-handed gun." In the movie, *Left-Handed Gun*, the main character, emerging from the saloon for the final shoot-out, cries out to his rival, "Moon . . . Moon!"[7]

These cowboy banalities then jolt into a description, tight-lipped and Hemingwayesque, of a lion stalking "a white woman, neither old nor young, and she had lost one of her shoes" (13). And this is followed, again without warning, by what seems to be some sort of Christian allegory until the "dark man with thick matted curls that hung down till they became a beard" (14) dismounts to kick his donkey in the genitals, hops round to hit it between the eyes, then sticks his fist under his armpit to dull the pain, whereupon "the donkey turned to look at him with an air of christ-like forbearance" (15). Jarring as these combinations are, certain details within each episode also confound our expectations: nothing is what it seems to be. This is particularly true of the next sequence, in which Jane is described, in purple Barbara-Cartlandese, "sitting at her toilette, as she called it in the French manner, dreaming of might-have-beens". Tricked by that turn of phrase, we envision a former world, London at "the height of the Season", and our golden heroine sighing in her boudoir. A rider approaches; Marie, the French maid, announces Monsieur Jones; the weeping Jane begs her to tell him she is not at home. Only after the importunate suitor has shot away the lock do we realize that Jane sits on the toilet, and Romance comes crashing down with the bathroom door.

Then, having returned us to Mr Moon (still interviewing himself), Stoppard describes the journey of the runaway coach so as to link the previous episodes into a more coherent shape, although why Moon should clutch a bomb and ride in a pink carriage through rows of parked cars has still to be divulged. The coach swerves right (shouldn't that read "left"?) along Piccadilly, and a protesting wall of oncoming traffic parts before it as a woman totters out from the colonnade of the Ritz Hotel and into Green Park: "'Laura!' shouted the ninth earl. 'Pull yourself together and go home!'" But Lady Malquist falls to the ground; "a long yellow animal" emerges from behind a bush, sniffs at her, and runs off: "'Rollo!' shouted the ninth early joyfully . . . 'she's found Rollo.'" Plunging against the one-way traffic of Park Lane, the coach sends two taxis careering into a bus: "From the ensuing fragmentation of glass and steel there bolted, with a completeness and an air of instant creation that suggested to Moon divine responsibility, a donkey with a white-robed rider sitting on its back" (21). Eventually, the galloping greys pull up beside a third horse tethered to the railings of a house in a mews off South Street. In the drawing-room lies Jane who may, for a moment, be taken for Malquist's mistress. But the elegant house is Moon's, the lady his wife, and the new puzzlement also his as he sees her stretched semi-naked upon a couch beside a kneeling cowboy, Jasper Jones, "rubbing cream into her left buttock".

If Moon never knows whether to believe Jane's story about having bruised herself when she fell in the bathroom, the reader never can be quite certain about what goes on *chez* Moon. "Dislocation of an audience's assumptions is an important part of what I like to write", Stoppard once told an interviewer; "I'm fascinated by the correspondence between easy stereotypes and truth."[8] Jane shares her name with the busty blonde heroine of a comic-strip which ran for years in the *Daily Mirror*. The cartoon shows Jane in the tightest of clothing or more usually in little or nothing; enticing though she may appear, she herself behaves with an innocent disregard for appearances. For his Jane, Stoppard elaborates upon the possibilities of this stereotype. At first she appears less than innocent, calculating the effect of her dishabille upon her visitors, and later she is discovered in a number of compromising situations with Malquist. On the other hand, her apology "that you should find me in this awfully undone state" (22) may be more innocent than its wording, and Malquist may in fact *be* testing her right breast for cancer, reading her fortune from the creases in her navel, or sharing the simple pleasures of a hot bath. What is certain is Jane's childlike nature. She also had a "terrible" family and suffers from epilepsy, the throes of which are made to appear like erotic frenzy. So her behaviour may be the result of sexual frustration, or a way to gain attention, or simply childlike innocence; whatever the case, the novel implies that the truth of her character is somewhat sadder than the outwardly comic stereotype suggests.

The comedy surrounding Marie has no such undertones. Stoppard plays with the naughty-postcard image of the French Maid to point up the deceptiveness of words as well as appearances. Moon's feelings towards her veer between the avuncular and the lascivious: " 'I'm glad you're living in my house because you are so – simple.' In a minute he would have to eat her. 'I mean, you're [*sic*] breasts are so *little* and –' *That is not what I meant at all*' (27). But Marie is not so "simple". Moon answers the phone to a man enquiring about her advertisement: "French lessons. Corrective." Oblivious to the possibility that this may be a prostitute's euphemism for sexual punishment, Moon tells him that Marie is not available (74). When the man asks if anyone else is there, Moon suggests Jane, although she only knows the French she learned at school; at this, the caller insists that "I'm all right, don't you worry" (not someone from the police). When Moon asks the caller's name, the man, after a garbled attempt, plumps "fiercely" for Brown, and we recall Moon's earlier memory of the friend at school who used to make indecent phone calls:

> One of his victims cunningly pretended interest in some obscene suggestion and asked for the caller's name, and Smith blurted out, "My name is Brown." There was a nuance in that which Moon had tried to pin down for years. (54)

The deceptive oddities of language fascinate Stoppard, too. Marie, who actually spends half the novel lying dead beneath a couch, is at one point accused of being a voyeur:

> "My dear Jane, we were sitting right on top of her. She could not possibly have seen anything to afford her any gratification, unless she's a foot-fetishist."
> "She was listening," said Jane.
> "An *écouteuse*! What a deliciously subtle refinement!" (48)

Sounds and sights prove so ambiguous at South Street, what with "uncles" arriving to see Marie and a General who wants to take photographs "at the usual rates", that they convince the donkey-man (if not the reader) he is in a brothel.

Much of the novel's verve evolves from the fun Stoppard has with stock characters and situations, subverting those hackneyed images and his readers' expectations: "What I like to do is take a stereotype and betray it.... All my best characters are clichés."9 L. J. and Jasper, it turns out, are not cowboys at all; they dress that way, as do several other clones, to represent "the Hungriest Gun in the West man with the porkiest beans straight out of the can" (158). But in having both of them play out that persona for real, Stoppard entertains us with every conceivable permutation of the Western while tripping up these two guns-for-hire with the ineptitude of their actual non-cowboy selves. The pair "mosey" through London, vie for the favours of "Fertility Jane", and talk (when they remember) with an excruciating Texas drawl, but their saddle-bags bulge with cans of beans, their maladjusted spurs play havoc with their inside legs, and their aim is inaccurate, though lethal, during their final hilarious shoot-out in Trafalgar Square. They also view the novel's other peculiarly dressed characters as potential interlopers on their sales-territory: "I don't care what you're selling, just piss off" (22). Apparently there are other salesmen at large in London. The fat lady who falls victim to Malquist's equipage recognizes the ninth earl as "Mr San, the Toilet Tissue Man, and I claim the five pounds". In that she is mistaken, for Mr Moon, in his dazed wanderings, stumbles upon a second pink coach with "a roll of pink toilet paper lying on the seat" (149).

The novel also admits more serious reasons for exploding a stereotype. To satirize the way prepackaged images so often lead to prejudice and bigotry, Stoppard creates O'Hara, Malquist's mustard-liveried coachman, out of a number of contradictory clichés whose collision defies all stock response. Having heard Malquist's remarks about his servant's cockney wit, Moon has unconsciously prepared himself for either a Sam Weller or, given the fact that O'Hara is Catholic and smokes a stubby pipe, someone "Irish, boozy and fat". O'Hara's defiantly music-hall-Jewish idiom disturbs Moon less than the sudden discovery that the coachman is black. Caught off guard by the collapse of all his presuppositions, Moon feels the way he used to as a schoolboy, after football, when he would find himself stuck half in and half out of his tight sweater and fighting to find some air-hole. In similar panic, he pours out a torrent of racial insults which are themselves the clichés of white hatred and fear. Then, pulling himself together, Moon apologizes:

"If I'd had time to prepare my words I would have given the other side too. I can see both sides . . . I distrust attitudes . . . because they claim to have appropriated the whole truth and pose as absolutes. And I distrust the opposite attitude for the same reason."   (52–3)

But this Jewish-accented black Irish Catholic has his own prejudices. Taking one look at the Risen Christ, he ignores the latter's stage-Irish patois and pronounces him "a Yid". Christ's Reincarnation has convinced himself of his identity because, though he does not fit the picture-book image of a tall, blue-eyed Jesus, "a class of a Russian of the name of Josephus" (he confuses the Jewish historian with Joseph S[talin]?) described Him as "a little dark feller . . . with a hook nose and eyebrows that met in the middle" (40). He also claims to have the stigmata. Though his palm is unscarred, he screams when Moon presses it with his thumb. So his claim may be true or it may not be, or perhaps the Risen Christ was once one of the two thieves, or one of the many anonymous thousands crucified by the Romans, or "Then again, it could be fibrositis" (41).

Because of the novel's many deceiving mirrors, it would be a mistake to see Mr Moon as a self-portrait. Although Stoppard has admitted "I'm a Moon myself",[10] he endows his protagonist with the same irony that colours his other characters. On occasions we move into Moon's mind and so get nearest to him, and many of his thoughts express views that Stoppard himself has subscribed to in interviews,[11] but we are also distanced from him by a self-dramatizing *Angst* that makes him a figure of fun. Moon is like Gladys Jenkins in having glimpsed the void; he too cannot look away nor can he cope with that vision. Moon's particular trouble is "the multitude". Overwhelmed by a feeling of people and things multiplying and expanding, he awaits the moment when modern civilization will go bang. So he clutches his mad Uncle Jackson's home-made bomb, determined to fight fire with fire and bring the world to its senses before it reaches its own explosion point. Stoppard objectifies Moon's profusely bleeding heart by having him accidentally cut himself on tins or broken glass so that, battered and bloody, he hobbles into Trafalgar Square where his idea of a ballooning creation which must eventually pop comes true in a comically literal way. As the bomb reaches the end of its twelve-hour time fuse, Moon hears a music-box tinkling the National Anthem; out of his uncle's toy comes an enormous balloon: "printed across its girth in black letters which expanded with it, a two-word message – familiar, unequivocal and obscene". *Go–od save* – the music-box reaches *Queen* and the balloon explodes: "A few people, obscurely moved, began to applaud" (165). Moon, then, is inadequate and paralysed, a comic exaggeration of a certain aspect of his creator, particularly evidenced by their shared delight in arguing both sides of an issue: "But I take both parts . . . leapfrogging myself along the great moral issues, refuting myself and rebutting the refutation towards a truth . . . And you never reach it because there is always something more to say" (53).[12]

In Lord Malquist, Stoppard argues the other side of many of Moon's attitudes, but both characters present half-truths and both parody Stoppard's own ideas. For the ninth earl, the multitude lack shape: "I long to impose some aesthetic discipline on them, re-arrange them into art" (10). Whereas Moon considers he stands for "substance" in opposing the ever-proliferating awfulness of mankind, Malquist retreats above the common herd into Style, a posture which exaggerates into egotistic dilettantism Stoppard's tongue-in-cheek remarks about his own stance as stylish dilettante. Compared with his creator's distrust of polemics – "I must stop compromising my plays with this whiff of social application . . . I should have the courage of my lack of convictions"[13] – Malquist's non-commitment stems, not from a knowledge that all attitudes are relative, but from the fact that "I am not frightfully interested in anything, except myself." Malquist is a hollow man. Though on occasion he can talk like a Yellow Book aesthete as, for example, when he discusses the colour scheme of various prospective coachmen, his contempt for humanity marks him as a relic of the *ancien régime*. If Moon feels too much, Malquist considers emotion a breach of good manners: "Since we cannot hope for order let us withdraw with style from the chaos" (21). However, behind that pose, Falcon, Earl of Malquist is as rapacious as his Christian name suggests; but his emotions are aroused only by his desire to stamp his mark on the English language, as Lord Sandwich or the Duke of Wellington did, so that his studied calm ruffles when the newspaper reports of his collision fail to describe his coach as a malquist. The ninth earl represents the stylist as victimizer and predatory egotist.

Viewed as a whole, the novel spins off on too many tangents. Stoppard finds great sport in trying on different hats, exuberantly switching from style to style, but he often pursues a joke for its own sake.[14] For instance, Moon, in search of a bottle of Scotch for Lady Malquist, comes across Birdboot, the butler, ironing *The Times*. When the latter protests at Moon's raid on a locked cupboard in the pantry, the two burst into a quick parody of P. G. Wodehouse (133). At times like these, Moon seems too self-assured and self-consciously literary to square with the earnest, confused bungler who has got no farther than the first line of his history of the world. Moon's role in the novel makes consistent sense, but his voice becomes difficult to place since it frequently overlaps with that of the omniscient narrator, and this presents a major problem.

Nevertheless, Stoppard does see the need for strong central threads to hold together the web of conflicting viewpoints. One of these is the state funeral of Winston Churchill, during which all the principal characters unintentionally tangle with each other in Trafalgar Square. Although the statesman is never actually named, the crowds gathered outside the dying man's house in Hyde Park Gate and the description of the procession itself reflect the events of January 1965. Those mourning crowds confirm Moon's vision of sprawling humanity, and on the day of Churchill's death, Malquist, writing to confirm Moon's appointment as biographer, sees the passing of an age when history was shaped by dedicated men of action:

"For this reason, his death might well mark a change in the heroic posture – to that of the Stylist, the spectator as hero, the man of inaction who would not dare roll up his sleeves for fear of creasing the cuffs." (79)

It is on the afternoon of the funeral that Moon is blown to pieces by an authentic anarchist.

The streets and parks of London, between Moon's house off South Street and Malquist's in Queen Anne's Gate, also provide a unity. Characteristically, Moon, with his passion for order and symmetry, ponders the relationship between one triangular area of land and another: "the labyrinthine riddle of London's streets might be subjected to a single mathematical formula, one of such sophistication that it would relate the whole hopeless mess into a coherent logic" (122). Malquist sees only the passing landmarks of himself:

the shop where he bought his braces; South Street, home of Beau Brummell. But the main effect of Stoppard's meticulous topography is to create a surreal counterpoint between the realistic, detailed landscape and the extraordinary figures who people it. London also reminds him of one glorious pun, so he makes Moon hobble past "the statue of Napier who captured Sind and sent back the message *Peccavi* [I have sinned]" (151).

A third motif, taken both directly and by implication from T. S. Eliot, weaves its way across and under the novel's surface. In burlesquing certain lines from "The Lovesong of J. Alfred Prufrock", Stoppard links Moon's stumbling protests against his world to the confusions and anti-heroics of which Prufrock is the modern archetype. Moon is himself partially aware of the parallel:

> (That is not it at all,
> that is not what I meant at all.

> But when I've got it in a formulated phrase, when I've got it formulated, sprawling on a pin, when it is pinned and wriggling on the wall, then how should I begin . . . ?)
> *And how should you presume?*   (23–4)

Later, while his bomb's time-fuse ticks away, he remembers with ironic appropriateness a line from *The Waste Land*: "Hurry up please, it's time." Alerted by these quotations, the reader makes still further connections. Moon's bomb represents his own attempt to squeeze "the universe into a ball / To roll it toward some overwhelming question"; but whereas Prufrock does not dare to put that question into words, Moon has either been asked the wrong questions all his life or cannot find the right words to answer the overwhelming question. Though "he would be presumptuous" (24), daring to press the time-fuse, he is still beset by "a hundred visions and revisions" because of the arbitrary nature of reality. And as he dances attendance on Lord Malquist and Jane, bleeds his way across London to retrieve Lady Malquist's lost shoe, or joins the crowd at Churchill's funeral, Moon comes to typify Prufrockian inadequacy: the "attendant lord" who is not Prince Hamlet but "almost, at times, the Fool". *The Waste Land*, too, has a general relevance to Moon's vision of a chaotic, degraded universe, and Stoppard's piecing together of quotation and parody could be considered a comic equivalent of Eliot's technique. Particular details from the poem also are reflected in the novel: the crowded city, Lord Malquist's fortune-telling, Lady Malquist's neurotic boredom, Jane's seduction in a punt on the Serpentine, the three pistol shots that thunder out in Trafalgar Square. But all these borrowings and distortions have been worked into Stoppard's own version of a sliding world in which all truths are relative and where eyes and ears deceive.

Lord Malquist and Mr Moon is his first walk on the water, but by early 1967 Stoppard's name was still not one to conjure with. The novel had sold only a few hundred copies,[15] the plays had not been seen on the London stage, and after the Royal Shakespeare Company had let their option lapse on *Rosencrantz and Guildenstern Are Dead*, Stoppard's agent had agreed to release the script to an Oxford student group who wanted to perform it on the "Fringe" of the 1966 Edinburgh Festival. What happened next reads like a Stoppard scenario, for what at first looked like one thing turned out to be its opposite:

The play was done in a church hall on a flat floor so that people couldn't actually see it. There was no scenery, student actors. The director didn't show up. Someone else filled in. I turned up for thirty-six hours and tried to put a few things right. It went on in some kind of state or other. . . .[16]

The production opened to tepid reviews, but on the Sunday, Ronald Bryden of the *Observer* singled it out as an "erudite comedy, punning, far-fetched, leaping from depth to dizziness . . . It's the most brilliant debut by a young playwright since John Arden's."[17] Had Bryden not had the acumen to see through to the text despite the performance's inadequacies, then, according to Stoppard, "I would have been said to have failed as a writer, with the same text . . . It's a nonsense."[18] Within a week of that momentous review, the National Theatre had acquired the rights to the play. After six years of trial and error, Stoppard achieved "overnight" success with the opening of the London production in April 1967.

Since then, the play has been the subject of all sorts of critical interpretations, notably as a statement of existential or absurdist intent or as a serious critique of Shakespeare's *Hamlet*, and those views have led to what might be called the *Catch 22* of Stoppardian criticism: his theatrical fireworks masquerade as important ideas; his important ideas are trivialized by theatrical trickery. The fallacy behind this comes from supposing that frivolity and seriousness are incompatible opposites (and Stoppard has always sought to unite the two) or, in the particular case of *Rosencrantz*, to mistake the farcical framework (derived from *Waiting for Godot* and *Hamlet*) as the play's serious thesis. What Stoppard does is to exploit the comic potential of Ros and Guil's situation in *Hamlet*, a confused paralysis most cogently expressed in modern terms by Estragon and Vladimir's circumstances in *Godot*, in order to arrive at a statement about death that is both serious and of universal application.

The reason such a strategy proves so difficult to come to terms with lies in the inadequacy of language. 'A play' has come to be understood as a very different experience from 'to play', which has overtones of an escape from serious business. And that distinction is particularly prevalent in Anglo-Saxon society, which separates the serious business of culture from the mindless pleasures of popular entertainment. Yet it is perfectly possible to play with ideas to serious intent – scientists and publicity men even make that their business – just as 'to play with' someone has different shades of meaning depending on whether the players are footballers or political opponents. Similarly, in Stoppard's work, games are not superficial, either for the author, his characters, or his audience, and *Rosencrantz* stands poised between both terms when described as "a serious play".

In that context, the genesis of *Rosencrantz* proves instructive. To cheer Stoppard on the drive back from an abortive conference that saw the refusal of *Samuel Boot*, Kenneth Ewing happened to remark that he had often wondered which king of England received Claudius' letter commanding Hamlet's destruction; keeping to the Shakespeare canon, was it Lear or Cymbeline? By the end of the ride, Stoppard was playing with the idea of *Rosencrantz and Guildenstern at the Court of King Lear*.[19] Some weeks later, Stoppard took up residence in West Berlin as the recipient of a Ford Foundation grant and developed that playful "What if Ros and Guil were to meet . . .?" into a one-act comedy which was given a single performance at the end of his six months' tenure. Encouraged by his colleagues to pursue the idea, Stoppard expanded the play into two Acts on his return to England. Like Mr Moon, who discovered that straightening his tie was "the culminating act of a sequence that fled back into pre-history and began with the shift of a glacier", Stoppard found himself moving steadily backwards into the two courtiers' history in order to explain their arrival in Britain:

The interesting thing was them at Elsinore . . . By this time I was not in the least interested in doing any sort of pastiche, for a start, or in doing a criticism of *Hamlet* – that was simply one of the by-products. The chief interest and objective was to exploit a situation which seemed to me to have enormous dramatic and comic potential – of these two guys who in Shakespeare's context don't really know what they're doing. The little they are told is mainly lies, and there's no reason to suppose that they ever find out why they are killed. And, probably more in the early 1960s than at any other time, that would strike a young playwright as being a pretty good thing to explore. I mean, it has the right combination of specificity and vague generality . . . That's why, when the play appeared, it got subjected to so many different kinds of interpretation, all of them plausible, but none of them calculated.[20]

What he did intend, he explains in the same interview, was "to entertain a roomful of people" with the combination of the two courtiers and the events at Elsinore; to do that, he sought "to inject some sort of interest and colour into every line, rather than counting on the general situation having a general interest . . ." That last remark discloses the lure of his fatal siren, for the play is overloaded with comic business and is consequently too long, but though the entertainment appears unrelenting until the last few minutes, it does not trivialize Stoppard's ideas.

One of the pleasures of a game is to pit oneself against a set of rules or conventions. The rule book here is *Hamlet*, and everyone knows the game except Ros and Guil, for should there be anyone in the theatre unfamiliar with Shakespeare's play, Stoppard's title supplies him with the crucial information. Ros and Guil are dead, even before the play begins:

PLAYER: There's a design at work in all art – surely you know that? Events must play themselves out to aesthetic, moral and logical conclusion.
GUIL: And what's that, in this case?
PLAYER: It never varies – we aim at the point where everyone who is marked for death dies.
GUIL: Marked?
PLAYER: Between "just desserts" and "tragic irony" we are given quite a lot of scope for our particular talent. Generally speaking, things have gone about as far as they can possibly go when things have got about as bad as they reasonably get. (*He switches on a smile.*)
GUIL: Who decides?
PLAYER (*switching off his smile*): Decides? It is *written.*[21]

But though the two courtiers know they are part of a game, they have not read this particular rule book; all they know is that they have been picked as part of the team.

So when we come upon them they are somewhere on the road to Elsinore, unsure as to directions, in the middle of a game of their own. But even this coin-tossing, while granting them some sense of purpose, defies the rules by which they expected to play when Heads comes up for the seventy-fifth time. This astonishingly simple image presents what seems to be a chance-ridden world and immediately distinguishes the one courtier from the other. Ros "is nice enough to feel a little embarrassed at taking so much money off his friend" but is not at all surprised at this unusual run of Heads (7). Guil, on the other hand, "is well alive to the oddity of it", and the chasm which those thoughts open up in front of him fills him with dread. To allay that fear, he searches somewhat despairingly for a logical pattern that will pull the coin-tossing back under the known rules; "One: I'm willing it . . . Two: time has stopped dead . . . Three: divine intervention" (10–11).

From their point of view – though Ros directs more thought to his toenails – the progress of their lives has no causal connection; they remember "a royal summons", but what comes next? When logic fails, Guil instigates a number of other games with which to bridge the chasm. Falling back on their intelligence ("being of so young days brought up with" a Prince), they try abstract word-play – anything to prove they have control over events. But they are not in control. When the Player and his troupe meet up with them, he confirms their feeling of being participants: "I recognized you at once . . . as fellow artists" (16). Once in Elsinore, other players come at them from all directions. Oddly, the pair know *how* to play, responding to their parts in the Shakespearean dialogue, but they do not know *what* they are playing. Eventually, like Gladys or Alfred's Constance, they prefer not to choose. Finding themselves with Hamlet on the boat to England, they can safely float with the tide, holding their position, as Guil puts it, "until the music starts" (72). But then the music does start. At the sound of a band, the theatrical players pop out of their barrel, the unknown game continues, and the boat has become a trap: "our movement is contained within a larger one . . ." (89).

From their own little corner, in which one thing obstinately refuses to lead to the next, Ros and Guil share the predicament of the two tramps in *Waiting for Godot*. But their world is not in fact an absurd one. Because we enter the theatre knowing the outcome of Ros and Guil's lives, the audience share the viewpoint of Godot – whoever he is! In the Beckett play there can be no answers; Godot may or may not exist and may or may not arrive; we know no more about him than do Vladimir and Estragon. In the Stoppard play, life only seems absurd because of the limitations of one's own particular angle. The audience who know *Hamlet* know the game Ros and Guil have to play and are assured, as is Shakespeare, that "There's a divinity that shapes our ends, / Rough-hew them how we will." Nevertheless, as part of his game plan for *Rosencrantz*, Stoppard dangles a second rule book before us, the script of *Godot*, at the same time that he invites us to perceive the differences between his pair of attendants and Beckett's. For the latter, time *has* stopped still, at least until Act 2, when Vladimir sees the leaves on the tree and recognizes Estragon's discarded boots and Lucky's hat. By the end of the play, Vladimir has acknowledged the truth in Pozzo's remark about being born astride the grave and, knowing that "we have time to grow old", is prepared to go on. But whereas *Godot* presents us with an entrapping circle, or a spiral at best, *Rosencrantz* is linear. Ros and Guil may sometimes behave like their *alter egos*, but a known end, execution by the British king, lies in wait for them, and the fact that a royal summons has led them from one step to the next gives their death a kind of sense.

Also the games they play while waiting for that end are not simply a means to fill time, and here Stoppard resolves a problem that *Godot* fails to answer. While, from a superior viewpoint, our little lives may seem purposeless as we busy ourselves between birth and death, from our *own* point of view that busyness seems both purposeful and genuinely diverting. Consequently, Ros and Guil are far more articulate and intelligent than their counterparts in *Godot*. Admittedly the two lords have been to the right school, but they also reflect our idea of the joys we find between womb and tomb. It is crucial to the meaning of the play that we should recognize both of them as fellow human beings, and the major problem with the parallels Stoppard constructs between his own play and *Godot* occurs when he has them forget their own names. In Beckett, the characters can answer to any name because a crazy world has robbed them of a sense of identity, but from an empirical perspective, when ordinary people feel so threatened and lost they tend to cling to their individuality; one's name is the essence of that self. So although the confusion between Ros and Guil also makes sense in terms of Shakespeare's text, since they are non-entities to the King and Queen and (in Stoppard) even to their former companion, Hamlet, that they should forget their own names fails to ring true.

Stoppard uses *Godot* as part of the game he plays with the audience, juxtaposing its rules with those of *Hamlet*. Until one understands that intention, *Rosencrantz* may seem to be Beckett diluted and sentimentalized; it has none of *Godot*'s taut spareness. But in the theatre we respond almost totally to the garrulous niceness of the two courtiers. We laugh at their confusion, from our omniscient vantage point, but we also acknowledge ourselves in them, and what starts out as an amusing evening at the expense of two friends ends with a sense of personal loss. That final empathy is essential if, after all the game playing has ended, we are to experience their deaths for ourselves:

Dying is not romantic, and death is not a game which will soon be over . . . Death is not anything . . . death is not . . . It's the absence of presence, nothing more . . . the endless time of never coming back . . . a gap you can't see, and when the wind blows through it, it makes no sound . . .   (90–1)

It has often been argued that in making his pair so likable Stoppard has been unfaithful to Shakespeare's concept. In *Hamlet* they are mere henchmen who betray their past friendship with the Prince, though they are too transparent ever to pose a threat to him. So expendable as to have been omitted from some productions of the play, so colourless as to have become theatrical bywords for anonymity, if we think about their personalities at all we can but agree with Hamlet's verdict: "Why, man, they did make love to this employment! / They are not near my conscience." Those who are fool enough to step between two powerful opponents deserve whatever they get. Villains by association with the corruption of Elsinore, Shakespeare's pair are at their worst in their first scene with Hamlet, when they fail to respond frankly to his appeal to "deal justly with me", and again after the entry of the players with recorders, which prompts Hamlet to accuse Guildenstern of thinking "I am easier to be played on than a pipe". To achieve his own more attractive ends, Stoppard concludes his Act 1 just as Hamlet first greets the pair, and when we return after the interval we hear only the final phrases of that interview. He omits the second episode completely, although some of the recorder lines are transposed to the sea voyage. Having established the convention whereby episodes from *Hamlet* come and go, Stoppard does not actually break the rules of his game; instead, he shows Shakespeare's home team playing away.

Though Ros and Guil can never be at home, we are their supporters, and it is through them that we come to feel what death is. We know they must die as must we, but like us they behave as if that were not the case. So inured are we to mortality that we have erased the moment when we first understood. As the Player tells Guil, "Relax. Respond. That's what people do. You can't go through life questioning your situation at every turn" (47). Yet when they do think of death they can only do so in terms of the living. In his jokey way, Ros rehearses the irrational fears of us all:

I mean, you'd never *know* you were in a box, would you? It would be just like being *asleep* in a box. Not that I'd like to sleep in a box, mind you, not without any air – you'd wake up dead, . . . (50)

As events finally close in on them, their reaction is a human "Why me?" They voice the self-pity we also feel regarding "the endless time of never coming back". We shall miss us.

Death is terrifying because it rarely makes sense. If we can perceive a pattern then there are certain consolations or platitudes: "light goes with life, and in the winter of your years the dark comes early". But when death seems arbitrary we can only react with a sense of injustice and fear at the reminder of our own vulnerability. We know all this, and Stoppard does not pretend to teach us anything. He plays with ideas we usually put away from us and then makes us live through "the absence of presence". When, after some three hours, Ros and Guil simply disappear and the entire stage immediately lights up to reveal the final tableau from *Hamlet*, we care nothing about those noble corpses and are angered by the final two Shakespearean speeches in which Ros and Guil are dismissed in a single line. This is death's "human position", the sense that things go on without regard to one's own important dramas. As Auden's "Musée des Beaux Arts" puts it:

> About suffering they were never wrong,
> The Old Masters: how well they understood
> Its human position: . . .

> They never forgot
> That even the dreadful martyrdom must run its course
> Anyhow in a corner, some untidy spot
> Where the dogs go on with their doggy life and the torturer's horse
> Scratches its innocent behind on a tree.

Behind the humour of *Rosencrantz* lies a genuine compassion, and the subtlety with which Stoppard works upon his audiences' emotions lifts the play's ideas out of the commonplace. In *Hamlet*, the skull beneath the skin becomes a metaphor for the corruption of a court where "one may smile, and smile, and be a villain". In Stoppard's play, death is an abrupt exit from one's own drama into a place incomprehensibly other, and the theatre itself becomes a metaphor for that. "Faith in one's uniqueness dies hard", says Mr Moon, and Ros and Guil, summoned to play parts they cannot predict, are made self-consciously aware that they are players on a stage, and their desire to remain so "dies hard".

Guil's first line, after five calls of "Heads" from Ros, immediately implants that theatricality: "There is an art to the building up of suspense." And at points throughout the play Stoppard breaks our sense of illusion to remind us that we are in a theatre watching actors. For example, after first meeting Hamlet, Ros and Guil discuss "his illuminating claim to tell a hawk from a handsaw . . . When the wind is southerly" (41). Seeking for their bearings, in several senses of the word, the pair move down to the front of the bare stage; Ros licks his finger, holds it up to the air, and the two stare out at the audience. In that embarrassing pause, we experience the anomaly between an empty, indoor stage and the demands the actors make of it. From where they stand, the auditorium "doesn't *look* southerly"; from where we sit, Guil's ramblings around the stage-space, as he wonders about the direction of the sun, do not look as though they happen in the open world. As the pair then make clear, the only wind comes up through the floorboards, stages are notoriously draughty places, and any lingering sense of illusion vanishes when, after a lengthy silence,

(. . . ROS *leaps up and bellows at the audience.*)

ROS: Fire!

(GUIL *jumps up.*)

GUIL: Where?

ROS: It's all right – I'm demonstrating the misuse of free speech. To prove that it exists. (*He regards the audience, that is the direction, with contempt – and other directions, then front again.*) Not a move. They should burn to death in their shoes. (43)

An estranging device like this not only emphasizes the way one's own drama appears differently to others, and allows us sufficient detachment to consider that truism, but it points up the nature of drama itself and the oddity in the fact that we should find pleasure in going to the theatre to watch life and death at work.

Like actors, all individuals need an audience. While waiting for the other characters to "come pouring in from every side", Ros and Guil improvise with each other, but were they to find themselves entirely alone, despite the fact that contact with others leads to a series of "obscure instructions . . . messing us about from here to breakfast" (62), their lives would hold no meaning at all. Even though the Player claims that "We're *actors* – we're the opposite of people" (45), Stoppard makes us see Ros and Guil as both actors and people. The moments of overt theatricality ensure this, as do certain moments which temporarily halt our sympathies and stop us from entirely losing ourselves in the pair as people until the dénouement. Our empathy towards them is not a sudden emotional outpouring but a process in which we give ourselves to them by degrees during the play, holding back whenever their cries of bewilderment become overinflated or when they use rhetoric to persuade themselves to dishonest ends such as allowing Hamlet to go to certain death. Because of that fluctuating state, our final and total empathy with the pair is neither uncritical nor sentimental.

These tensions between detachment and attachment are similar to those which, at any play, allow us to bear and find pleasure in the sight of death on the stage. The remarkable thing about *Rosencrantz* is that it leads us intellectually through all the peculiarities of staged death yet still causes us to surrender to it emotionally. "There's nothing more unconvincing than an unconvincing death", says the Player, and yet if we *were* to be entirely convinced we would run screaming from the theatre. We remain there because at the back of our minds we have agreed to certain conventions, and it is only when those are broken that the imitation of death becomes un- or too convincing. What we expect is that the action on stage should have a convincing level of reality, a delicate balance between the unreal and the too real.

Staged death must be clean so that we may see in it a pattern, an appropriateness, which we rarely perceive in actuality. If there are no jarring details in the rhythms of the actor or in his dying words, we are able to emote towards him while remaining subconsciously assured, under the agreed conventions, that the actor will get up afterwards and live to do the whole thing another day. If the performance appears exaggerated in a mechanical way, we detach ourselves completely and laugh. If it appears bloody, that delicate balance tips towards complete attachment and we react in horror. However, a complicating factor, as anyone who has been to a schools' matinée knows, is that the level of reality differs from one member of an audience to another. *Hamlet* offers a good example of this. Claudius brings to the performance of the play-within-the-play his own perceptions; he is the only member of the court who has experienced murder "i' th' garden", and so he finds the players' imitation too real and calls for lights.

A further complication stems from the actor and the way he presents death's picture. To enable an audience to remain safe in their seats, the actor must present death neatly. He must achieve a degree of objectivity; that is what rehearsals are for, so that, while he dies, a part of him consciously draws death in lines that seem both elegant and substantial:

GUIL (*fear, derision*): Actors! The mechanics of cheap melodrama! That isn't *death*! (*More quietly*) You scream and choke and sink to your knees, but it doesn't bring death home to anyone . . . You die so many times; how can you expect them to believe in your death?

PLAYER: On the contrary, it's the only kind they do believe. They're conditioned to it. I had an actor once who was condemned to hang for stealing a sheep – or a lamb, I forget which – so I got permission to have him hanged in the middle of a play – had to change the plot a bit but I thought it would be effective, you know – and you wouldn't believe it, he just *wasn't* convincing! It was impossible to suspend one's disbelief – and what with the audience jeering and throwing peanuts, the whole thing was a *disaster*! – he did nothing but cry all the time – right out of character – just stood there and cried . . .   (61)

The condemned actor, suspended from his rope, could not feel objective; unable to suspend his belief in what was about to happen, he performed without the artifice that would have made his death seem real to his audience. The ironies of that naturally appeal to Stoppard, for here again point of view is everything. The credibility of an acted death depends upon the perceptions that both the actor and each member of the audience bring to it.

Consequently, as Guil becomes increasingly aware that some disaster awaits him, he grows less tolerant of the actors' played-out versions of death which do not square with his new perception of its reality:

No, no, no . . . you've got it all wrong . . . you can't act death. The *fact* of it is nothing to do with seeing it happen – it's not gasps and blood and falling about – that isn't what makes it death. It's just a man failing to reappear, that's all – now you see him, now you don't, that's the only thing that's real: here one minute and gone the next and never coming back – an exit, unobtrusive and unannounced, a disappearance gathering weight as it goes on, until, finally, it is heavy with death. (61–2)

Death for him means the pain and loss to those who survive. In Act 3, after having read the letter which condemns him to death, Guil experiences the pain of his own abrupt and final exit with an "intensity which squeezes out life . . . and [his] blood runs cold" (89) with a terror he thinks no actor could convey. In rage, he pushes on the dagger he has been holding to the Player's throat. The actor staggers and falls, and, for a moment, Guil thinks he has killed him – so do the audience until the Tragedians applaud and the Player rises to take a modest bow. In spite of his former protests, Guil believes in the Player's death because he believes in the dagger, and the Player acts in a way that answers those expectations; Guil was not to know that the dagger, a stage property, had a retractable blade. At the same time, the audience also suspend their disbelief, suddenly caught up by the actor's skilful gestures, which match their expectations of what dying should look like. In the daring theatricality of this moment, Stoppard makes us live through the illusion despite all the play's reminders that it *is* just an illusion. Then as Ros and Guil make their final abrupt exit, "Now you see me, now you –", we are left to bear the weight of loss and to experience the pain of absence that Guil has identified as death.

The whole play exemplifies, in a sympathetic way, the egoism which causes us to fear death. When we think of dying, we think of what it is like to lose a friend or of how much worse it would be to lose ourselves. If death is absence, absence is also a kind of death: Hamlet has disappeared, so he is 'dead' as far as Ros and Guil are concerned, or they are, from his point of view (86–7). The collision between the muddled striving of Ros and Guil and the purposefulness of those at Elsinore dramatizes that sense of life's going on without us which makes the thought of death so painful. As the pair stumble their way through the court, they try to obey Claudius' vague instructions concerning Hamlet, "glean what afflicts him". To do that effectively, they try to pick up whatever clues they can in order to feel themselves masters of the situation – secure at the centre of their lives. But the other characters keep on coming at them from the wings, talking purposefully, making demands on them, leaving them with the feeling that the centre of events lies elsewhere, and it is that feeling that the audience are left with at the play's end, when Ros and Guil are dead and the survivors at Elsinore only concern themselves with state affairs.

The action on stage punches home a sense of injustice which we share with the two lost wanderers. Lighting changes and the sudden shifts from the contemporary to the Shakespearean mode lurch us from one world to another in as unsettling a way as that experienced by Ros and Guil. That we, who know *Hamlet*, are able to interpret the invading action may make the situation somewhat less terrifying, but we too are jolted by the Player's all-knowing attitude (in the original production at the Old Vic his tone and manner were peculiarly sinister), and by the alarm that grips Ros and Guil when the characters from *Hamlet* bear down on them, smoothly and determinedly, and then sail off again. The pair simply cannot control the traffic, even when they act like policemen:

ROS: (*. . . wheels again to face into the wings*) Keep out, then! I forbid anyone to enter! (*No one comes – Breathing heavily.*) That's better . . . (*Immediately, behind him a grand procession enters . . .*) (52)

Yet in spite of the seeming inconsequence of their lives and our sympathy with the pair's bewilderment, from a wider angle *Rosencrantz* presumes a coherent world. In Elizabethan tragedy, death had greater significance than the Player (via Wilde's Miss Prism) would allow: "The bad end unhappily, the good unluckily. That is what tragedy means" (58). Hamlet's death makes sense, unlucky though it is, because it is the logical outcome of the step-by-step progression of the previous action: "There's a design at work in all art", as the Player also says. Tragedy explains death, making it part of a coherent pattern which one rarely perceives in actuality, and Hamlet's death, if undeserved, proceeds in a satisfying way out of a hard-won self-knowledge. Unable to cope emotionally with his father's murder and his mother's o'erhasty and incestuous marriage to the murderer, Hamlet has busied himself with elaborate plans to test the ghost's veracity and Claudius' guilt. But by the final Act, though Horatio offers him a perfectly reasonable excuse to avoid the duel with Laertes, Hamlet has come to the realization that he must meet the fate that cried out to him when the apparition of his murdered father first appeared. He goes to his death open-eyed, with a new and genuine sense of himself: ". . . if it be not now, yet it will come: the readiness is all". Stoppard's characters also have an appointment with destiny: "You are Rosencrantz and Guildenstern. That's enough" (89). But their journey brings them no new knowledge. Though they succumb to their fate, they have no idea why they do so: "To be told so little – to such an end – and still, finally, to be denied an explanation . . ." They are little, like us, and are more moving, because more pathetic, than the heroic Hamlet (Ros considers tales of royalty "escapism"), but they are not tragic figures because they cannot meet death on their own terms. Yet though their deaths are neither satisfying nor heroic they are not absurd, for the play offers an explanation to us, if not to them.

Just before Guil disappears for ever, he unknowingly approaches the truth: "There must have been a moment, at the beginning, where we could have said – no. But somehow we missed it" (91). He is wrong if he thinks they could have said "no" to the messenger who summoned them or to Claudius' requests; had they done so they could not have been Ros and Guil. But Stoppard adds two details which point up their blindness and give us a reason for their deaths beside the fact that, as Ros and Guil, they had to die. In Act 2, the Player's troupe rehearses for what in *Hamlet* is the play-within-the play. However, their dumbshow extends beyond "The Mousetrap" to include a mime of Shakespeare's "closet scene", in which Hamlet stabs Polonius, and a commentary whereby the Player explains how the Prince is then sent to England under the care of "two smiling accomplices" who arrive, minus Hamlet, with "a letter that seals their deaths" (59–60). As the tragedians who play the two spies stand ready for their execution, Ros and Guil stare at them, unable to understand why the two, who are dressed in identical coats to theirs, should seem so familiar. The fact that the troupe performs all this with an easy fluidity surrounds these future events with a fatal inevitability, a feeling that deepens as the well-known incidents from *Hamlet* criss-cross the rehearsal. At one point Ophelia and Hamlet burst in to enact the last lines of the "nunnery scene", and as the two prophetic accomplices mime out their execution with splendid efficiency, the stage lights dim slowly to a blackout, then voices off-stage break the silence with calls for lights, calls which in Shakespeare break off the actual performance of "The Mousetrap".

The rehearsed quality and the dramatic telescoping of the action enable Stoppard to have things both ways. Ros and Guil's destiny appears unstoppable, yet as they stare at their doubles we are shown a road not taken. As Guil once said, this combination of "the ordained" and "the fortuitous" creates a "kind of harmony and a kind of confidence" (12). Doomed as they are, the pair still seem free to choose, and their refusal to seize that opportunity is nowhere more apparent than when they read the letter condemning them to death.

In adding this detail, Stoppard provides them with an unequivocal moment when they could have said "no". But though they now know their destiny in no uncertain terms, they refuse to act on that knowledge and stand "appalled and mesmerised" as the tragedians surround them in "a casually menacing circle" (89).

Although he sports with the techniques of the absurdists, Stoppard's universe is not their mechanistic one. Ros and Guil's loquacity may occasionally seem glib, but the play contains at its centre an affecting exploration of what death means. The master stroke is the creation of the Player, a world-weary actor-manager down on his luck because of the current vogue for child actors, and willing to stoop to any scurrility in order to make a living. By having him meet Ros and Guil on the road to Elsinore and by making the troupe stowaways after their play has displeased Claudius, Stoppard creates the circumstances for an ongoing debate about life as drama, a debate whose very theatricality persuades us emotionally as well as intellectually.

Chapter 3

Victims of perspective

The idea for *The Real Inspector Hound*,[1] the one-act play that opened in London in June of 1968, also originated during the years of apprenticeship. Many of the jokes have a Goon-Show stamp, or they parody familiar clichés. Though Stoppard began the play while still in Bristol,[2] the final version develops in purely farcical terms the ambivalence between truth and illusion that informs both *Lord Malquist* and *Rosencrantz*. But where the novel's many distorting mirrors create some narrative confusion, both plays work clearly in and out of a known structure, in this case the "who-killed-thing" plot best exemplified by Agatha Christie's *The Mousetrap*, which was then a mere fifteen years into its West End run. "I have enormous difficulty in working out plots, so actually to use *Hamlet*, or a classical whodunnit . . . for a basic structure, takes a lot of the pressure off me."[3] *Hamlet* itself is a sort of thriller and has its Mousetrap scene. Lord Malquist's "slim and useless volume bound in calf and marked with a ribbon" investigates *Hamlet* as a source of book titles ("Her Privates We") and Moon thinks "something is rotten" with modern life. *Hound* has its two drama critics Birdboot and Moon, whose names echo the novel and whose attitudes are not all that far removed from the First Player's Boot and from Ros and Guil's full and half Moon. Yet all Stoppard's characters up to this point appear to have some freedom of choice. In *Hound* they are puppets pulled by the strings of the whodunnit or, in the critics' case, by an overwhelming ambition.

The play was always planned as an entertainment, a "nuts-and-bolts comedy"[4] and nothing more:

I originally conceived a play . . . with simply two members of an audience getting involved in the play-within-the-play. But when it comes actually to writing something down which has integral entertainment value . . . it very quickly occurred to me that it would be a lot easier to do it with critics, because you've got something known and defined to parody . . . If one wishes to say that it is a play about something more than that, then it's about the dangers of wish-fulfilment.[5]

Stoppard confesses his own fondness for the play because it is "very, very carefully constructed . . . and I knew that I wanted it somehow to resolve itself in a breathtakingly neat, complex but utterly comprehensible way."[6] Two drama critics attend the first night of "a sort of a thriller" with a patently meaningless plot. But as the action, such as it is, unfolds, the two impose their own meaning upon the hand-me-down materials. The sensual Birdboot emerges from his box of Black Magic to savour the charms of the actress playing Felicity, to whom he has promised a critical puff in return for services rendered, but finds himself bowled over by a different actress so that he associates himself with Simon in the play, who also rejects Felicity for Cynthia. Moon, the second-string critic of another national daily, sits brooding about the removal of his senior colleague. He therefore sees the murder plot as peculiarly inviting, even though "it is not enough to wax at another's wane" (19).

Halfway through the play, a phone rings on the empty set; Moon answers it, and both critics become part of a play-within-the-play, which then loops back to what went on before. In a sense, nothing in the second half of *Hound* actually happens, since the actors repeat their lines but with an appropriateness that seems new in the context of the critics' projected desires. Accordingly, the set is intended to implicate the audience; in the theatre, we also have a tendency to bring our own meanings to a staged action. At the outset, Stoppard calls for "a huge mirror" in which the audience seem to see themselves: "Impossible. However, back there in the gloom – not at the footlights – a bank of plush seats . . . one of which is now occupied by Moon" (9). But Stoppard is nothing if not pragmatic: "it's always worked much better with the critics at the front".[7] The mirror image does not matter much anyway; if the critics sit downstage with their backs angled towards the audience, they will still suggest the front row of a group that includes us.

The problem with *Hound*, and why it seems the least satisfactory of all Stoppard's plays, is that the theatrical whodunnit tends to be transparently banal in the first place, so that to parody its emptiness simply restates the obvious. The plot of the actual *Mousetrap* appears so contrived and its characters such ludicrous stereotypes that audiences have for years taken the play as a comic send-up of the genre, so all Stoppard's burlesque does is to underline the banalities in a rather schoolboy manner.

The Christie play, set in the Great Hall of Monkswell Manor, begins with a number of melodramatic sound-effects followed by a radio report of a murder, regarding which the police "are anxious to interview a man seen in the vicinity, wearing a dark overcoat, light scarf, and a soft felt hat".[8] Some minutes later, Giles arrives home and removes his overcoat, hat and scarf. It goes on like that, trailing blood-red herrings and heavy-handed coincidences in its wake. So a parody cannot achieve much in the way of witty or subtle insights. Stoppard adds Mrs Drudge, the turbanned charlady, to switch on the radio and react in overdrawn alarm to the announcement that an escaped madman, described in the vaguest of terms, has been seen near Muldoon Manor: enter a man "answering this description. . . . He is acting suspiciously." Christie's hotel guests are cut off from outside help by a snowstorm; all Stoppard does is to multiply that lumbering device by surrounding his manor with "desolate marshes", "treacherous swamps", and a "fog . . . shrouding the cliffs in a deadly mantle of blind man's buff", though he does make the point more wittily through Mrs Drudge:

Yes, many visitors have remarked on the topographical quirk in the local strata whereby there are no roads leading from the Manor, though there *are* ways of getting *to* it, weather allowing. (16)

His most successful lampoon occurs at the entrance of Inspector Hound who has reached the Manor on swamp boots: "These are two inflatable – and inflated – pontoons with flat bottoms about two feet across" (30). This ridicules the not-so-directly outlandish arrival of Christie's Detective Sergeant Trotter on skis.

The silliness of all this, until the two critics enter the scene, is relieved occasionally by ripples in the dialogue:

SIMON (*to* MAGNUS): So you're the crippled half-brother of Lord Muldoon who turned up out of the blue from Canada just the other day, are you? It's taken you a long time to get here. What did you do – walk? Oh, I say, I'm most frightfully sorry! (25)

And the arrival of Hound occasions a splendid sequence of verbal and visual booby-traps (30). But generally the watchword here is "nothing succeeds like excess" as Stoppard doubles and triples the clichés which, presented singly and straight, would still create a preposterous situation for the critics to inflate with their individual ambitions.

The comedy surrounding the two critics is more successfully pointed. Both Birdboot and Moon provide a range of styles to parody, as opposed to the whodunnit's creaking plot, and Stoppard's ear for rhythms, turns of phrase, and idiom renders their intellectual pretensions in lethal detail. Birdboot writes for a popular audience: "[The author] has created a real situation, and few will doubt his ability to resolve it with a startling dénouement. . . . For this let us give thanks, and double thanks for a good clean show without a trace of smut" (35). Moon directs himself to élitist readers, even when he examines Birdboot's colour slides of a review which has been blazoned in neon outside a theatre: "Large as it is, it is a small masterpiece – I would go so far as to say – kinetic without being pop, and having said that, I think it must be said that here we have a review that adds a new dimension to the critical scene" (15). And as he draws attention to his own cleverness by evoking a host of influences upon the ridiculous play, from Dante to Dorothy L. Sayers, he completely overlooks Agatha Christie. With the two critics, Stoppard can reveal the comic pretensions of their personalities in addition to parodying their jargon.

Birdboot's desire impels him into Simon's role until the point where, as his predecessor did, he looks down at the body on the drawing-room floor. It has lain there from the outset, unnoticed by the characters in the whodunnit and uncommented upon by the two critics. The corpse, at stage-front, initiates much comic business as the characters in the murder mystery steadfastly overlook what is so apparent to us and what is usually the central piece of evidence in a thriller. As far as they are concerned there has been no murder for Hound to investigate, so there is some relief when the Inspector eventually notices the corpse – "Is there anything you have forgotten to tell me?" – though his enquiries then revolve around the identity of the victim rather than the killer. But when, in his turn, Birdboot chances to look down, he recognizes the corpse as Higgs, the senior critic whom Moon envies so much, and that moment allows a light-hearted glance at the theatrical paradoxes so central to *Rosencrantz*. The audience has presumed the corpse to be part of the play (as, in a different sense, they continue to do). The actors in the thriller now appear to have been purposely avoiding a *real* body for, when Simon looked at it, his surprise and "alarm" might not have been part of the script. The critics, too, see the body as "really" dead. Shocked though he is, Moon finds his desires have been realized by Higgs' death, while Birdboot, catapulted from his fantasy-world by the discovery, tries to tell Moon 'who dunnit'. But the clichés of that world envelop him again when, just as he is about to name the murderer, a shot rings out and Birdboot falls dead.

The mechanics of the farce structure have swept both critics into circumstances beyond their control. Someone in the play is no longer play-acting, as Moon, leaping to the stage, discovers his friend is also *really* dead: "That's a bit rough, isn't it? – a bit extreme!" *Hound* does resolve "in a breathtakingly neat" way when Moon takes on the role of the Inspector only to be accused of murder by Magnus, who tears off his moustache to reveal himself, to the actors, as the "real" Inspector Hound and, to Moon, as his paper's third-string theatre critic, Puckeridge, whose own ambitions are the last to be fulfilled, as he shoots his competitor and returns us to a wickedly faithful parody of the dénouement of *The Mousetrap*: "Yes! – it is me, Albert! – who lost his memory and joined the force, rising by merit to the rank of Inspector, his past blotted out – until fate cast him back into the home he left behind" (48).

But though contrivance is essential to farce, the undisguised mechanics of the action must appear to be self-propelled along a mad, logical trajectory. After the two critics enter the thriller, Simon and the first Inspector Hound can have no place in it, so Stoppard has them leave the stage to sit in the critics' seats and deliver their own reviews of the ensuing events. The logic behind this seems tenuous at best, an actor's revenge upon the critics, and those critiques have not been sufficiently worked into the escalating plot as further instances of obsessive wish-fulfillment. In their few comments, the actor–reviewers tear down the play itself and only fleetingly criticize Moon's acting. This results in contrivance of a different order: these two characters appear to be controlled by the playwright's ends rather than by the necessities of the action.

The play most associated with *Hound*, since they were revived together as a double bill in 1972, was also "an attempt to bring off a sort of comic coup in pure mechanistic terms".[9] *After Magritte*,[10] first presented by the Ambiance Lunch-hour Theatre Club in 1970, depends absolutely on a carefully contrived structure. With no ulterior purpose beyond the brilliant solution of its own seemingly in-soluble problems, it has the self-conscious artifice of a Malquistian equipage. In fact, the puzzles with which this one-act play challenges its audiences appear as disruptive as the seemingly chaotic collision of events and characters in the opening chapter of the novel, with the advantage that in the theatre the conflicting details can all be display-ed instantly at one and the same time. *Hound* seems to avoid all mystery until at least its half-way point, since everyone ignores the body and we do not realize the irony behind Moon's remarks about "waiting for Higgs to die. . . . I wonder if it's the same for Puck-eridge?" (17) or Birdboot's guess as to the villain of the piece: "It's Magnus a mile off" (27). *After Magritte*, which has no real plot – "The activities in this room today have broadly speaking been of a mundane and domestic nature bordering on cliché" (44) – presents puzzle upon puzzle in the assurance that "There is obviously a perfectly logical reason for everything" (32).

We perceive the opening tableau of the play without the means to connect cause and effect, just as the paintings of René Magritte rearrange ordinary objects, such as a rock, a train, a bowler hat, in ways that divorce them from their expected roles. But whereas the play's business is to restore the links in the causal chain, Magritte's paintings are meant to admit no such resolution:

The images must be seen *such as they are* . . . The mind loves the unknown. It loves images whose meaning is unknown, since the meaning of the mind itself is unknown. The mind doesn't understand its own *raison d'être*, and without understanding *that* (or why it knows what it knows), the problems it poses have no *raison d'être* either.[11]

Accordingly, Magritte's *L'Assassin menacé*, the picture which prompted Stoppard's initial tableau, simply presents "the mystery".[12]

Two large respectably-dressed figures in overcoats and bowler hats stand on either side of what amounts to a proscenium, which frames a bare, uncarpeted room. The man on the left grasps a club whose knob resembles a human knee-cap; the one on the right holds a net at the ready; both stare abstractedly outwards, although, because their faces and bodies are angled slightly towards the opening, they could be listening to movements in the room behind them. Immediately beyond the opening, to the right, a wooden table with a simple cloth supports a gramophone into the horn of which a man gazes as if listening to the record as he leans against the table. Behind him lies a naked woman on a couch whose shape and unyielding surface suggests a coffin; a towel draped across her neck isolates her rather masculine-looking, bloodstained head. Beyond her is another opening which duplicates the foreground's proscenium; this is blocked by the grille of a balcony above which rise the heads and shoulders of three impassive male observers against a background of mountains. The mystery arises from the peculiar isolation of each of the figures, linked though they are by the ascending lines of the floorboards and by a moulding which runs from the front of the proscenium and right round the room at exactly the height of the balcony's balustrade. Though the painting has – untypically – a narrative coherence, its air of brooding quietude disturbs the mind.

Stoppard's picture mystifies but is not mysterious. The room is also bare, for nearly all the furniture, including "a wind-up gramophone with an old-fashioned horn", is piled up against the door in the rear wall. At the centre hangs a light with a heavy metal lampshade and, about a yard away, a basket of fruit dangles from another cord. Mother lies face up on an ironing-board with one foot against the surface of an upturned iron; she is swathed in a bath towel, wears a black rubber bathing cap, and on her stomach rests a bowler hat. Reginald Harris stands on a wooden chair in order to blow into the lampshade; stripped to the waist, he wears evening dress trousers under green rubber fishing-waders. Thelma Harris, with elegant *coiffure* and dressed in a ball-gown, crawls about on all fours, looking down at the floor "and giving vent to an occasional sniff". A large window at the back reveals the helmet, face and shoulders of P C Holmes; he "might be a cut-out figure; but is not". Though the narrative links in this picture seem much more opaque, the ensuing dialogue and action reveal in a casual way the logic behind this ordinary, if eccentric, household.

The Harrises have been practising for a professional dance competition, hence the stacked-up furniture. Mother rests on the ironing-board because the extra height saves Thelma's back while she gives the old lady a massage before her bath. Reginald blows on the light bulb so that he can remove it and plug in the iron for his dress shirt; he wears waders because he has also had to change the light bulb above the bath already drawn for Mother. His bowler hat lies within reach so that he can place it on the fruit-basket once he removes the bulb, for the fixture's proper counterweight has broken, scattering metal pellets over the floor; Thelma, who has a cold, searches for the last of these. However, once the room and its people have been restored to order and the audience put in the know, enter PC Holmes and his superior, Inspector Foot, with interpretations of their own:

FOOT: (*without punctuation*) I have reason to believe that within the last hour in this room you performed without anaesthetic an illegal operation on a bald nigger minstrel about five-foot-two or Pakistani and that is only the beginning! (31)

Although *After Magritte*, like *Lord Malquist* and *Rosencrantz*, works towards a rational order beneath life's sometimes confusing surface, Stoppard does share a kinship with the Belgian painter. Both of them question the nature of perception. Magritte pictures the impossibility of knowing, since objective reality, projected as something outside ourselves, can only be perceived by the subjective sense. Stoppard constantly emphasizes the second part of that paradox by showing the way our subjective desires limit or distort our angle of vision. As Wittgenstein put it:

I ask you, is the subject-experimenter observing one thing or two things? (Don't say that he is observing one thing both from the inside and from the outside; for this does not remove the difficulty.)

I can say "in my visual field I see the image of the tree to the right of the image of the tower" or "I see the image of the tree in the middle of the visual field." And now we are inclined to ask "and where do you see the visual field?"[3]

The two also share Wittgenstein's concept of the unreality of language, for words can have no meaning apart from the way they are used. For Magritte, to label the picture of a pipe as "a Pipe" represents an abuse of language; one cannot smoke it, for instance, and so he writes "this is not a pipe" under its picture or inscribes "door" under the picture of a horse. For Stoppard, the meaning of words depends on a learned code which continually blinds us to its inherent unreliability, as illustrated by the opening fracas between Thelma and Reginald:

(HARRIS *blows into the lampshade.*)
THELMA: It's electric, dear.
HARRIS: (*mildly*) I didn't think it was a flaming torch.
THELMA: There's no need to use language. That's what I always say.

(11)

Presumably, like the Harrises, Stoppard visited the Magritte retrospective held at the Tate Gallery (in 1969). Mother Harris, a fanatic for the tuba, thought the exhibition was "rubbish": "Tubas on fire, tubas stuck to lions and naked women, tubas hanging in the sky . . . if you ask me the man must have been some kind of lunatic" (37). Thelma's verdict speaks for all of them: "it just wasn't life-like". But Stoppard himself must have been struck by the theatricality of Magritte's pictures, which are often framed by stage-wings, and by the way the painter repeatedly takes up motifs, as he himself does, in a continuing effort to resolve the technical problems they pose. And as far back as *Lord Malquist*, Stoppard had toyed with the deceptions of painted landscapes. Mr Moon looking out of his kitchen window feels soothed by the gracious prospect of distant hills; later he goes out only to find himself in a walled yard smelling of rotting garbage. But this contradiction also has its solution. Moon turns to discover the kitchen window has been sealed by a huge painting; the label on the back reads "*Panachrome Murals give you a New Outlook*. Moon was intensely grateful. Perhaps there was an explanation for everything" (56).

In *After Magritte* there are *conflicting* explanations for everything. While rearranging "this bizarre spectacle" in their living-room, the Harrises argue about a one-legged man who hobbled up to their car as they drove away from the Tate. Each person's picture of reality bears a different descriptive label. Ironically, in explaining this to Inspector Foot, who interprets the figure as their accomplice in the Crippled Minstrel Caper, each person gives one detail that accords with the actual facts: Reg saw the man in pyjamas; Thelma noted shaving foam on his face; Mother saw the alligator handbag. Yet none of these actual facts seems any less fantastic than the distorted ones.

Their muddle also extends from the language they use, since words like "operation", "practice", and "caper" vary in meaning according to their context:

MOTHER: Is it all right for me to practice?
FOOT: No, it is not all right! Ministry standards may be lax but we draw the line at Home Surgery to bring in the little luxuries of life.

MOTHER: I only practice on the tuba.

FOOT: Tuba, femur, fibula – it takes more than a penchant for rubber gloves
to get a licence nowadays. (33)

As this passage shows, Inspector Foot's perceptions are further
distorted by personal vanities; like the critics in *Hound*, he has his own
ambitions. A stickler for detail and precision, he ties himself into
mental knots in his anxiety to have his enquiries fit with a precon-
ceived and complicated theory that will bring him glory down at the
police station. Foot's overbearing determination parodies Joe
Orton's Inspector Truscott, who will stop at nothing, search-warrant
or no, to bring in his man, though Stoppard's version eschews the
self-serving ruthlessness of *Loot*. Here his policemen, however comically exaggerated, never resort to violence.

Such entangling complications unravel with a smoothness that
makes the farcical details of *After Magritte* seem utterly inevitable.
Having created a cartoon-like tableau to begin with, Stoppard can
afford to launch his cardboard characters into their arguments about
the one-legged man with the same cut-out artifice: "For some
reason, my mind keeps returning to that one-legged footballer . . ."
At the same time that those arguments escalate, the confusing
appearances in the living-room become grounded in logic; even the
potentially awkward stage-business of returning the furniture to its
normal place is neatly covered by Mother's jaunty tune as she prac-
tises on her tuba. But though the stage picture now makes sense, the
arrival of the Inspector propels the confusions over the Crippled
Minstrel Caper still faster until everyone is in the dark, metaphorically and literally, before the light bulb can be returned to its fixture.
During that blackout, the Inspector unknowingly discloses to us, but
to none of the characters, that it was he who hobbled up to the
Harrises' departing car, and upon that 'illuminating' information the
light comes on again to reveal the characters in another set of
postures, which would seem as grotesque as their earlier ones had the
audience not been privy to the causes behind these latest effects.
Only PC Holmes lacks the means to interpret the new picture. After
entering the room and switching on the light, he "recoils" and the
lampshade descends onto the table (or into the tuba). Like that light
at centre stage, the whole play balances on a fulcrum. As we solve the
puzzle of the introductory tableau so, like a counterweight, the
identity of the one-legged man who hopped up to the Harrises' car
grows more and more mystifying. When that mix-up is solved, the
final tableau, clear as light to us, plunges PC Holmes into darkest
confusion and the stage light also glides downwards to its extinction.

From the early radio plays on into *Lord Malquist* and *Rosencrantz* and these two one-act farces, the contradiction between distorting perspectives pits the characters (sometimes unwittingly) against each other and involves the audience in a similar counterpoint, perceiving or misperceiving the action. These ambushes had become second nature to Stoppard and they now provided him with a way of using the intimacy of the television camera to advantage.

Teeth, transmitted in early 1967, has a less outlandish logic than his other farces, but those entrapping perspectives at last allow Stoppard to impose his personality upon the small screen. He starts by persuading us that George is having an affair with his dentist's receptionist–wife, and then, half-way through, we discover that the receptionist is George's own wife. However, since George's actual *inamorata* does happen to be the dentist's wife, he has every reason to be terrified of the chair, the drill, and the pincers. In this way, the script makes farce out of the fears nearly everybody has of dentists, terrors which the cameras emphasize in close-up. All Stoppard's early plots, when they are not evolved from other plays, either build out of joke ideas that are a part of modern folklore, like the human TIM voice or, in this play, the dangers of offending one's dentist, or they centre upon a recent event: the first moon landing, the deaths of Marilyn Monroe and Winston Churchill, the Magritte retrospective at the Tate. Those ideas then seem to trigger a fantasy which divides off into many seemingly contradictory directions but which finally comes together in the neatest and tightest of knots.

The half-hour of *Teeth*[14] begins realistically with the sort of conversation one might overhear on a London bus, as the cameras focus on a *Woman's Own* magazine and the eyes of George, the eavesdropper, behind it. As he listens to conspiratorial whispers from two ladies seated on the couch opposite, we share his view of the dingy waiting-room, and the two voices become clearer and louder as his concentration on them deepens. Agnes is in the middle of explaining to Flora how she had thought of killing herself. The word-play suggests the semi-literate minds of the two women – "Plenty of fish in the sea, I say" . . . "Different kettle altogether" – stuffed with the phraseology of advertisements and pulp literature: "I wouldn't be here today if we hadn't been all-electric." But once we notice that George "has been studying a bra-and-panty ad" in his magazine, this may act as a filter that colours the way we interpret the next part of Agnes' narrative as she explains how Jack Stevens burst in on her while she was in the bathroom, though this slight frisson soon resolves into the play's controlling motif. Agnes had been caught with her two front teeth out and, as the toothpaste advertisements proclaim, flashing smiles have sex-appeal. This prelude ends with a shot of George's "great white smile" in deference to the two women's sudden awareness that he has been listening.

The audience find themselves the victims of perspective when an elaborate false trail opens up as the dentist's receptionist enters. From her surprise at seeing George and from their whispered conversation once they are in the ante-room, it would seem that this smiling Lothario has come to chat up his girl friend after having forgotten her birthday. The trail leads farther astray when George, enquiring about her new ear-rings, is told they were a gift from "a very good friend". "Don't give me that", he replies; "you're a respectable married woman. It was Harry, was it?" Presumably, then, they came from her husband, Harry, whom George feels sure he can play false with his winning smile. The trap at the end of the trail clicks shut when George makes a grab for the wife, who backs away anxiously, and through the surgery door comes Harry. Since he simply smiles and jokes with the embarrassed pair, we wonder how much he knows as he ushers George into the surgery and the camera focuses on the instruments of torture, "silent, waiting, ready . . ." (75). By these means, Stoppard has built up a game of now-you-see-it, now-you-don't, which will control the rest of the play, putting us as much in suspense as George is. And the cameras ensure that point of view, with close-ups of George's terrified eyes as Harry probes away at his mouth and his treachery.

However, this game of cat-and-mouse starts pleasantly enough, except that Harry's camaraderie implies that George's life as a travelling salesman lives up to its stag-party reputation, "lovely work if you can get it", and his conversation takes on a double edge as he complains about his wife's frequent absences from home. So much of what Harry says could either refer to dentistry or adultery as he prods deeper into George's mouth and situation:

HARRY: You've been letting yourself go a bit, haven't you?
(GEORGE's *worried eyes*)
> I'm glad you came in today – this is a serious warning, George; you think what people can't see isn't happening – but it all comes out in the end. Your sins always find you out.
(GEORGE's *eyes:* HARRY *probes.*) (77)

These *double-entendres* broaden into farce as Harry punctuates his game with nicks to George's mouth or fiddles with a hypodermic syringe and a concoction which stains the teeth green but which will be excellent for George's "condition". Casually mentioning the way he dealt with his wife's previous indiscretion – "Oh yes. Collins wouldn't be showing his face around the fair sex for quite a while to come . . . and a real smiler, he was" (80) – Harry then approaches with a fiendish-looking mallet and chisel only to pass by the terror-stricken George and adjust the head-rest with a thumping whack.

Eventually, Harry calls for 'Mary', the name of George's wife, and in walks the receptionist who had seemed to be Prudence. As the viewer readjusts to that relationship, Harry's torture takes a psychological twist. While George's wife, Mary, mixes the green paste, the dentist comments brightly about the odd places salesmen go to. Then the camera zooms in on George's worried eyes and gaping mouth while off-screen we hear Harry and Mary flirtatiously adjusting her new ear-rings. An extensive silence follows, during which George's eyes swivel as he tries to see what the two are doing. When they come back into his view, Harry's tie and Mary's white cap are noticeably adrift, and when Harry, "humming softly", moves to fit the oxygen mask on George, the picture dissolves back to the waiting-room and more *double entendre*:

AGNES: That's it, I wouldn't have a man without them on principle –
FLORA: Because if *they've* gone already, what'll go next, I said.
AGNES: That's the point.
FLORA: (*Pause: sighs.*) Mind you, I was sorry. Six months later mine turned black. I would've had *any*body.   (88)

Whereupon the door opens from the ante-room into which George is emerging, "a stricken man". As he passes through, Mary coolly asks if he will be late again that night, and, since Prudence has her dressmaking class, Harry wonders "if I could ask Mary to stay behind a while – as she knows the ropes". Faced with the stares of a now-crowded waiting-room, George "*lets out a thin smile which is more like a wince. His middle tooth is missing. At this, all the patients smile at him, as one of their own. All around there are smiles like broken-down brooms.*"

No other screenplay from this period depends so neatly on opposed perspectives or uses the cameras so effectively. In *Another Moon Called Earth* (1967), about which more later, and *The Engagement* (1970), a fifty-minute expansion of *Dominic Boot* for an American network, the eccentricity and theatricality seem disconcertingly artificial and tend to overwhelm the screen. The short stage farces are too frenzied to allow their audiences to linger over the meaning of those battling points of view. Only in the radio plays does Stoppard explore the possibilities of the union between farce and philosophy which *Jumpers* would eventually ceremonize. *Albert's Bridge*, broadcast in July 1967, like *If You're Glad* (with which it was to be paired in a stage production on the Edinburgh Fringe in 1969), contains characters who are overwhelmed by their own peculiar vision of humanity. Three years later, *Where Are They Now?* suggests, in a strangely moving and more naturalistic way, how most of our perspectives on the past are determined by our need to stay happy in the present.

Aptly, the protagonist of *Albert's Bridge*[15] had been a philosophy student and had wanted to stay on at university, "but they wouldn't have me". During his final vacation he takes a temporary job painting Clufton Bay Bridge, "the fourth biggest single-span double-track shore-to-shore railway bridge in the world bar none –" (12). Albert feels happy there above the crowded town. Although he shares none of the ninth earl's effete cynicism, he retires from the farce below, devoting himself to what he considers a work of art. From up there, the town and its people look like bricks, dots and beetles: "I saw the context. It reduced philosophy and everything else" (17). When the town council's Bridge Committee decides upon a long-lasting paint which will eliminate the need for more than one painter, Albert applies for that job and dabs away in sublime isolation until his eyrie is invaded by Fraser, who has climbed there "because up was the only direction left" (31). Fraser's nightmare, like Mr Moon's, derives from a ballooning population in a limited world. He intends to jump from the bridge, but after some time up there everything below seems ordered and bearable: "each square a function, each dot a functionary. I really think it might work. Yes, from a vantage point like this, the idea of society is just about tenable" (34). Once down in the town Fraser again feels suicidal, yet when he climbs back up he again wants to live: "I'm forced up and coaxed down. I'm a victim of perspective" (37).

There are other intersecting perspectives. In an amusing variant of the vestibule-door sequence at the beginning of *If You're Glad*, the four bridge-painters are first heard clambering down after their day's work. Their calls to each other, at different distances from the microphone, grow closer until the men come together in a descending line. "Dad", who has been doing the job for twenty years, has had enough and will not be starting again at the other end of the bridge for a further two-year stint, whereas Albert sees the endless task as a finite achievement:

DAD: I've spread my life over those girders, and in five minutes I could
     scrape down to the iron, I could scratch down to my prime.
ALBERT: Simplicity – so . . . contained; neat; your bargain with the world,
     your wages, your time, your energy, your property . . . all contained there
     in ten layers of paint, accounted for.   (11)

Back home, Albert's mother views his university career as a waste of time; he could already have been a trainee executive in his father's factory: "That university has held you back." Nothing practical can come from a study of philosophy: "You're thinking all the time. It's not like you, Albert" (16). Up on the bridge, Albert's thoughts are what make his job exciting, and the impracticality of sliding paint in behind the rivets is a challenge: "No one will see that from the ground; I could cheat up here. But I'd know . . ." (10). His father, "Chairman of Metal Alloys and Allied Metals", wants him to work his way up from the bottom, but Albert prefers to start up top because "there are no consequences to a coat of paint. That's more than you can say for a factory man; his bits and pieces scatter" (11).

Despite his lofty, detached perspective, Albert is no spectator hero. Gladys, who shares his sense of man's littleness, half wants Frank to rescue her from that isolation; Brown, painting his murals in solitude, still cares about the lives of the hospital staff. Albert eventually cares for nobody and nothing but *his* bridge. His detachment starts out as disarming vagueness; he neglects to tell his mother he had a vacation and tumbles into marrying Kate, the maid, because he happened to be still in bed when she came to clean his room. In the early months of his job, he wants Kate to wheel their baby girl to the bridge so that he can see them, and he contemplates his assimilation into society as "the honest working man, father of three . . . content in his obscurity" (24). But "don't wave, don't look down" becomes more than a safety motto as his obsession for the bridge grows. A comic Icarus – "I'm the bridge man" – Albert comes to see his family as two more dots. So the baby's rattle annoys him; he starts working on Saturdays; he is unaware of his neighbours' names.

Kate, a simple soul who wants only Albert's happiness, though that includes Allied Metals, persuades him to take a holiday. Albert considers Scotland and the Forth Bridge, but he agrees to go to Paris where he is just as obsessed:

ALBERT: . . . The pointlessness takes one's breath away – a tower connects nothing, it stands only so that one can go up and look down. Bridge-builders have none of this audacity, compromise themselves with function. Monsieur Eiffel, poet and philosopher, every eight years I'll scratch your name in the silver of Clufton Bay Bridge. (29)

For Kate "life is all close up" (25); for him it is dots, bricks and beetles, so he stays up there all night or races off each morning without a goodbye. Albert never regrets having married Kate, yet when she takes the baby and leaves him, his mind is on the bridge. As Fraser remarks when he hears Albert singing away at his work, "Very nice, very nice. The egotist school of songwriting" (31), and by this time Albert regards any visitor as a threat, so if Fraser intends to jump he had better do so: "And you're holding me up. I've got to paint where you're standing" (33).

Albert/Icarus eventually falls because of the Committee's miscalculations. Mr Fitch, the City Engineer, loves efficiency as much as Albert does, "It's poetry to me – a perfect equation of space, time and energy" (20). Despite the new long-lasting paint, if one man takes eight years to complete the bridge, "in two years' time he'd only be a quarter of the way along, so the old paint would be ready for another coat" (35). Anxious to save his reputation in the town, the Chairman demands action, so seventeen-hundred-and-ninety-nine painters are deputed to join Albert and finish the bridge in a day. Albert may see himself "as the centre" of things, but he had not thought they would "go to such lengths". From his perspective, the men represent an army "flung against me by a madman! Was I so important?" (40), whereas Fraser sees them as the vanguards of an overspilling populace who, like him, have nowhere to go but up. But, as Albert once said of the bridge, there are "rules that make it stay up", and the engineering department has forgotten to tell the painters to break step. As they march onward, whistling "Colonel Bogey", in a spoof of *The Bridge on the River Kwai*, and their rhythmic steps begin to ring metallically as they reach the bridge, we hear the sounds of creaking, wrenching, "rivets starting to pop".

The play spans its sixty minutes of air time with all the logical simplicity of a (non-collapsed) bridge. Its characters, blinkered or made grandiose by a particular view of things, rigidly pursue their individual ends. Despite its rich texture, the main thread of the plot arcs through the air with none of the diversionary tangents of those plays which set out to snare the audience along the way. We begin placed at Albert's shoulder, listening to the close-up slosh of his paint-brush and the distant shouts of his workmates from various levels below, then "very close", so that we share Albert's self-contained happiness as he croons softly to himself. Each ensuing scene is riveted to its neighbour either by a linking sound-effect or by an abrupt cross-fade so that the play's forward momentum undulates with a pleasing delicacy. These transitions telescope the time scheme, as Albert flies higher in his pride and Kate sinks lower into despair. Within those clear lines of development, Albert has Gladys-like soliloquies whose lyricism, while not so metaphysically complex, is particularly suited to the creation of radio's mind-pictures. Reminiscent of the broad humour and poetic scene-painting of Dylan Thomas' *Under Milk Wood*, the play seizes all the opportunities the medium has to offer. Not surprisingly, it won the Prix Italia (1968) for radio drama.

Having taken the *brio* style to its limits in *Albert's Bridge*, Stoppard switched to a patterned realism in his next play for radio. The characters of *Where Are They Now?* (1970)[16] are not cartoon stereotypes, though they are distinctive social types; consequently, most of their remarks seem to come from within, pulled out of them in dialogue which people of that class or occupation might actually speak. They are no longer propelled by a manic situation or by a single, heightened obsession. The comic collision of perspectives still matters, indeed the play is about perspective, but because the characters no longer collide full tilt into one another there emerges a subtle interplay of attitudes, none of which can be said to stand as Stoppard's final statement, and the play contains a range of feeling that is both wider and more heartfelt than the radio farces and more penetratingly ambiguous than *'M' Is for Moon*.

Symptomatically, the engendering aphorism here is not a mildly diverting idea, like the ceaseless painting of the world's large bridges, but that "schooldays are the happiest days of our lives", a sentiment to which many of his audience may feel passionately committed or, since the play was originally written for Schools' Broadcasting, passionately antipathetic. To juggle the perspectives, Stoppard sets an Old Boys' Dinner in 1969 against a lunch scene in that school twenty-four years earlier. At the outset we hear the hum of adult male voices which subsides into an expectant silence. An authoritative voice delivers the Grace, and a scraping of chairs, as the gentlemen take their seats, leads with no division whatsoever into a young boy's "Eurgh!" and we are back in 1945 at a table in a school hall, where the boys are not thankful for the wartime rations they "are about to receive". By the play's end, that irony has come to include the whole of their school lives and whether or not the men around the hotel table should feel "truly grateful" for having had those boyhood experiences.

As the play moves back and forth across time, we are set wondering how the boys got to where they now are, and within the naturalistic limits of the dialogue Stoppard plants one of his booby-traps. The school lunch involves Mr Dobson, the former Latin master, and three boys in particular who are referred to, both by him and by each other, as Groucho, Chico and Harpo. The conversation soon reveals that Chico's actual name is Brindley, whose older self chats with Mr Dobson at the beginning of the second scene. However, for the major part of the play we are kept guessing as to the adult identities of the other two, although the fact that Harpo murmurs a single "Yes, sir" during the school scenes and an Old Boy called Gale says one quiet "No" to repeated attempts to draw him into the adult table-talk encourages us to put those two together and therefore to deduce that the talkative Groucho has grown up into the voluble Mr Marks. The device is an aural equivalent of the "find the lady" game Stoppard plays in *Rosencrantz* during the pirate episode when Hamlet leaps into the left barrel, the Player into the right one, and Ros and Guil hide in the middle one. When the lights come back up after a blackout, only two barrels remain on stage; the centre one is missing, but out of the Player's come Ros and Guil while out of Hamlet's comes the Player. Similarly, the boy we think to be Marks eventually turns out to be Gale, and until that game resolves itself it ensures that we continually measure the boys against the men, thus enforcing that part of the play's meaning.

Brindley, whose identity we do learn quickly, contains no mystery; in his case, "the boy is father to the man". As Chico, he can always be relied upon to give Mr Dobson the answer he requires or to trot out the roots of Latin nouns and verbs on demand. The sort of boy who delights in precise detail, he readily volunteers whose turn it is to serve at table or that the rice pudding is bound to have been made with Klim, a powdered milk-substitute. As the Reverend Mr Brindley, he still defers to "Mr Dobson" and has grown even more precise, instructing Marks on the appropriate ways to address a vicar, correcting him on English usage, explaining to Dobson that Gale, whom none of them has met for years, has just returned from Lagos.

The Latin master, too, has simply become more set in his ways. In Dobson's benevolent sarcasm and donnish wit, Stoppard has captured that British schoolmasterly habit of always performing to the gallery, usually at one pupil's expense, in order to display a deliberately cultivated, endearing (?) eccentricity as he scores off Harpo and invites the boys to share a waggish joke built out of the Ministry of Food's propensity for using reversed names for their products:

DOBSON: Nothing wrong with Klim. Fresh from the Ministry of Food's prize herd of Jersey wocs. I have just said something extremely risible – Root, boy!
CHICO: Rido – ridere – risi, I laugh! (129)

The reality of this studied eccentricity enables Stoppard to savour the peculiarities and nuance of language without unnaturalistic exaggeration. Mr Dobson calls the boys by their nicknames and shares their slang as part of the school's private world and mode of speech: he wonders why Anderson did not go to "Staggers [report sick] this morning", "who's on tucker today", and whether Harpo has a "mog chit [an excuse note]". At the Dinner, among near-equals, he can afford a joking reference to his Welsh ex-colleague as "Jenkins the

French". At lunch, among lesser mortals, his jokes tend to have a pretended ferocity which nevertheless contains a genuine dismissiveness: "[French] will prove invaluable to you in later life should you join the Foreign Legion, which most of you will probably have to" (129).

This ambiguous mixture of bullying and comradeship, ferocity and concern explains why some boys like school while others do not, or why schooldays can be miserable to live through but wonderful in memory. The play shows happiness itself as a relative emotion. A master's behaviour, however hateful at the time, becomes part of a private and shared world of slang, nicknames, hard knocks, as one looks back through rose-coloured spectacles. This is especially possible if, like Mr Marks, one needs those roseate memories as part of one's present self-image.

At the Dinner, the "Corpulent Marks" reveals himself to be a vain, patronizing snob whose limited intelligence flickers behind an insensitive, hearty façade. Believing himself a connoisseur of the good life, he commands the waiter to leave the wine near them on the table, "there's a good fellow", and complains that the menu is "pretty unimaginative". The bottle contains "pretty poor chablis but I'll have another crack at it" (125) and "as for the turkey, I wouldn't give it to my chow" (130). This gives him a chance to explain that he keeps this dog, "an absolute brute", to guard the "bit of decent silver, you know . . .", that he happens to own. But that bluff manner only draws attention to his empty-headed awfulness.

Stoppard injects phrases like "old man" into Marks' patter and allows him to chortle over their schoolboy slang, which still infects his adult vocabulary, because Marks has invented for himself the sort of persona that *needs* to have had a rip-roaring boyhood. Convinced by that fiction, he professes genuine shock that Crawford, last term's head boy, should seem such a greenhorn: "The Upper Henty must be full of children!" (128). Brindley excuses the remark as "heavily ironic", but Marks is incapable of that; he sincerely remembers his schoolboy superiors as larger than life. To some extent we all share that perspective, though Marks' legend of himself requires that those who made him tremble should have been kings, like Mr Jenkins with "his famous Bruiser". Brindley hopes "that sort of thing no longer exists", but Marks has converted the master's harshness into the necessary school of hard knocks, and to confirm the legend has sent his son to his old school.

Through that boy, Stoppard lets us see the nicknames, the slang, and young Mr Crawford (so out of place and naive at the Old Boys' Dinner) from an altered perspective. Mr Marks asks Crawford "how's Gerald buckling down?" Crawford wonders whom he means; Christian names are not the form at school. Marks blunders on; naturally not, all well-liked boys have nicknames: "You haven't been accepted till you've got a nickname" (132). True, and not true, since Crawford, sharing his name with a well-known brand of biscuits, is sometimes known as "Crackers". In sudden flashback, we hear him "viciously" reacting to that name and accusing his juniors of being "wet, stinky boys". Nicknames can be degrading; kings can be tyrants; schoolboy jargon can itself become an instrument of torture. The episode after this reveals Gale's identity and makes us also realize that Mr Marks was formerly as intimidated a "wet" as his son now is. The ebullient ass who doubts whether "I was actually *afraid*" of the fearsome French master once had "the frits" at the mere thought of French class. Yet Marks does not consciously lie. His son will probably grow up to be just as expansive about the old school.

Gale, who has sat through this reminiscent talk with singular reticence, bursts out in bitter criticism upon the Headmaster's rising to ask the gathering to pay a minute or two's silent tribute to Mr Jenkins, whose death occurred a few days before the Annual Dinner. We know that Gale had specifically requested to sit at the same table as the French master, and now he explains that he has attended this reunion, after years of absence and refusal "to contribute to the [School] Magazine's 'Where Are They Now?' page", because he knows how memory plays tricks with actuality: "I wanted to see if I'd got him right" (136). In his opinion, the master was a *stupid* bully: "I think we would have liked French. It is not, after all, a complex language" (135).

From the Head's viewpoint, Jenkins was a "selfless worker for the school" in the twenty years he was French master and after his retirement. We can read between the lines to allow for the softening that usually accompanies a eulogy for the dead, when the Head describes his colleague's "dapper figure, with gown billowing and moustache bristling" or his dominating baritone in Chapel (134). "Billowing ... bristling ... hurrying ... shaming younger men" are words that could describe a holy terror to those on the receiving end. Mr Dobson can only wonder why Gale bothered to come there: he neither confirms nor denies these two views of Jenkins. From his perspective, to interrupt the Dinner for any sort of tribute is "Ridiculous fuss" since "Every master dies in the twelve months preceding one Old Boys' Dinner or another – except for that appalling man Grimes who actually died during one" (126).

With such conflicting memories, Groucho, Chico, Harpo and the Headmaster might have been at different schools. To highlight this,

Stoppard implants a comic subplot, if one may so dignify a single strand in a thirty-five-minute script. Throughout the Dinner, a running *contretemps* occurs between Dobson and an equally elderly gentleman, also called Jenkins, who sits at the place apparently intended for the dead French master. Dobson tries to place this man, who was his junior at school, but fails to understand why the stranger should say he was a weekday boarder – "No such thing" – or why he did not belong to a House. For a moment, Dobson is too annoyed to play his expected self: "You're mad! I may be senile but I'm not completely loco" (127). Jenkins, equally piqued, complains to his neighbour that Dobson "must have been a complete nonentity. If he was there at all" (131). At the end of the evening, those assembled rise to sing the school song, and, after an introductory chord, Jenkins sings out . . . alone. The piano falters; Jenkins stops: "I say, have they changed the Song?" He has mistaken the Old Hovians' Dinner for that of his own "Oakleigh House for the Sons of Merchant Seamen's Widows" (138).

This outrageous comedy of errors defines the comic extreme of a range of contradictory memories; Gale's bitterness stands at the other extremity, and Stoppard carefully relates the two by having the 'false' Jenkins describe his memories to that silent neighbour at table. The interloper also moves the play from its focus on the French master's character to a commentary on the nature of happiness itself.

None of the verdicts is precisely Stoppard's own. Gale's diatribe stands out, owing to the concrete and specific way he dismisses the dreamdays of Billy Bunter, "the incorruptible Steerforth", cricket and "your best friend's beribboned sister" with an anguished portrait of loneliness and boredom unprotected by literary models:

God, I wish there was a way to let small boys know that it doesn't really matter. I wish I could give them the scorn to ride them out – those momentous trivialities and tiny desolations. I suppose it's not very important, but at least we would have been happier children, and childhood is Last Chance Gulch for happiness. After that, you know too much.   (136–7)

This seems like the play's bedrock of feeling, and its placement just before the final deflation of the Dobson–Jenkins muddle makes it something of a climax. Nothing has felt so autobiographical since the short stories; Stoppard has described his own schooldays with a similar dislike:

I left school thoroughly bored by the idea of anything intellectual, and gladly sold all my Greek and Latin classics to George's Bookshop in Park Street. I'd been totally bored and alienated by everyone from Shakespeare to Dickens besides . . . I was seventeen, and it took about another five years for me to start buying them back – not the same books, but books.[17]

That this disaffected youth should turn out to be the most bookish of contemporary playwrights or that Gale should become a "crusading journalist" chimes with the ironies of the play's shifting perspectives.

But if the force of Gale's remarks strikes lethally at the sentiments of the concluding school song which urges all fellow Hovians to "Spread the flag of Britain / All around the globe! / And the lesson we have learned / In happy days at Hove", a final cross-fade conjures up Gale's shouts and laughter as he plays ball "on an open windy field . . . It is a day he has forgotten, but clearly he was very happy" (139). He himself had admitted to only one moment of perfect happiness, and not at Hove either, in prep school as he walked down a corridor, running a finger along the moulding of a wall:

> . . . I mean I experienced happiness as a state of being: everywhere I looked, in my mind, *nothing was wrong*. You never get that back when you grow up; it's a condition of maturity that almost *everything* is wrong, *all the time*, and happiness is a borrowed word for something else – a passing change of emphasis . . . Maturity is a high price to pay for growing up. (137)

A second aspect of the song is vindicated by Jenkins, who may have gone to a lesser school – Brindley calls them "the lot having dinner downstairs" and Marks had dismissed them as "the lower decks" – but his days there have given him standards to live by. For one thing, he sees through Marks' attitudinizing. For another, though it would have been impossible in 1970 not to shudder at the Imperial bravado of the song, Jenkins' British standards kept him going through his years in up-country Malaya, and when his England disappeared after the Second War,

> It wasn't home any more, you see, not as I knew it . . . Once I'd retired and life was *all* leave, well I began to feel I was *abroad* again. Dammit, I was homesick. (*Chuckles*.) Or schoolsick. I think I came back just to attend this dinner, for the first time. Like you, I believe. (130)

Jenkins *is* like Gale. Both men's youth has shaped their lives and both are aware that memory falsifies, yet both cannot but let it do so.

"'What is Truth?' said jesting [Thomas]; and would not stay for an answer." There can be no answer concerning the true nature of happiness. In 1965, the actual John Gale, a journalist whose reports on events in Egypt and Algeria during the 1950s revealed the under-side of Empire, produced an autobiography wryly entitled *Clean Young Englishman*. Though Stoppard's Gale makes no comment on the Imperial theme, John Gale's experiences turned him into "what they like to call a manic-depressive". Writing cursorily about his own schooldays, towards which he is generally dismissive, he too remembers them as a sequence of storied events, like the cricket match in which he hit the ball "square off the front foot past point for four: it went like butter. I have never hit a ball better. Cricket was worth playing for that shot alone." He notes his disillusion when he moved up from prep school: "I had believed that all public school boys were witty, cynical and enlightened, leading dazzling lives . . . the school seemed a lifeless cardboard sham in comparison with my prep school." There are no memories of magisterial sadism. When he is ironic about a master's foibles, though, his critique inevitably turns into an appreciation of eccentricity:

[The Headmaster] was always kind and gracious to me, but since I was neither an aristocrat nor a scholar, I was scarcely to his taste. He took each form once a week, and addressed even the smallest boys as "gentlemen". After beating a boy he would sometimes offer him sherry.[18]

Even for this detached observer, looking back after having witnessed policies that exposed the sham behind imperial benevolence, irony becomes tinged with sentiment.

Our memories colour and are coloured by the persons we are; happiness comes at the most unexpected moments. Far from being a criticism of the school system, Stoppard's play accepts and explores these ambiguities. Unlike his previous plays, *Where Are They Now?* does not demand that its audience make a first leap up to an intellectually amusing or provocative premise. Each character views an inescapable fact of life with about as much accuracy as his fellows. In other plays, one character's frantic obsession collides with another's, which can also sometimes represent the daft systems of society, or all the characters hold contradictory ideas about a particular event. Like *Rosencrantz* and, in its minor way, *'M' Is for Moon*, this play illumines the human condition. Here, though, each character seems impelled completely from within. Only once does Stoppard impose a jokey *aperçu* – when he makes Marks giggle after the final Grace, having had the unlikely thought (for him) that after thanking the Lord three times a day at school "we lost touch . . . *where is He now?*" (137). A small masterpiece, this script implicates the listener beyond the momentary trap created by the boys' identities. Its tricks of memory resonate against the truth of our own experience to remind us that we too are the victims of perspective.

Chapter 4

Trapped in language

At one point in the first Act of *Jumpers*, George Moore complains to Inspector Bones about the difficulty he has experienced organizing the paper he intends to deliver at a philosophers' symposium: "the words betray the thoughts they are supposed to express. Even the most generalized truth begins to look like special pleading as soon as you trap it in language" (46). The idea derives from Wittgenstein's *Philosophical Investigations*, but such 'influence' is a complicated matter. Stoppard constantly reminds interviewers and critics alike that what a person writes about is largely a matter of temperament. His novelist friend, Derek Marlowe, commenting on Stoppard's work habits, gets them wrong:

For Tom, writing a play is like sitting for an examination. He spends ages on research, does all the necessary cramming, reads all the relevant books, and then gestates the results. Once he's passed the exam – with the public and the critics – he forgets all about it and moves on to the next subject.[1]

Far from forgetting his homework, Stoppard used it to advantage in *Dogg's Our Pet*, while waiting for the first rehearsals of *Jumpers*, and would return to that material some years later, transforming *Pet*'s game-playing into political statement.

In addition, what a writer swots up for his public exam is bound to have a personal significance. One cannot be sure exactly when Stoppard began reading the Austrian philosopher, but as early as *Free Man* Linda talks casually about there being "two of everyone. You see you need that, and if the two of him's the same, I mean if [her father is] the same in the pub as he is with us, then he's had it." Similar ideas abound in *Rosencrantz*, in terms of the deceptiveness of symbols and language. One of the philosopher's thoughts, unpublished at the time of the play, will serve to illustrate the sympathetic bond between the two thinkers:

A hero looks death in the face, real death, not just the image of death. Behaving honourably in a crisis doesn't mean being able to act the part of a hero well, as in the theatre, it means rather being able to look death *itself* in the eye.

For an actor may play lots of different roles, but at the end of it all *he himself*, the human being, is the one who has to die.[2]

Quite independently, this thought delves to the play's emotional centre.

Throughout his career, Stoppard seems to come upon outside influences – Beckett and T. S. Eliot were "the twin syringes" of his early self[3] – which confirm ideas he has already been toying with. *Jumpers*, for instance, is the result of a lengthy gestation, rather than a couple of years' reading. Two thematic strands in that play exemplify this process, and their transformation over the years epitomizes the way he returns to old ideas and reworks them until he has mined their theatrical potential.

The relationship in *Jumpers* between George Moore and his wife, Dotty, began life in *Lord Malquist*, and the 1967 television play, *Another Moon Called Earth*,[4] presents another, closer version. In the novel, Mr Moon agonizes over the provocative yet equivocal liaison between his wife and the ninth earl, giving vent to his feelings with a despairing "I just don't care". In the television play, Bone, like Mr Moon, constructs human history: "I dissect it – lay bare the logic which other men have taken to be an arbitrary sequence of accidents" (93). Sitting in his study he is interrupted by cries of "Wolves! Look out!! Rape! Rape! Rape!" coming from his wife's room. Penelope, like Dotty after her, has obviously cried "Wolf!" too many times, for Bone reacts by criticizing the logic of the outrage she pretends to. Wolves are unlikely to rape their victims. When Penelope acts out the rape for her distant husband – "it's too lovely – oh – don't stop – ah – I don't care if he comes in – ", Bone "weakens" and storms into her bedroom (91).

The eccentricity of this first scene demands too much of its television audience, lulled by the realism of the Bones' surroundings. Dilettantism needs an equally outlandish vehicle to carry it successfully into one's living-room, and the television play suffers from an uneasy union between cartoon characters and a three-dimensional setting. In *Lord Malquist* the surrounding circumstances were imaginary though 'real' as we read of them; here, the same ideas sound less acceptable, given the normality of the Bones' flat. Where *Jumpers* will open with an extraordinary tableau which forces its audience to leap out of everyday reality into the play's particular world, the television script has no such launching pad, so its dialogue seems to sputter into madness too precipitously.

A second salvo from what will become *Jumpers*' battery also misfires in *Another Moon*. Penelope has taken to her bed because the first man to reach the moon "stood off the world with his feet on solid ground, and brought everything into question" (92). The lunanaut has seen "the whole thing for what it is . . . he's made it all random" (108). In contrast, her husband's historical opus, in which he has struggled as far as the third century BC, provides a way of "discovering the patterns – exposing the fallacy of chance – there are no impulsive acts – nothing random – everything is logical and connects into the grand design" (101). The idea of a revolutionary perspective, which alters everything, goes back at least as far as Gladys Jenkins who, from her eminence in the Post Office, has seen "such distance, / such disappearing tininess so far away, / rushing away, / reducing the life-size to nothing" (50).

Although Stoppard denied any familiarity with existentialism, the influence on him at the time must surely have been Sartre's *Nausea*. In that novel, Antoine Roquentin has been working on a biography of the eighteenth-century Marquis de Rollebon (reverse the "de Rol", change "bon" to its opposite, "mal", add the "quis" and one has something like Lord Malquist – though a less complicated derivation may simply be "my lord Marquis"). Despite his having private means and no personal ties, Roquentin is neither free nor happy; the world preys on his nerves and creates within him a feeling of vertigo, "the Nausea". In a universe whose laws are arbitrary, anything is possible; one's tongue might turn into a centipede, and the thought terrifies him. The biography had helped him forget his own existence, but he eventually comes to accept that an unpredictable universe throws the onus for living upon each individual: "All is free," he discovers, "this park, this city, and myself."[5] Climbing a hill above the town of Bouville gives him a sudden and new perspective, and his vision is particularly relevant to *Albert's Bridge*[6] for he, too, sees the people as little black dots amidst the patterned geometry of the streets below. The way Albert finds his life's purpose in the artistic symmetry of steel gently parodies *Nausea*'s final moment when Roquentin decides to take his life in his own hands by writing a novel. His illumination comes as he listens to a scratchy old recording of "Some of These Days" and imagines a Jewish musician in his stifling apartment twenty floors above New York composing this song and so creating a reason for his having lived. Roquentin decides to create something which never existed before; he will find salvation through art, producing a novel which, like Albert's bridge, "would be as beautiful and hard as steel".

In Stoppard, the possibility of a mind-bending shift of perspective had struck other characters besides Gladys and Albert. In *Lord Malquist*, Moon feels "that reality was just outside his perception. If he made a certain move, changed the angle of his existence to the common ground, logic and absurdity would separate. As it was he couldn't pin them down" (32). In *Rosencrantz*, Guil ponders the fact that one lives "so close to truth, it becomes a permanent blur in the corner of your eye, and when something nudges it into outline it is like being ambushed by the grotesque" (28). None of them has seen the world from beyond its boundaries as Penelope's lunanaut has, but that landing, long one of Stoppard's personal fantasies, alters the logic of all things. Wittgenstein's *Tractatus* explains the limits of logic:

Logic pervades the world: the limits of the world are also its limits.

So we cannot say in logic, "the world has this in it, and this, but not that".... since it would require that logic should go beyond the limits of the world; for only in that way could it view those limits from the other side as well.

The sense of the world must lie outside the world. In the world everything is as it is, and everything happens as it does happen: *in* it no value exists...[7]

As Stoppard once suggested, "There's an element of coincidence in what's usually called influence. One's appetites and predilections are obviously not unique. They overlap with those of countless other people, ..."[8]

The moon-landing idea does not work well in *Another Moon* because for Penelope it remains only an idea; it has no connections – as it will have in *Jumpers* – with the state of things beyond the bedroom. So Penelope's peculiar view of the lunanaut appears as just another symptom of this child-wife's neurotic behaviour, and the play merely pits the wife's eccentric logic against her husband's, while it unravels her none-too-mystifying claim to have given her old Nanny "the push". Neither Bone nor his wife provokes in us much interest: he retreats to his private pursuit of the world's history; she has taken to her bed ten days before because the lunanaut has spoiled things, just like Nanny Pinkerton who would keep winning at cards or at noughts and crosses. The dialogue, crisp and clever though it is, skitters across a void, unable to mask the play's jejune plot and tiresome characters. Yet their situation is such that, what with her emotional breakdown and his confused malaise, we should want to feel for them.

Just as emotions are trivialized, so the word-traps and deceptive appearances are reduced to comic misunderstanding as the characters dance their dance, stumbling occasionally over one another's feet:

BONE: Well, this way! She won't keep you a moment . . . I'm Mrs Bone's husband.
ALBERT: Mr Bone.
BONE: Yes . . . I'm something of a logician myself.
ALBERT: Really? Sawing ladies in half – that kind of thing?
BONE: Logician . . .   (100)

The games here fail to satisfy because the players themselves do not take those pastimes seriously. Penelope's charades with Albert have as little impetus behind them as has the game of battleships she plays with her husband, so the viewer does not feel pressed to investigate the relationship between the wife and her doctor. The latter, too, behaves in a totally casual manner, whereas Malquist, in a similar situation, throws all his ingenuity into appearing casual. The situation in Bone's household is simply good for a pun or two.

Apart from the dialogue, there are moments of technical ingenuity. During the game of battleships, the sounds of the astronaut's celebration parade drift in from outside so that when Penelope hits one of her husband's submarines the imagined depth charges are made concrete by the actual booms from the ceremonial canon and, as the military bands reach the house and jets scream overhead, those noises orchestrate Penelope's mounting hysteria. Yet that very brittleness, a neurosis which Penelope tries to forestall by playing games and pushing Nanny through the window because she "felt like it", takes away all force from her view of what the lunanaut has done. When Bone enters the bedroom to find her at the window gazing down on the parade, having walked there despite her own and the doctor's insistence that she has lost the use of her legs, her words are simply words: "There goes God in his golden capsule. You'd think that he was sane, to look at him, but he doesn't smile because he has seen the whole thing for what it is ... he's made it all random" (108).

Some five years after this short television script, Stoppard had transformed these ideas into *Jumpers*, the play which, up to the present moment at least, stands as his most completely achieved stage work. Everything knits together in *Jumpers*: stage-picture, dialogue, lighting, sound-effects, action combine into an ultra-theatrical game that matters deeply. George and Dotty Moore, fumbling and lost to each other, yet hanging on for dear life, are under siege. The astronaut's yellow uniform, so literal in the television script, has become the symbol of a cynical and manipulative pragmatism made concrete in the persons of Sir Archibald Jumper and the Radical Liberals: "I have seen the future", said the late Professor McFee, "and it's yellow." Doing his homework for this play led Stoppard to understand how words, which he had always seen as sliding, ambiguous and confusing, can, because of those inadequacies, be deliberately used to deceive, persuade or undermine. *Jumpers* therefore marks the turning-point in Stoppard's career as he moves towards the political implications of words that ensnare. The play is also very funny (ha-ha and peculiar) from beginning to end.

The relationship between the Moores, like that between the Moons or the Bones before them, is larger than life. So to propel his audience into a heightened world, Stoppard begins with a daring and extravagantly theatrical flourish. From the completely darkened stage, a voice grandiloquently announces the return of "the much-missed, much-loved star of the musical stage, the incomparable, magnetic Dorothy Moore!"[9] Dotty (aptly named, it soon turns out) walks into a spotlight to the sound of applause but fails to pick up on the musical introduction to "Shine on Harvest Moon". Re-introducing herself as "incomparable, unreliable, neurotic", she asks her unseen audience for the cues and rapidly becomes entangled in a jumble of moon tunes; unable to continue, she apologizes and leaves the stage. The public disintegration of a beautiful star – and Dotty must look like a goddess – is oddly disturbing, especially when it comes without warning, but the next events prove still more unsettling.

A loud drum-roll introduces a female stripper seated on a swing attached to a chandelier which arcs in and out of the spotlight's beam. We now feel as disoriented as Dotty and as confused as the waiter who then stumbles with his tray of drinks into the light. The stage-audience protests vociferously at his blocking the view. Every time he looks in their direction, the stripper flies in, having shed more and more of her clothes; every time he looks behind him to see what the fuss is about, the stage is empty. Eventually he "backs into the path of the swing and is knocked arse over tip by a naked lady. BLACKOUT and crash of broken glass" (18). Instantly, the off-stage voice proclaims "the INCREDIBLE – RADICAL! – LIBERAL!! – JUMPERS!!"; spotlight, music, and eight yellow-clad figures come leaping and tumbling from both sides of the stage. Dotty wanders on to complain that the jumpers are certainly not incredible. Calling for someone truly unbelievable, she turns to find George, a rumpled, shabby figure, clutching a sheaf of papers: "Promptness I like." George protests about the noise, but is furiously dismissed: "It's my bloody party, George!"

Several muddled moon-songs follow as Dotty strolls amidst the jumpers, who have begun to form a human pyramid until, obscured from our view, she sneers, "Jumpers I've *had* – yellow, I've had them all! *In*credible, *barely* credible, credible and all too bloody likely – When I say jump, *jump*!" A gun-shot sends one of the figures reeling from the base of the pyramid. Dotty walks through the gap and looks down in surprise as the dying jumper tries to pull himself up by her dress. After a few precarious seconds, the pyramid collapses away into the surrounding darkness. The party is over. Isolated in the spotlight and calling out for "Archie", Dotty stands in her now blood-soaked dress while the units of the Moores' apartment assemble around her. When the stage is fully lit, the immobile Dotty is discovered to be in her bedroom still clutching the dead jumper. The hyperbole of this opening assault prepares the audience to accept any event that may follow; the overt theatricality of the action and set-change forbids our settling into the Moores' apartment with a cosy sense of everyday life. An idiom has been established that will support the most outlandish of fables.

But this opening has also established a bond of confusion between ourselves and the Moores. Although they know why their party takes place, by the end of this prelude Dotty stands paralysed, George has been excluded, and we are also in the dark. The rest of the staging keeps us at varying levels of knowledge and ignorance, groping along with the Moores for enlightenment of one sort or another. The entire set, two rooms separated by a reversed-L-shaped corridor, creates a paradigm of the sort of world all Stoppard's characters inhabit. Like their predecessors, George and Dotty live inside the boundaries of their own special view of the world. What goes on in one box may or may not mean something to the inhabitant of the other box, and, if it does, then that something is likely to appear different.

One of Stoppard's favourite stories concerns a friend who kept peacocks.[10] Seeing one disappear over the garden wall, he interrupted his shaving and dashed out after it. Recovering the bird, he waited to cross a busy road. What, Stoppard wonders, can the occupants of the passing cars have made of a man standing at the roadside in a dressing-gown with shaving lather on his face and a peacock tucked firmly under one arm? A similar vision of Inspector Foot of the Yard had puzzled the Harrises in *After Magritte*. A replay occurs in *Jumpers* when George answers the door to Inspector Bones. George is somewhat surprised to see a man with a bunch of flowers, since he had expected to confront Archie. Bones "recoils" as from a madman, since George has forgotten to remove his shaving cream and carries a bow-and-arrow and a tortoise, having been interrupted in the middle of demonstrating a fallacy in logic.

Jumpers' set evokes exactly this interdependent independence. George's study, to the right of the hall as we look at the stage, presents his ivory tower: a trifle sterile, especially when furnished in the stark, modernist outlines of the National's original production, and cluttered with books, papers, and the paraphernalia he uses to demonstrate his ideas. Dotty's bedroom, confined by the reversed-L shape, exudes luxury and femininity with its lush carpets and curtains, elegant furniture, record-player, huge television set and four-poster bed. Their separate lives are suggested by this contrasting décor, by the fact that George's study includes a monastic-looking day-bed, and by the actual barrier of the corridor between the two rooms, although once the action starts we realize that this apartness is more extensive than any of the staging proclaims. Dotty, alone in her room and now calmly considering what to do with the corpse, hears somebody singing "Sentimental Journey" to himself. Things get off to a false start as she addresses the voice as "Darling!" and Crouch, the hall porter whom we last saw employed as the waiter at the party, explains her mistake. Crouch leaves; George's secretary, the previous night's stripper, hurries in; life at the Moores' moves into its 9 a.m. routine, except that from the bedroom Dotty calls "Help!" first quietly then "slightly louder". George looks up at the imaginary mirror between us and him; he may or may not have heard the distress call as the lights go to black in Dotty's room.

The intermittent disappearance of that area of the set is essential to the play's effect and meaning. The device ensures that the audience will focus primarily on George, awarding him a large proportion of their sympathies despite his muddle-headed inadequacy. At other times, when we see both rooms, we understand more than George can or, owing to a previous blackout, we are for a moment more muddled than he is. For example, since we have already seen the dead jumper in Dotty's bedroom, her cries of "murder" out of the darkness have a more complicated effect on us than Penelope's to Bone. We can understand why George thinks them an irritating distraction, yet we can also sympathize with Dotty's panic and suspect that she refers to the whole state of their marriage with her "*is anybody there?*" On the other hand, Stoppard may have been a shade too clever when he makes her quote *Macbeth*:

DOTTY (*off. Panic*): Help! Murder!
(GEORGE *throws his manuscript on the desk and marches angrily to the door.*)
(*Off*) Oh, horror, horror, horror! Confusion now hath made its masterpiece ... most sacriligious murder! – (*Different voice.*) Woe, alas! What, in our house?
(GEORGE, *with his hand on the door handle, pauses. He returns to his desk and picks up his papers.*) (24)

The general reference to murder and the aptness of "in our house" are amusing enough, but the literariness may mislead us into thinking Dotty callous and so not truly horror-struck. Only later do we learn the dead acrobat's identity, Duncan McFee, but by then we have no time in the theatre to connect back to these lines on the murder of Duncan[11] and so change our minds about Dotty's lack of feeling.

When the lights come back up on the bedroom as George enters to look for his pet hare, Thumper, we have lost our overview entirely, for during the blackout the corpse has vanished. In another respect we are even less in the know than George who, after a glance around the room, ignores Dotty's apparently lifeless body, face down and naked on the bed. Stoppard allows us a moment to misread that picture while George searches in the off-stage bathroom for Thumper. Emerging, he casually asks whether Dotty is a proverb – "No, I'm a book" – whereupon he guesses *The Naked and the Dead* and we suddenly leap ahead of George, who cannot know that title's appropriateness. When he leaves, the lights stay up to reveal the jumper hanging from a hook on the door George has closed (at the National the door synchronized with a trick cupboard to disclose or conceal the corpse).

The habitual charades between husband and wife lead up to the enigma of Archie's behaviour with Dotty. George's suspicions and her defence are partly taken from *Another Moon* but now the lines have more emotional force, since for the past twenty minutes or so George has been shown battling with questions of logic, and the now-you-see-it-now-you-don't quality of the action and staging has created a context for what is possibly a misunderstanding or possibly a half-truth:

> GEORGE (*reckless, committed*): I can put two and two together, you know. Putting two and two together is my *subject*. I do not leap to hasty conclusions. I do not deal in suspicion and wild surmise. I examine the data; I look for logical inferences . . .
> (*He has lapsed into a calm suavity.*)
> Now let us see. What can we make of it all? Wife in bed, daily visits by gentleman caller. Does anything suggest itself?
> DOTTY (*calmly*): Sounds to me he's the doctor. (32)

If Dotty is deceiving George, and we never do know for sure, then the charade is a most elaborate one. At the end of Act 1, Archie and the jumpers bring in "a machine of ambiguous purpose" and a number of lights on stands. This machine, supposedly a dermatograph, connects to Dotty's television screen. When the bedroom lights up for the first time in Act 2 it appears to be empty until voices sound from behind the closed curtains of the four-poster:

> (*These sounds are consistent with a proper doctor–patient relationship. If* DOTTY *has a tendency to gasp slightly it is probably because the stethoscope is cold.* ARCHIE *on the other hand, might be getting rather overheated under the blaze of the dermatograph lights.*)
> ARCHIE (*within*): Excuse me . . .
> (ARCHIE's *coat comes sailing over the drapes.* GEORGE *retreats, closing the door.*)
> (60)

At this stage of the play, it is crucial that we should also find it impossible to know the truth of the situation. When George goes back into the study, his "How the hell does one know what to believe?" (71) refers us to his confusion over the discussion paper, in which he seeks to prove that God exists, and to the Archie–Dotty axis which fills us with a similar confusion and so dramatizes what would otherwise remain an abstract philosophical conundrum. Stoppard draws those parallels together in the dialogue. Trying to deal, or to put off dealing with Dotty's neurosis, for which Archie purportedly attends her, George ("facing away, out front, emotionless") tells the story of how Wittgenstein asked a friend why "it was *natural*" to suppose the sun moves round the earth. The friend replied that it *looked* as if it did, to which the philosopher answered, "what would it have looked like if it had looked as if the earth was rotating?" (75).[12] Moments later that same philosophical problem is applied to events in the bedroom. George sees a close-up picture magnified on the television screen. Depending on how magnified it is, the audience may for a moment believe they see a view of the moon's surface as they did in Act 1. However, George recognizes it as his wife's naked body and angrily switches off the set:

GEORGE: You must think I'm a bloody fool!
ARCHIE: What do you mean?
GEORGE: Well, everything you do makes it *look* as if you're . . .
(*Pause.*)
ARCHIE: Well, what would it have *looked* like if it had *looked* as if I were making a dermatographical examination? (78)

"Confusion now hath made its masterpiece" indeed. Experiencing that, the audience participate in the sexual and philosophical battle between George and Archie.

The play's most elaborately deceptive moment takes its effect from a combination of lighting, dialogue, action, and sound-cues. After Inspector Bones, who confesses that "show business is my main interest, closely followed by crime detection" (46), has been established as an ardent fan of Dotty's, he prepares to question her about the previous evening's party: "after which, I will take my leave, perhaps with her autograph on the cover of this much played much loved gramophone record" (45). We see him standing outside the darkened bedroom, sprucing himself up and fishing for Dotty's gramophone record as he balances his tributary flowers, now in a vase. Tapping respectfully on the door, he enters, and the bedroom glows romantically:

. . . *pink curtains have been drawn across the french window, and there is a rosy hue to the lighting.* DOTTY, *gowned, coiffed, stunning, rises to face the Inspector. Music is heard . . . romantic Mozartian trumpets, triumphant.* DOTTY *and* BONES *face each other, frozen like lovers in a dream.* BONES *raises his head*

slightly, and the trumpets are succeeded by a loud animal bray, a mating call.
DOTTY, *her arms out towards him, breathes, "Inspector . . ." like a verbal*
caress. From BONES's *lifeless fingers, the vase drops. There is a noise such as*
would have been made had he dropped it down a long flight of stone stairs.
BONES *is dumbstruck.*
DOTTY *lets go a long slow smile: "Inspector. . . ."*
From behind the closed curtains, the stiff dead JUMPER *falls into the room like a*
too-hastily-leaned plank. (52)

Although the trumpets create an appropriate, if comically exaggerated, sound-track for the Inspector's sense of triumph and Dotty's
enchantment of her public, the action appears to shift into farce at the
"mating call" and goes hilariously awry when the vase falls loudly on
the thick carpet. The sequence builds to the sudden and unexpected
appearance of the corpse and an instant blackout. However, we may
have noticed George testing his tape-recorder, and now that our
focus moves over to his study we watch him launch once more into
dictating his paper. Arguing that beauty is "an aesthetic absolute"
just as goodness is a moral one, he turns to the recorder to illustrate
three different kinds of trumpet sounds. In this new context, we again
hear the snippet of Mozart which George invites his opponents to
compare aesthetically with the trumpeting of an elephant (the "loud
animal bray") and with "the sound made by a trumpet falling down a
flight of stone stairs" (the vase effect).

In *Jumpers*, Stoppard's characteristic tricksiness has sinister implications behind it. This is particularly so during the charades. The
pleasing irony of *The Naked and the Dead* turns darker and more
cynical when, in order to cover up the dead body as George returns to
the bedroom, Dotty "calmly lets her robe slip down her back" and, as
a further clue, "turns to look at him coquettishly over her shoulder":
"*Lulu*'s back! – in town – Very good!" (43). Consistently, throughout
the play, the jokes sour. Amidst the bedroom's pink romance, Dotty
tests her charms on an admirer, but she may be trying particularly
hard because she knows he is a policeman. Once the corpse falls to
the floor, her charms are all she has to save the situation: when the
blackout ends, "Music! Lights! Dorothy Moore – in person" is
discovered swinging and miming to her recording of "Sentimental
Journey" for her audience-of-one.

At the start of Act 2, Bones appears from the kitchen with a
dinner-trolley complete with an elegant meal for two; halting in the
corridor, he listens to the sound of Dotty's voice "rather as a man
might pause in St Peter's on hearing choristers" (57). To George he
describes her as a vulnerable, nervous little bird and suggests that any
psychiatric expert would be prepared, at a price, to say on the witness

stand that Dotty had snapped "under the strain". George does not yet know about the murder, but Archie, who has already had the evidence spirited away in a large plastic bag, is only too eager to manipulate Dotty's compliant fan. Treating him like a manservant, Archie hands him the coat from the bedroom floor "and then readies himself to put his arms in the sleeves". Archie *is* a psychiatric expert (she needs a lawyer!) and Dotty's legal adviser (a man has been murdered!); being a coroner as well, he hands Bones a death certificate and a suicide note which suggests McFee had a nervous breakdown and shot himself inside a plastic bag (64).

Bones is impressed by the expertise, but not enough to contemplate "offers of large sums of money for favours rendered". Archie tries the psychological approach, suggesting that Bones looks like a man whose services to the Force have not been truly appreciated and, as a University Chancellor, offers him the Chair of Divinity along with "prestige, the respect of your peers and almost unlimited credit among the local shopkeepers". Then comes the fist from beneath the glove: "a professorship will still be regarded as a distinction come the day – early next week, in all probability – when the Police Force will be thinned out to a ceremonial front for the peace-keeping activities of the Army" (65). Since Bones cannot be deflected from enquiring what became of the gun if McFee shot himself inside a bag – "Very good thinking indeed! On consideration I can give you the Chair of Logic" – the problem is left to Dotty as he races into her darkened room in answer to her calls of distress. Stoppard keeps us all in the dark for the next few minutes. Only one loud "Darling!" impinges upon the two philosophers' conversation until an urgent cry of "Rape . . . Rape!" sends Archie gleefully into the bedroom to find Dotty sobbing on the bed and Bones looking guilty. No doubt some "arrangement" could save the incorruptible officer. After the next blackout Bones has gone for good and the victorious pair sit eating a civilized lunch from the trolley.

That Archie can talk glibly about the Army's "peace-keeping activities" exposes the cynical power the new Rad-Lib regime has with words, and the huge television screen in Dotty's room acts as our window to those political realities in the outside world. Also, since the screen later registers whatever the dermatograph has scanned, this stage-property serves to underline Archie's connections with Yellow Power. The television is on when the bedroom set first slides in behind Dotty and the jumper. The white spotlight moves from her to the screen, where it changes into a satellite picture of the moon, then to close-ups of an astronaut, rocket, and moon-vehicle, the accoutrements of the first British moon mission. This event and the Rad-

Libs' victory parade, televised on a second channel, establish a context which will govern our reactions to George's philosophical paper.

In landing upon the moon, the two-man space-capsule had suffered damage to its booster rockets. When the time came for lift-off, millions of home viewers watched the commander, Captain Scott, knock Astronaut Oates off the foot of the ladder then pull it up and close the hatch. Stoppard names his explorers after the two most famous members of Scott's ill-fated Antarctic Expedition in 1910. The historical Oates, incapacitated by frost-bite and not wishing to hamper his already hard-pressed companions, walked off into the snows. His act of self-sacrifice has become the stuff of legend, but in *Jumpers* Oates' actual last words, "I am going out now. I may be gone some time", are transferred to Astronaut Scott, "I am going up now . . .," as he saves his own skin at his partner's expense. By converting an archetype of heroic sacrifice into an image of expediency, Stoppard prepares us for the main argument in George's paper which will take human altruism as man's saving grace and as "proof" that goodness is not simply a matter of social convention. On the contrary, as George will also point out, the conventions of society can change or be manipulated, and it is that fact which makes the other happenings on the television screen so important to the play's central relationships and meaning.

The enormous screen dominates Dotty's bedroom. Pictured there, from time to time in Act 1, are shots of a long procession of a decidedly military character. George finds the noise of the brass bands disconcerting as he dictates his paper, turns the set off on entering the bedroom, and only notes some sort of parade once the sounds of jets come screaming over the house. Through those reactions, Stoppard pinpoints the weakness in George's moral position, for though he is disturbed by the Rad-Lib victory his concern is never strong enough to pull him away from his intellectual pursuits. Yet for us, the pictures and sounds from the screen and the screaming jets overhead project all that the Rad-Libs stand for out into the auditorium and vivify the details of the dialogue. Because of this, we are unlikely to share George's naive faith in democracy. The Party have juggled the votes, taken over the broadcasting system, arrested the leading newspaper proprietors, and intend to "rationalize" the Church and, as Archie implied, establish the military State that the nature of their victory parade suggests. Yet George only bursts out in protest over the idea that Sam Clegthorpe, the Party's spokesman for agriculture, has been made the Archbishop of Canterbury. Even then, he soon retreats into irony:

DOTTY: Do you find it incredible that a man with a scientific background should be Archbishop of Canterbury?

GEORGE: How the hell do *I* know what I find incredible? Credibility is an expanding field . . . Sheer disbelief hardly registers on the face before the head is nodding with all the wisdom of instant hindsight. "Archbishop Clegthorpe? Of course! The inevitable capstone to a career in veterinary medicine!" What happened to the old Archbishop?

DOTTY: He abdicated . . . or resigned or uncoped himself –

GEORGE (*thoughtfully*): Dis-mantled himself, perhaps. (38)

In having George joke like this, Stoppard nevertheless illustrates the way the most intelligent can slide into acceptance and become an easy prey to powermongers. One of *Jumpers'* main points is that credibility *does* expand.

If the theatricality of *Jumpers* dramatizes the Moores' mental confusion and the cynical expediency of the world around them, the same can be said of the play's two major plot lines. The one, Archie's confusing relationship with Dotty, has a great deal to do with the other, the murder of Duncan McFee. That George should be oblivious for most of the play to the murder that takes place in his flat underlines his withdrawal from the actualities of life, in addition to creating many comic misunderstandings. But knowing that one of the jumpers died at the party, we may be inclined to suspect Dotty as his murderer from her position behind the human pyramid. Her look of surprise as the dying man clings to her might confirm that suspicion but then it might also point to her innocence. However, because so much else goes on at the Moores' we would probably not dwell upon this until well into the first Act, when Dotty fleetingly admits to being "in a bit of a spot" (34). The whodunnit only becomes central upon the arrival of Inspector Bones, and, cleverly, with no sign of forcing things, Stoppard keeps us in ignorance as to the victim's identity by having Bones mention everything about the previous night's party except the fact of a dead body, so enamoured is he of Dotty's aura and of the theatrics of his role as investigator. In his conversation with George we hear the name of McFee for the first time as one who attended the party held to celebrate the Rad-Lib victory. From George's explanation of his colleague's ethical stance, the audience might even suspect McFee of being a potential murderer:

GEORGE: He thinks good and bad aren't actually *good* and *bad* in any absolute or metaphysical sense, he believes them to be categories of our own making . . . For example, McFee would hold that when we speak of, say, telling the truth as being "good", and, er, casual murder as being "bad", you don't really want to go into all this, do you?

BONES (*his pencil poised, his eyes wide*): I am enthralled. (48)

Stoppard forces us into this guessing game so that we may feel for ourselves how difficult it is to verify *anything*, let alone the good and the bad. At the end of Act 2, when George finally learns about the murder, he too believes that Dotty shot Duncan:

GEORGE: Crouch says – You can't hide! – Dorothy – it's not a game! Crouch says he *saw* – For God's sake – I don't know what to do –

ARCHIE: Crouch says he saw *what*, George?

GEORGE: Well, he didn't actually *see* . . .

ARCHIE: Quite. We just don't *know*.

GEORGE: There are many things I know which are not verifiable but nobody can tell me I don't know them, and I think that I know that something happened to poor Dotty and she somehow killed McFee, as sure as she killed my poor Thumper. (78)

But Dotty, despite appearances, has not killed Thumper. Minutes later George finds out that he himself killed the hare with an arrow he inadvertently let loose on an instinctive reaction to Dotty's cry of "Fire!" from the bedroom.

In the mean time, we have witnessed a crucial conversation between Crouch and Archie in which the porter explains his friendship with McFee and how the latter had been stunned by the behaviour of the astronauts on the moon. As the spokesman for the logical positivists, Duncan had come to the conclusion he was "giving philosophical respectability to a new pragmatism in public life" (79). The contrast between these new explorers and the former Oates and Scott had convinced him that there is an absolute good:

If altruism is a possibility, he said, my argument is up a gum-tree . . . Duncan, I said, Duncan,[13] don't you worry your head about all that. That astronaut yobbo is good for twenty years hard. Yes, he said, yes *maybe*, but when he comes out, he's going to find he was only twenty years ahead of his time. (80)

If Archie knew of Duncan's conversion – Crouch says, "he no doubt told you" – then on his own admission he had a motive for murder. Earlier, while dealing with Inspector Bones, Archie had suggested that, apart from the jumpers themselves, anyone at the party could have fired the shot, including himself. When Bones asks him why he should have wanted to do that, Archie's hypothetical answer that perhaps "my faithful protégé had secretly turned against me" (63) leads to his saying that if the "figurehead of philosophical orthodoxy" had gone astray, "I'm afraid it would certainly have been an ice-pick in the back of the skull" (64). Considering the Rad-Libs' victory parade, this reference to the elimination of Trotsky is apt. We recall, too, that Archie "had a furious row last night" with McFee and was anxious to know from George whether the Inspector had asked him about it (68). Whether or not Archie did in fact kill Duncan, the moment we suspect him of that crime opens a new view onto his relationship with Dotty. Knowing that Bones, Crouch and George think her guilty, Archie is quite willing to let them do so, whereas she, thinking all along that Archie had done it, has been trying to protect him.

Having let us see the manipulative Archie as a second Astronaut Scott, Stoppard immediately plants a further possibility as he makes Crouch go on to explain how he and Duncan used to talk philosophy while he waited to pick up his girl. As Crouch speaks, the secretary, who has sat wordlessly in the study throughout the play, "comes down stage to make use of the imaginary mirror . . . a grim, tense, unsmiling young woman, staring at the audience" (80). It transpires that she and Duncan had been secretly engaged for three years. He had dreaded telling her he had a wife, though his wife knew about the secretary, but his decision to relinquish the Chair of Logic had left him no alternative. On that awesome thought, the secretary clicks her handbag shut and briskly takes her coat from a cupboard. The strategic click and her unyielding grimness both point to what Crouch calls "a certain kind of girl". It was she who swung from the trapeze and, as she puts on her coat and goes out for lunch, it is she who has "a bright splash of blood" down her back. Seeing that stain, George then discovers that the blood has trickled down from the top of the wardrobe and so finds that his own pet jumper lies dead. As Archie has said,

The truth to us philosophers, Mr Crouch, is always an interim judgment. We will never even know for certain who did shoot McFee. Unlike mystery novels, life does not guarantee a denouement; and if it came, how would one know whether to believe it?
(81)

This elaborate, interlocking superstructure of stage devices and plot may seem cumbersome when described like this, but in perform-ance the theatrical razzle-dazzle along with the impenetrability of Archie's "professional" behaviour and the mysterious murder com-bine to create in us the vertigo that also threatens George and Dotty. The game-playing here dramatically conveys the issue at the play's centre, the inadequacy and danger of words in a society which considers all truths to be relative. There, at that centre, the most human of Stoppard's flawed protagonists, George and Dotty, struggle to express, in inefficient words, what they instinctively know to be right, and it is their battle which makes the outward games a matter of burning concern. What to believe? As George muddles his way through his paper on "Man – good, bad or indifferent" or as Dotty attempts to cope with the fact that the first moon-landings have reduced mankind and his morals to something limited and arbitrary, the dice may be loaded against them but, sentimental though this sounds, their hearts are somehow in the right place. In a scientific world, there must be more to Man than meets the microscope.

Archie regards George as he would the Dodo. In a "rationalized" society, what was once the University chapel has become the gymnasium, a place where "the more philosophical members of the university gymnastics team and the more gymnastic members of the Philosophy School" (51) can learn to jump, to expand their political and intellectual credibility at Archie's command. But George refuses to "jump along with the rest", because in his view British moral philosophy "went off the rails" roughly forty years ago. Hoping to put things back on track, George prepares his attack on the "mainstream" logical positivists, a school of thinkers who insist that the only factual statements are those which can be proved through observation. "Truth" must be capable of scientific verification, and anything which falls outside this area of fact is not philosophical.

Logical positivism goes back to the 1920s when the 'Vienna Circle' sought to extract all mystery from philosophic investigation and to rationalize it in accordance with science, "the sum of all meaningful statements".[14] In Cambridge, Wittgenstein had concluded that "what we cannot speak about we must consign to silence",[15] a statement which seemed to banish everything beyond the realm of "atomic facts" to irrelevance. Accordingly, A. J. Ayer in his *Language, Truth and Logic*, the orthodox bible of British logical positivism, maintains that "all utterances about the nature of God are nonsensical". For Ayer, "moral judgements do not say anything. They are pure expressions of feeling and as such do not come under the category of truth and falsehood."[16] For its opponents, logical positivism simply circumvents the problems of human ethics: "they disappear not because they have been solved but because they are dismissed"[17] or, as *Jumpers* puts it, "no problem is insoluble given a big enough plastic bag" into which to sweep it. Wittgenstein himself in his *Philosophical Investigations* came to revise his view about the nature of factual propositions by suggesting that language itself determines what is real, because we perceive things through language. In consequence, all objective fact is an illusion.

But instead of building an argument which would point out the subjectivity of all scientific verification, George tries to meet the opposition on their own "logical" ground. An intuitionist like his namesake, G. E. Moore, George "insist[s] that goodness [is] a fact, and on his right to recognize it when he [sees] it" (67). But in the first part of his paper George traps himself, because words can only go so far in describing the indescribable; after a certain point one has to leave "proof" behind and take the leap of faith, a jump into the void, and George is no jumper. Wittgenstein's thoughts on this are helpful:

If someone who believes in God looks round and asks "Where does everything I see come from?", "Where does all this come from?", he is *not* craving for a (causal) explanation; and his question gets its point from being the expression of a certain craving. He is, namely, expressing an attitude to all explanations. – But how is this manifested in his life?

The attitude that's in question is that of taking a certain matter seriously and then, beyond a certain point, no longer regarding it as serious, but maintaining that something else is even more important.[18]

As he gathers together his random notes to dictate his paper, George runs into immediate trouble over the way to pose the question of whether God exists. The linguistic tangles of the first part of his paper unintentionally illustrate how "language is an approximation of meaning":

... why we should believe that existence could be asserted of the author of "Principia Mathematica" but not of Bertrand Russell, he never had time, despite his punctuality, not to mention his existence, to explain, very good, keep to the point, to begin at the beginning: *is God*? (*To* SECRETARY) Leave a space.   (25)

George can never jump that space. He feels he needs God – or preferably two – to account for the Creation and for the moral behaviour of His creations. But as he thrashes about with First Causes, Zeno, bows and arrows, the tortoise and the ... but Thumper is missing ... his paper becomes a ludicrous Whodunnit on a cosmic scale.

However, when George turns to moral absolutes, Stoppard builds up his long speech into the climax of the first Act. Despite the comic counterpoint between Dotty's seduction of the Inspector and the recorded trumpet sounds or the running jibes about McFee's jumping skills (to which at one point the secretary raises her head), George begins to find the words to mount a vigorous attack. The positivists would say that "good" means different things to different people; George does not dispute that, since it is not a statement about values but about the use of language. But when the argument does move on to human behaviour, George wins our sympathy because of the sudden force and clarity of his thesis and because we have seen from the rest of the Act where man-made values can lead:

... Professor McFee should not be surprised that the notion of honour should manifest itself so differently in peoples so far removed in clime and culture. What is surely more surprising is that notions such as honour should manifest themselves at all.   (54–5)

In Act 2, Stoppard changes tack from argument to satire. Bones presses George to spare no expense in Dotty's defence; George assumes he is talking about his own phone-call of complaint to the police about the noise at the party. Having calmed down since then, he regrets his action. Bones suggests that George has concocted this story to shield Dotty, but George argues that as the householder he must be held responsible for any disturbance that occurred in the flat: "It was just a bit of *fun*! Where's your sense of humour, man?" (59). To the Inspector's ears, George talks like the acrobatic jumpers in the sort of doublespeak on which the Rad-Libs' policies depend. For if "good" means different things to different people, people can be persuaded to accept new conceptions of good, and a murder can be defined as "a bit of fun".

The comedy of this episode leads directly to the core of George's argument when he returns to his paper. Picking up on the vagaries of language, "a finite instrument crudely applied to an infinity of ideas" (63), George addresses himself to the distinctions between "a good bacon sandwich" and "the Good Samaritan". In the first expression, "good" can be described in other terms, "such as crisp, lean and unadulterated by tomato sauce". The goodness of that sandwich would not be apparent to someone who liked his bacon "underdone, fatty and smothered in ketchup". In the second expression, however, there is no getting away from the fact of the Samaritan's goodness; it is an absolute value, to be expressed in no other way, and not, as the positivists would have it, a mere statement about "feeling, taste or vested interest":

... when we say that the Good Samaritan acted well, we are surely expressing more than a circular prejudice about behaviour. We mean he acted kindly – selflessly – *well*. And what is our approval of kindness based on if not on the intuition that kindness is simply good in itself and cruelty is not?   (66–7)

"Intuition" also saves Dotty, though in her case she would prefer to have her problems spirited away in words. In the first Act, one of Dotty's functions is to voice the positivist opinions of Archie who, apart from his off-stage announcements at the party, makes his silent first entrance at the very end of the Act in order to choreograph the disposal of the inconvenient corpse. In consequence, Dotty might appear as another of Archie's creatures; she would indeed like him to dispose of her inconvenient moon-madness, but something within her resists his linguistic plastic bag. For example, when she begs George to stay with her, "I don't want to be left, to cope . . ." (with Duncan's body or her own mind), he pleads work and assures her "things will get better", a phrase which spins her Archie-wards. But her recital is cross-cut by personal reservations and finally undercut by her actual circumstance, which will not simply disappear because "Archie says" it should. Furthermore, in repeating the positivist "line" she adopts the same detached, ironic tone towards it that George uses in his paper. At one point, George asks her what she meant by "God help you and the Government", a question she deliberately and wittily takes as a philosophic one: "I only mentioned God reflexively." Nevertheless that leads her to ponder why God refuses to disappear despite the positivists and their political arm, the Rad-Libs:

DOTTY (*still merry*): And yet, Professor, one can't help wondering at the persistence of the reflex, the universal constant unthinking appeal to the non-existent God who is presumed dead. Perhaps he's only missing in action, shot down behind the thin yellow lines of advancing Rad-Libs and getting himself together to go BOO! (35)

The note of bright hysteria under her irony stems from Dotty's psychotic reaction to the very first moon-landing. But Man's foot-steps on the moon did more than spoil the romance of Moon–spoon –June songs and wreck her stage career. Dotty suffers from another of those mind-warping perspectives. For her, men on the moon have seen mankind "all in one go, *little – local,*" so that all human values which "never had edges before" have been seen to have limits. The behaviour of the astronauts during the latest mission confirms what happens when absolute values are perceived as relative values, and Dotty feels certain that when the rest of the world catches up with that view chaos is come again (75). Actually, then, she shares George's faith in the rightness of the Ten Commandments, whose rules, unlike those of tennis, cannot be changed. Were Archie able to convince her that there are no absolutes, then the moon-landings would have no significance. Instead, she is torn between wanting to believe in Archie's logic and knowing intuitively that things are otherwise.

Both she and McFee are disciples who cannot become apostles of the positivist creed. Although George never knows that McFee's crisis was also the result of moon happenings, convinced instead that the jumper was a smug time-server, he reacts to the news of Duncan's "suicide" with mild surprise:

Where did he find the despair . . .? I thought the whole *point* of denying the Absolute was to reduce the scale, instantly, to the inconsequential behaviour of inconsequential animals; that nothing could ever be that important . . . (69)

Dotty knows that despair but, oddly, that knowledge marks her as her own mistress and not Archie's puppet.

Dotty and George's concern over absolute values is more than abstract word-play. Neither of them takes a moral stand, yet the ideas they give voice to have urgency because of Archie's manœuvrings within the flat and the Rad-Libs' manipulations outside it and on the screen. But if *Jumpers* has darker undertones than any of its predecessors, it is also the first of Stoppard's works (apart from "Reunion") to explore a human relationship in any depth. The Malquists and the Moons, Constance and Alfred, Glad and Frank, Albert and Kate, even Ros and Guil for that matter, all talk past each other from within their self-absorbed enclosures. The Moores do that too, but they also make convincing attempts to reach each other, and the failure of those efforts creates a poignant, human drama at the centre of this verbal and theatrical whirligig. The fact that they are both intelligent people with a dry sense of their own inadequacies and absurdity gives them an unsentimental view of themselves and each other, but their intellect ultimately destroys their will. Dotty, shut away in her bedroom, takes refuge in her trauma when the going gets rough. George, buried in his notes or wandering purblind through the flat clutching his paraphernalia for his defence of love and goodness, takes cover amongst "matters of universal import" whenever demands are made on him. Yet the two do have moments of desolate or furious contact, and those episodes establish an ironic picture of two people who seem unable to put their well-meaning intuitions about universals into personal practice.

In the first of these episodes, the audience receive an immediate impression of a shared life from the way George can take Dotty's charade-playing for granted. Stoppard has frequently been accused of not understanding women or of failing to create a complex, believable female character, and Dotty has been singled out as the major weakness of *Jumpers*, but her behaviour here, though eccentric and stamped with her creator's own personality, has corners to it, facets and angles which make her a complicated, interesting and – given the play's established idiom – credible individual. All Stoppard's women characters have a sort of inner mysteriousness, an untouchable knowingness which makes them puzzling to their Moon-partners or provocative when allied with the worldly poise of a Harry (in pub or dental surgery), a Malquist or an Archie. Perhaps this impenetrability is the mark of what Stoppard cannot understand, but in *Jumpers* those hidden areas of personality make a dramatic impact. Dotty's external vibrance and neurotically destructive tendencies allow us to feel there is more to her than meets the eye, and Stoppard has given her moments with George in which we glimpse that inner self. In addition, he makes Dotty aware of her own mystery as a woman and a star – a mystery which she deliberately uses on George and later, quite lethally, on the Inspector.

Her first actions in the play as neurotic moon-singer, critic, and commander of the acrobats, or as a histrionic attention-seeker (with a penchant for Shakespeare) and player of ambiguous charades all present the threatening puzzle behind the glamour. But as the scene with George continues, she veers from behaviour which could seem acted out into a desperation that arises from a genuine annoyance at not being able to reach her husband. Since we do not yet know about her *Angst* over the astronauts, this sequence between the Moores re-creates a fairly normal thrust-and-parry between two people with a shared history and a fair knowledge of each other's habits and weaknesses but with insufficient regard for each other's inner bewilderment. This scene works because Stoppard has made Dotty George's intellectual match. As we soon discover, she had once been his student and she can laugh at her former career: "not at all bad for a one-time student amateur bored with keeping house for her professor" (39). Moreover, that intelligence and sense-of-self inform most of her remarks so that the characters pierce each other's guard and then, after a feint or two, resume the attack. Dotty's mind, and the energy it generates, makes her verbal thrusts seem entirely her own. Having dismissed George's claim to friendship with Bertrand Russell, she quickly stabs at his "living in a dreamland", and when he defensively turns that aside, she falls back dejectedly on the bed: "Oh God . . . if only Archie would come"(31).

But it is their moments of stillness, rare in Stoppard, as the two reach across the gap between them, that move us nearest to who they are and persuade us that Dotty would not need Archie were George less unavailable. The stage-directions indicate the characters' genuine feeling:

DOTTY: I won't see him any more, if you like. (*Turns to him.*) I'll see you. If you like.
(GEORGE *examines the new tone, and decides the moment is genuine.*)
GEORGE (*softening*): Oh, Dotty . . . The first day you walked into my class . . . I thought, "*That's* better!" . . . It was a wet day . . . your hair was wet . . . and I thought, "The hyacinth girl" . . . and "How my hair is growing thin."
(33)

Granted that the mood lasts only an instant, since George protects himself with bits from T. S. Eliot which Dotty picks up in gentle mockery, it does lead to their frankest interchange so far (Dotty is "in a bit of a spot") and to a relaxed affection. The climax of this scene, after more rounds of fencing, depends on a further instant of repose after Dotty bursts into hysteria and pictures George and herself under the moon of songwriters and poets. In tears, she clings to George who, bewildered and silent, can do nothing but stroke her hair, until it occurs to him that she may have seen Thumper. The question ruins the tenderness between them and, shamed though he is by his gaucherie, he has thrown one more chance away (41–2). However, in Act 2, an angry exchange proves just as convincing an indicator of the depth of feeling between them. That episode also adds to our sense of Dotty as her own person and qualifies our hitherto unreserved sympathies towards George who, from this point on, appears alarmingly naive and indecisive.

Oblivious to murder in his house and to repression on the streets, George emerges from the bathroom holding a dead goldfish whose bowl Dotty had commandeered for an earlier charade. Interestingly, the fish is called 'Archie', which suggests a shared joke at the latter's expense and fits well with the sort of detachment towards the whole psychiatric game that Dotty has displayed throughout the play. Shaking with rage, George calls Dotty a "murderous bitch", lamenting that the fish should have been murdered for the sake of a game:

DOTTY (*angrily*): Murdered? Don't you dare splash *me* with your sentimental rhetoric! It's a bloody goldfish! Do you think every *sole meunière* comes to you untouched by suffering?
GEORGE: The monk who won't walk in the garden for fear of treading on an ant does not have to be a vegetarian . . .
DOTTY: Brilliant! You must publish your findings in some suitable place like the *Good Food Guide*.
GEORGE: No doubt your rebuttal would look well in the *Meccano Magazine*.
DOTTY: You bloody humbug! – the last of the metaphysical egocentrics! You're probably still shaking from the four-hundred-year-old news that the sun doesn't go round *you*! (74)

The way Dotty cuts through George's finer feelings and the way he delivers an equally smarting attack on what he takes to be her mechanistic views transform the play's philosophic debate into a lively marital quarrel, and Dotty's tirade leads naturally into her speech about the moon-landing's reduction of mankind, making it appear a spontaneous perception which wells up out of her anger (in *Another Moon* virtually the same speech had seemed imposed on Penelope). The irrationality behind their rage gives the clever dialogue a heartfelt drive. Had George listened to remarks like Dotty's "it's impossible to imagine anyone building a church on the moon" (39), he would know that her universe is not a mechanistic one; on the other hand, she is hardly the one to accuse George of being numbed by the planets. This sequence also ends in a climax of tears. Archie dismisses Dotty's emotion as mere emotion, "When did you first become aware of these feelings?" (75), yet Dotty calls out to "Geor-gie" – "*But* GEORGE *won't or can't* . . ." Another chance of *rapproche-ment* has flown away on the winds.

At the end of the Act, George's remark about the monk who feared to step on an ant returns to plague him. Climbing down from his desk after discovering Thumper's fate, George accidentally steps back onto the carapace of Pat, the tortoise: "CRRRRRUNCH!!!" With one foot on the desk and one on Pat, he "puts up his head and cries out, 'Dotty! Help! Murder!'" (81). So the patterns of the play's main action are rounded off in the same way that they began, when George, faced with a corpse, cries out for help to a partner who makes no answer. Then, as George falls sobbing to the ground, *Jumpers* shifts into a dream sequence, just as it began with a seeming-ly surreal ritual.

This dream coda, a Georgie-through-the-looking-glass night-mare version of the philosophical symposium, has earned about as much critical disfavour as Dotty has. Yet it is perfectly attuned to the play's idiom, balancing the extravagance of the opening scene on either side of the musically choreographed bagging of Duncan McFee which occurs at the close of Act 1. In addition, the coda directly articulates the philosophic and moral points at issue in George's rambling paper and Dotty's hysterical or angry outbursts. Stoppard's original plan for the coda made his meaning still plainer.[19] As George lies on his study floor, the Symposium assem-bles behind him with Crouch enthroned as Chairman, Archie at his side, and three jumpers dressed in yellow gowns as gentlemen-ushers backed by projected slides of the gym–chapel's magnificent stained glass. After "approximately two minutes of approximate silence" to the memory of Duncan, Archie is called upon to begin the debate, "Man – good, bad or indifferent?" Following an unreal-sounding burst of applause, Archie, ever the suave magician, whirls down words on George's confused brain to turn his questions about God and existence into ridicule:

> . . . If the necessary being isn't, surely mother of invention as Voltaire said, not to mention Darwin different from the origin of the specious – to sum up: Super, both natural and stitious, sexual ergo cogito er go-go some-times, as Descartes said, and who are we? Thank you.
> (*Shattering applause.*
> *The* USHERS *hold up score cards*: '9.7' – '9.9' – '9.8'.) (83)

At this point in the first version of *Jumpers*, Archie summons Captain Scott, who then enters ceremonially. The symposium has become a court of law, and Archie, aping the sentence structure and loaded wording of a defending counsel, would like Scott "to imagine if you will the scene of events last Thursday morning". His casual phrasing makes the fight on the moon sound like a street accident, and he prompts his client to describe his "instinctive" reactions on knowing that the capsule had only enough power to lift one passenger. This whole speech provides an overt example of the way Archie's doublespeak translates self-interest into a public good as he praises Scott's "rational assessment" of his usefulness to society back on earth (84). This episode was cut in order to streamline the finale and because it simply underlines what happens in the rest of the coda. The cut makes good sense dramatically, since George has nowhere shown concern about the moon landing, so would be unlikely to dream about Scott, but, more significantly, the later text delays George's failure to take action until the murder of Clegthorpe, whereas the earlier version weakens this climax by having him lamely refuse to question the witness: "Why should I cross-examine the figures of my dreams? If that is the real Captain Scott, then I am the Archbishop of Canterbury."

The two texts then converge to reveal another of Archie's doubting disciples. The rationalization of the Church has moved too fast for the people, who still clamour for the sacraments; their unreasonable fancies, like Dotty's, cannot be talked away, though Clegthorpe pleads that "surely belief in man could find room for man's beliefs" (84). Stoppard then has Archie quote from *Richard III* and from the story of Thomas à Becket's murder to give focus to this new clash between a tyrant and his former friend: between State and Church. To the opening bars of "Sentimental Journey", the jumpers menace Clegthorpe and hustle him upstage until they have made him part of their pyramid:

GEORGE: Point of order, Mr Chairman.
CLEGTHORPE: Professor – it's not right. George – help.
CROUCH: Do you have any questions for this witness, Professor?
GEORGE: Er . . . no, I don't think so.
CROUCH: Thank you.
(*The music goes louder.*)
GEORGE: Well, this seems to be a political quarrel. . . . Surely only a proper
    respect for absolute values . . . universal truths – *philosophy* – (85)

George's dream of his own moral failure in letting Clegthorpe die suggests that deep down he knows he has failed Dotty in a similar way, and it is she who now appears. In George's dream, she sits high above him and the chanting jumpers on her silver moon, a cool commentator towards whom no man could possibly remain indifferent, as opposed to that word's rationalistic meaning (neither good nor bad). As George imagines her, Dotty can only believe that "two and two make roughly four" whereas, in reality, she suffers from the fact that they can no longer be *relied* on to make four. Again, the pair of them drift pathetically apart.

The coda emphasizes the fact that, despite his failure, George has the right ideas although he is unable to use them to meet life head on. The audience is bound to sympathize with his insistence on an innate goodness in mankind, yet the play as a whole and the coda in particular are designed to show that simply to be well-meaning is not enough. It is characteristic and endearing of George to find goodness in something as inconsequential as "the exchange of signals between two long-distance lorry-drivers in the black sleet of a god-awful night on the old A1" (71); in fact, he immediately sees how that could make him "sound like a joke vicar". However, he has no such reservations about defending the basic value of such inconsequence; if rationality were the be-all and end-all, "the world would be one gigantic field of soya beans" (40). The irrational stamps us as human.

Jumpers may proclaim the forces of whimsy, in that George, Dotty, Crouch and Bones all live fiercely eccentric lives; but Archie and the grim secretary are also eccentrics, so Stoppard's own view is more complicated than that. At the end of the coda he makes George point to the irrationality of the logical positivists themselves, who can say that knowledge is only that which can be proved but who "claim to *know* that life is better than death, that love is better than hate ..." (87). Yet since words can make the rational seem irrational (and vice versa), whimsy offers no real defence against the likes of Archie, whose final speech reduces disease, war, pollution, famine and cruelty to relatively minor mishaps. His last comic flourish converts the pessimism of *Waiting for Godot* ("Astride of a grave and a difficult birth. Down in the hole, lingeringly, the grave-digger puts on the forceps. We have time to grow old") into a jaunty sexual encounter as he cocks a snook at Sam (Beckett and Clegthorpe): "At the graveside the undertaker doffs his top hat and impregnates the prettiest mourner. Wham, bam, thank you Sam."

George in his eccentric pursuit of "universal truths" considers himself beyond politics, both inside and outside his home, and will not fight to maintain the standards he values. Consequently the final comment belongs to Dotty, spotlit on her silver crescent, who sings farewell to the world of lovers' vows and irrational dreams: "Goodbye spoony Juney Moon." But even if he will not defend himself, alone and calling out in the dark, George like Dotty will not join the jumpers. Though Archie would rationalize away injustice and pain, and though Dotty (as George dreams her) would toss aside romantic fancy, the play does leave us with an irreducible sense of individualism. The very illogic of George's failure to help Clegthorpe when he *knows* the good in the Samaritan, those moments when he and Dotty cling to each other inarticulately – these incongruities defy the tidy reasonableness of Archie and his plastic bag. Foolish, bewildered, blind, and inconsistent, George and Dotty are finally too much themselves to let the system and the soya beans take over.

Chapter 5

What did *you* do, Dada?

The period between *Jumpers* (1972) and *Travesties* (1974) established Stoppard in the minds of West End audiences as a name that ensured an evening's laughter mixed with a satisfying sense of intellectual challenge, whether or not his plays proved fully comprehensible. At the same time, an increasing number of professional critics were beginning to see him as a showman whose theatrical precocity did not quite mask the fact that his ideas, though clever, were not, in their opinion, sufficiently thought through. Others who *were* prepared to take Stoppard's thoughts seriously, felt nonetheless that weighty subjects should, somewhere along the way, arrive at sober statement. Still others clicked their tongues over Stoppard's refusal to commit himself to one point of view, contenting himself with airy structures of ingenious and amusing complexity instead of disturbing his audience's view of themselves.[1]

From his beginnings as a writer, Stoppard always seems to have been looking over his own shoulder, conscious of his weaknesses (as regards plot or characterization) or of the temperamental bent which attracted him to particular ideas and authors. His reaction to these public criticisms was equally self-conscious and was apt to lead him into statements which defensively stressed the artifice of his work: "I'm not impressed by art *because* it's political, I believe in art being good or bad art, not relevant art or irrelevant art."[2] The polish and quotability of such statements had the effect of blinding his detractors to the impulse behind this artifice. Looking back in a 1981 interview at his public performance as the disengaged artist, Stoppard analysed his reaction:

> . . . I began writing at a time when the climate was such that theatre seemed to exist for the specific purpose of commenting on our own society directly. Temperamentally this didn't suit me, because I would much rather have written *The Importance of Being Earnest* than . . . than . . .
> INTERVIEWER: (*breaking in*) Than *Look Back in Anger*?
> STOPPARD: Yes. Well, hang on, that's more complicated because *Look Back in Anger* is full of wonderful speeches which I would like to have been able to write.[3]

It is characteristic that having taken a position he should immediately backtrack, determined to be fair to what he admires in Osborne's play. Even here, Stoppard has to shade things, to argue one point and then its opposite, because simple statement *is* too simple. Clearing that away, he goes on to explain his early defensiveness: "I took on a sort of 'travelling pose' which exaggerated my insecurity about not being able to fit into this scheme, and I tended to overcorrect, as though in some peculiar way *Earnest* was actually more important than a play which grappled."

Beneath the pose, Stoppard clung to a sincere distrust of easy argument or of head-on commitment to ideas which, when thought twice about, need not be as true as they first seemed. Yet his urge to remain objective did not mean that he held no personal views. Like his own George Moore, if Stoppard could not prove things to be true or false, given the inadequacy of words and the deceptiveness of appearances, he still "knows that he knows" certain basic truths. In consequence, he goes back over the same themes and situations, trying to reach the ultimate statement about them, or he will weave a detective story into his plots to show how this most deductive of literary structures can fall victim to the treachery of ear and eye just as more abstract detective work, such as political or philosophical theory, frequently does. In the 1981 interview, arguing after the fact, he could claim that "I had to change as time went by, and began looking for marriage between the play of ideas and the work of wit." The marriage idea, first voiced to interviewers in 1974, does represent a change of pose, but it did not require a change of heart. For example, *Albert's Bridge*, from the mid-sixties, can be interpreted as a study of artistic detachment, with Albert, increasingly absorbed in his own art at the expense of his commitment to life, versus Fraser, only able to cope with living in Clufton after having viewed it from above. In the end, both come crashing down.

Jumpers and *Travesties* made it possible for Stoppard to lower his defences and publicly announce the marriage of two sides of himself; they did not alter his views about politics and art. *Jumpers*, in that it upholds standards of human behaviour, is a political statement: "the play reflects my belief that all political acts have a moral basis to them and are meaningless without it".[4] Stoppard's strategy had always been to show how one viewpoint and its opposite were simply restatements of each other, but in *Jumpers* he presents this duality more forcefully. Instead of withdrawing from the impasse with a smile, he implies a third, superior principle against which both arguments may be measured. He has seen how important "it is to set each one up against a moral standard, a consistent idea of what constitutes good and bad in the way human beings treat each other regardless of class, colour or ideology, and at least my poor professor in *Jumpers* got *that* right".[5]

Ideas and wit go together for Stoppard because only through that union can he achieve the objectivity needed to rein in his volatile, impressionable senses. Yet the marriage is never a placid one since part of him (51 per cent by his count) would be perfectly content to drift along, courting adulation for his inventive cleverness, while another part of him, the serious thinker, tries to pinpoint the way things are. Scared of being over-serious – "It's not a condition of good art that you sit in a brown study" – yet "catching" himself in too much admiration of the "sort of eclectic, trivial person who's very gifted",[6] Stoppard pursues a middle path with integrity and intellectual humility, although he can sometimes be pulled out of centre in one direction or the other. *Dogg's Our Pet*,[7] the short piece he wrote for Ed Berman while waiting for *Jumpers* to go into rehearsal at the Old Vic, exemplifies the way he responds intellectually to what for others might seem an entirely light-hearted occasion and how that serious idea then leads to a flourish of playful cadenzas.

The play celebrates the inauguration of The Almost Free Theatre in Soho as a permanent home for the multifarious enterprises of Ed Berman, the theatrical entrepreneur for whose Ambiance Theatre Stoppard had already written *After Magritte*. But the germinal idea derived from the reading he had done for *Jumpers*: Wittgenstein's thesis about a man who calls for particularly-shaped pieces of wood from another man standing some yards away; when he calls for a block, he receives a block, and so on. As Stoppard explains in a note to *Dogg's Our Pet*,

A stranger who did not know the language, coming upon this scene, would conclude that, probably, the different words described different shapes and sizes of wood. But this is not the only possible interpretation.

Suppose, for example, the second man knows in advance which pieces Charlie needs, and in what order. In such a case there would be no need for Charlie to 'name' the pieces he wants, but only to indicate when he is ready for the next one. (81)

The two men need never discover they speak different languages unless a third person were to use one of their codes: "in the play it is Charlie who finds himself outnumbered". The point then is to educate the audience and, to a certain extent, Charlie in a language which sounds like English but which means something else. Charlie's simple, monosyllabic words no longer express what they are supposed to; the Magrittean divorce between description and picture has become an intricate puzzle. When Charlie, "some kind of workman or caretaker", calls out "Plank!", a plank zooms from the wings; he catches it and starts to build a platform. When he shouts the word a second time, he is surprised by a football; this is followed by a schoolboy, Baker, hopping from foot to foot in readiness for Charlie's return throw. A glare "freezes him to a standstill". Charlie then tosses the ball to Baker and calls out "Plank!"; a plank comes and he places it beside the first one; a third plank is dispatched in the same way. Then another schoolboy, Able, comes on stage yelling "Plank!" to Baker, who throws him the ball. They throw it back and forth, calling out "Plank!" (meaning "Here!") to each other until Charlie "freezes them to a standstill" (82). As Charlie continues building with slabs and blocks, the audience come to realize from the boys' counter-actions that "slab" and "block" could also mean "ready" and "next". At the entrance of a fourth character, Dogg, the head-master, we glimpse yet another lingo: the military method of naming the letters of the alphabet – Able, Baker, Charlie, Dog.

The playfulness generated by this investigation into the frail codes of meaning derives as much from the celebratory occasion and the circumstances of the play's production as it does from the accumulat-ing misunderstanding between the characters. For one of his many guises, Berman had adopted the soubriquet 'Prof. R. L. Dogg' in order to cheer "dry academics who leaf through library index cards in the never-ending search for permanence"; his poems for children would one day be listed under 'Dogg, R. L.'[8] More immediately, the pseudonym had launched a group of actors into the streets and schools as Dogg's Troupe; *Dogg's Our Pet* creates a cheery anagram out of that name. In shaping his idea to the demands of an opening ceremony, Stoppard orchestrates a celebration between actors and audience by formalizing the sort of improvisational games actors play to sharpen their technique – he pays tribute to the Troupe's inven-tiveness and calls the script "a description of an event collectively arrived at"[9] – moulding them into a situation which would appeal to both adults and schoolchildren.

The piece starts rousingly to establish a sense of occasion as a march tune blares out from the wings of an empty stage. The entrance of Charlie in overalls and carrying a radio creates an anti-climactic counterpoint, and this contrapuntal movement governs the rest of the action as the audience oscillates between participation and bewilderment. When the bustling headmaster enters, he hurries along the front row of the audience handing out miniature flags in the school colours to be waved by everybody at the climax of events, and he involves them still further by providing what amounts to a brief lesson in Dogg Maths as he counts out the flags. He hands flowers to the boys and later stretches a ribbon in the same school colours from one side of the stage to the other so that it passes a few feet above the now-completed platform. Watching this activity, we try to deduce its purpose, just as we attempt to discover meaning behind the verbal symbols. Ultimately, we perceive the point when Dogg rolls a red carpet towards the foot of the platform and smirkingly ushers in a gracious-looking lady: "perhaps she is the Queen, or perhaps the wife of the Chairman of the Governors". But having arrived at the idea of an opening ceremony, we again flounder when the Lady reads her dedication address "nicely" but in language which makes coherent sense yet whose unpleasant meaning destroys our expectations: "Sad fact, brats pule puke crap-pot stink, spit; grow up dunces crooks . . . nick swag, swig coke, bank kickbacks; frankly cant stick kids" (92–3). After this, however, situation and dialogue move in tandem as the Lady cuts the ribbon and Dogg and the boys sing the school song, "Floreat Cane", over and over. For a time, our world and Dogg's find common ground in a third, ancient (and ironically obsolete) code.

Simultaneously, Stoppard uses this simplest of dramatic structures – the building of a platform with differently shaped pieces of wood, the cutting of a ribbon, the singing of an anthem – to demonstrate varying ways in which we derive meaning from physical and verbal gesture. At one point, seeking some respite from the surrounding confusion, Charlie switches his radio on again and so initiates a sequence which points to the fact that intonation alone can often convey a fair amount of information. One of the most familiar rhythms to a British audience is the particular rise and fall of an announcer's voice as he reads out the weekly football results. Vocal inflection and our previous exposure to Dogg numbers make an immediate impact, and Stoppard expects that his audience may even come to deduce that one or other of "Clock" and "Foglamp" corresponds to "City" and "United": "Tube Clock dock, Handbag dock; Haddock Clock quite, Haddock Foglamp trog; Wonder quite, Picknicking pan . . ." (89). Stoppard also builds a joke from written symbols whose significance neither we nor Charlie understand. The slogans the boys create out of the "indecipherable signs" scrawled over the spare slabs and blocks they use to make a wall, centre stage, have a somewhat strangled idiom in English. The only way we can guess what they mean to Dogg is by observing his physical reaction. Seeing DOGG POUT THERE ENDS, the headmaster gives Charlie a slight tap on the cheek, but when that leads to protest he knocks him through the wall. After this happens a second time, Charlie deduces that practically anything he says will arouse the master's anger. After Dogg returns from escorting the Lady off stage, he glares at Charlie for having presented her with a bouquet while "respectfully" murmuring "Yob", a word he has come to think means "flowers" in Dogg. Charlie, seeing him fuming, makes another deduction and, borrowing a trick of Stan Laurel's, "dutifully hurls himself through the wall" (93).

Watching *Dogg's Our Pet* is like viewing an intermittently familiar ritual through a thick pane of glass. Throughout it all, Charlie functions as our confused interlocutor. Though we laugh at his slapstick antics with blocks, slabs, and wall, we also share his bewilderment and make many of the same logical assumptions. Stoppard relies on that sympathy in laying the final trap, for ultimately he reveals that the one person we thought we understood completely does not, after all, speak quite the same 'language'. Picking himself up out of the wall, Charlie mounts the platform to address the audience. For the first time in the play, what is said on stage makes sequential and unequivocal sense, and yet, because Charlie has not been a neutral observer of the previous action, but is in fact the school caretaker, he has a different interpretation from ours, one which surprises and yet brings everything back to normality. From his point of view, the footballs, the words on the wall, the 'language' the boys use are all part of the behaviour that makes his job harder:

Three points only while I have the platform. Firstly, just because it's been opened, there's no need to run amok kicking footballs through windows and writing on the walls. It's me who's got to keep this place looking new so let's start by leaving it as we find it. Secondly, I can take a joke a well as any man, but I've noticed a lot of language about the place and if there's one thing I can't stand it's language. I forget what the third point is.

The speech also works economically to tie up the investigation of language and the opening of the actual theatre. But Stoppard goes further by turning the 'language' of the theatre games in on itself. We automatically accept the empty stage-space as some sort of area inside or (more probably) outside the school but we have not seen the objects coming from the wings as flying through windows nor have we been able to see the building blocks as an actual wall or the slogans as schoolboy graffiti. Stoppard then has Charlie descend from the podium to tidy both the place and the play by rebuilding the wall so that the fourth side of each of its pieces assembles to read DOGGS TROUPE THE END.

Seriousness and frivolity balance neatly here upon a central pivot, a third ingredient which has not received much attention from Stoppard or his commentators. The major characters in all his work experience various degrees of agony. Charlie's pain is of the lightest sort; the play's knockabout confusion presents it frivolously and his final speech, in which he takes a 'serious' view of the goings-on around him restores the balance. But in plays like *Rosencrantz* and *Jumpers* the anguish grows increasingly desperate and that sort of pain is completely foreign to the unfeeling mechanics of farce, the label so often attached mistakenly to Stoppard's plays.

It is this pain which eventually tips the balance towards seriousness in *Artist Descending a Staircase*,[10] the radio play commissioned by a consortium of European broadcasting companies and aired by the BBC in November 1972. In the abstract design of its controlling idea the play has a certain kinship with *Dogg's Our Pet*, but emotionally it leads on from *Jumpers*, while thematically it offers what Stoppard himself called "a dry run" for ideas that will appear more expansively in *Travesties*.

The play's design follows a precisely worked time-pattern. Beginning in the present, it moves back in five irregular stages to 1914, and then the next five scenes repeat those stages in an upwards direction on into the present: "So the play is set temporally in six parts, in the sequence ABCDEFEDCBA" (73). In this way, all three artists of the play descend a time-staircase back to their innocent youth before they took up the fashions of modern art. Like Marcel Duchamp's cubist painting, "Nude Descending a Staircase", the script breaks that descent into separate moments and, like cubism itself, it then reassembles the captured parts. The title refers literally to the rapid descent of one of the trio, Donner, who has fallen through the rickety balustrade at the top of the stairs to their attic studio. But the V pattern sends the listener back into the past in search of clues which might explain what appears to be Donner's murder in the first scene; however, when the action moves up to the present once more the journey turns out to have been a wild-goose chase. Again Stoppard adopts the logic of a detective story to show how deduction often leads us weirdly astray. Naturally in a radio play we base those assumptions on aural evidence, and Stoppard has tailored his design to take advantage of the materials the medium provides in order to embroider upon the idea that "people have been taught to expect certain kinds of insight but not others" (82).

The script's middle scene, the flashback to 1914, illustrates the way Stoppard plays on our expectations through sound-effects. The three friends, Beauchamp, Martello and Donner, are on a walking tour in France, but along with the sound of feet which establishes this scene we hear the clip-clop of what we take to be a horse. Beauchamp's opening declamation also paints the picture: "All my life I have wanted to ride through the French countryside in summer, with my two best friends, and make indefensible statements about art" (104). Although this encourages us to interpret events in a particular manner, Stoppard plays scrupulously fair, for one of Beauchamp's "indefensible" remarks warns us that "Art should break its promises." So, despite the pile-up of such commands as "Whoa, boy, whoa" and the sound of skittering hooves when anything startling occurs, Stoppard plants other clues to suggest the 'horse' may not be what it seems. By this time in the play, we have already experienced a host of deceiving sounds so we should be alert to the hint he slips into Donner's complaint about their holiday, "I've had nothing to eat today except for half a coconut", a menu odd enough to draw our attention, especially since coconuts have a reputation as a sound-effect. We might also notice that Donner tells Beauchamp to "shut up" whenever he starts his "Whoa, boy" routine and that Beauchamp claims "this horse only believes in me" (106). This break between sign and meaning has much to do with the friends' own interpretation of their surroundings ("There's a discrepancy between the map and the last signpost", says Martello), so that once he has revealed the truth about the 'horse' ("For God's sake, Beauchamp, will you get rid of that coconut!") Stoppard moves on to the serious business of the scene and of the entire play: how do we know what we 'know'?

One answer is that we tend to arrive at verdicts which justify our personal prejudices. The friends have continued with their planned holiday, even after the Serbs "shot that absurd Archduke Ferdinand of Ruritania", because Martello's uncle in the Foreign Office, blind to anything beyond Britain's interests, has assured them there will be no war because "His Majesty's Government is not *ready* to go to war, and it will be six months at least before we are strong enough to beat the French" (109). Uncle Rupert may be a ludicrous relic of the Napoleonic Wars, but with the hindsight of history we can appreciate the sombre reality behind his obsolete ideas. Martello's aunt exhibits a similarly Edwardian certainty: "You live in a sane and beautiful world, my auntie said, and the least you can do, if you must be a painter, is to paint appropriately sane and beautiful pictures." Martello does not satirize either relative, for the three innocents abroad share this confident Britishness and so misinterpret, or refuse to see clearly, the evidence before them. However, the listener, again because of history's perspective, will not now misunderstand the sound of lorries, explosions, and passing cavalry in the high summer of 1914 which the travellers, blithely joking on about Beauchamp's Tenth Horse, prefer to reason away, because "if a man can't go for a walk on the Continent nowadays, what is the world coming to?" (108). This sort of statement accounts for the bite under the scene's tricksy surface: we already know that the three carefree young men will grow up to be ridiculous old fools, but now we see this fall from innocence in the wider context of what the world is coming to. Each scene in the play contains its drop or two of acid, and Stoppard lures us towards them with his disarming games.

This taste of bitter-sweet which makes the play so effective comes particularly from Stoppard's manipulation of his characters down and up the V pattern. The old men of the first scenes still talk about Sophie, the only other character in the play, as if she were part of their lives. By the time we actually meet her in the fourth episode we know she has died after a "sad enough life". Stoppard effects the transition back to 1922 through the elderly Donner's yearning cry so that she enters the play like a faded souvenir from the past:

> Oh Sophie . . . I try to shut out the memory but it needs only . . . a ribbon . . .
> a flower . . . a phrase of music . . . a river flowing beneath ancient bridges
> . . . the scent of summertime . . .
> (*Cliché Paris music, accordion* . . .)   (91)

The sentimentality quickly disappears, however, when Sophie complains that the accordion player downstairs drives her mad. We are not in Paris but in Lambeth, and after that trick of sound Stoppard pits Sophie's brave voice against the noise of a suitcase being strapped up and the young Beauchamp's half-hearted attempts to explain that he has finished with her. The girl's desperate cheerfulness as she quips with Martello maintains a tenseness until she can pretend no longer: "He doesn't know what to do with me, does he?" (94). Even then she finds refuge in irony so that the scene's pathos comes from her attempt to clamp back her emotion rather than from the fact that she is blind and rejected by the man she has loved for two years: "Perhaps he was going to leave a note on the mantelpiece. As a sort of joke" (95). Stoppard then moves us back to 1920, knowing that the aftertaste of Sophie's pain will affect our attitude to the polite gaiety of the moment when she first meets the three friends. Since we know what will transpire, Beauchamp's intense concentration upon his experiments with sound in this scene and the next (with the coconut) now seem to signpost an innate lack of feeling.

Sophie's blindness does eventually command our sympathies, but at first Stoppard uses it to delineate her lack of self-pity and, since she too must rely on sound, he can thereby involve his audience in still more games. As Martello guides her up the stairs we hear a ping-pong game in progress, and this becomes louder as they enter the room. At the sound of a winning shot, Sophie offers congratulations but is somewhat taken aback when the play resumes. She cannot see Beauchamp's recording, just as he and Donner have not seen her blindness. After explanations all round, Sophie reacts cautiously to the whistling tea-kettle: "Is that the gramophone again?" (97). She then insists on serving their tea, a process which necessitates further sound pictures. By the time we return to this scene after experiencing the French walking tour, all four are involved in another guessing-game. Sophie has apparently said to the three that she never loses her bearings, so we hear them instructing her to step this way and that until they call a halt: "I am exactly where I started, standing with my back to my chair" (110). They might have moved the chair, in which case she would have deduced wrongly, as indeed happens when she bumps against the misplaced tea-table. Here the deductive game has become part of the polite banter that controls the scene, a formal exuberance which conveys a period flavour but rings hollow the nearer we come to the betrayal of two years later.

The fading laughter, as Beauchamp guides Sophie downstairs, and Donner's reiterated warning, "don't fall", ensure a mood of ill omen as we move forward via the repeated accordion music and the sound of receding footsteps on the stairs to the barely audible slam of a door. The listener is now as blind as Sophie, sharing her focus and her vulnerability in close-up. Donner wants to stay with her, but in the first part of the scene she had explained that "I can't love you back . . . I have lost the capability of falling in love" (95). Now, as she lays her desperation bare ("I feel more blind than I did the first day, when I came to tea"), neither she nor we can be sure that Donner is still in the room. Her speech, which takes up the whole scene, builds in intensity as she tells him they cannot live as brother and sister and that she will not accept his pity: "Am I to weave you endless tablemats and antimacassars in return for life?" (111). But neither can she live alone in the dark, and here Stoppard's adroit use of the medium forces us into Sophie's imagination as she envisions day-to-day obstacles of a poignant triviality: who will be there to find a missing shoe, make sure her clothes match, or do up the back of her dress? Her panic at the silence in the room adds to her sense of helplessness and exposure. As she loses her self-control, the mounting rhythms of her speech convert the script's predominant sportiveness – were "Mouse" (Donner's nickname) still there he would be playing a cruel trick – into a moment of complete terror which culminates in a violent sound of smashing glass as she throws herself through a window down to the courtyard below.

The irony of Sophie's fall darkens as we move up to the present and Martello's opening comment: "She would have killed you, Donner." The girl's helpless dependency probably would have killed him, since he truly loved her yet could not have made her happy, but Martello means that, had she fallen a few feet to the right, her body would have struck him as he waved goodbye to his friends. Donner did intend to stay and care for her, and his constancy towards her memory creates the play's second centre of pain. On our way down the V pattern, we have heard Martello's patronizing dismissal, "Poor Donner, he never had much luck with Sophie" (79), and how the latter burst out weeping when Beauchamp criticized his post-Pop, pre-Raphaelite portrait of her: "Shut up, damn you! – how dare you talk of her?! – how dare you" (84). Stoppard has also distinguished Donner's relatively clear-eyed thoughtfulness from his friends' flippant egotism; even in France, it was he who eventually interpreted the sights and sounds around them as acts of war: "They might think we're spies . . . and kill us. That would be ridiculous. I don't want to die *ridiculously*" (108).

In the continuation of the scene between the two old men, Martello shows his utter blindness to Donner's feelings as he mulls the flavour of "defenestration" or idly toys with "de-escalate" and "influence" as words to describe "people being pushed downstairs or stuffed up chimneys" (112–13). Sophie's fall simply meant the end of "a nice girl who was due for a sad life", and the friends are "no doubt due for our own [fall] one way or another" (nice that, considering Donner's death) so that he views the fifty years since then as "a brief delay between the fall of one body and another". Martello can also chat on about a missing tooth from his own Pop portrait of Sophie – at which Donner sighs, "Her teeth were broken too, smashed, scattered" – so the listener may find it hard to decide whether Martello's decision to tell Donner that Sophie possibly singled Beauchamp out by mistake is meant to bring comfort or is yet another instance of his heedlessness. Whatever the motive, the revelation proves devastating and reduces Donner to moans of "Oh my God". Yet despite this threnody of pain, one week later, just before his own fall, Donner is happily at work on a realistic portrait of Sophie in a garden with a unicorn. Fired by his love, he has deserted "that child's garden of easy victories known as the avant garde" (81), remembering how she first spoke about her blindness: "I can put a unicorn in the garden and no one can open my eyes against it and say it isn't true" (103).

Martello's motives, Donner's pain, even Sophie's fall (which Beauchamp insists was an accident) all show themselves capable of interpretation and misinterpretation, as do the play's equivocal sound-effects. Stoppard encapsulates all this in a misleading tape-recording which seems to point to Donner's murder. The elderly Beauchamp, still enraptured by his recordings, had persuaded Donner to switch on the recorder as he worked silently and alone, but instead of the silence Beauchamp had expected to ensnare as his tape went round in a loop, he had captured a sound-picture of Donner's last moments. When the play begins, we hear "an irregular droning" and the noise of stealthy footsteps. A floorboard creaks; the droning suddenly breaks off; the footsteps cease; then across the expectant hush comes Donner's calm voice: "Ah! There you are!" This is followed by two rapid steps and a thump before Donner cries out and falls through the bannisters to his death. Listening to the tape, Beauchamp and Martello accuse each other of having crept up on the sleeping Donner and of striking him. One of the two must be his murderer, since Donner's calm greeting as he woke suggests that the footsteps could only have been those of a friend, and he had no other friends. The listener may share that verdict, even though the two crotchety old men continually disagree in their interpretation of other, past events:

MARTELLO: . . . Remember how John used to say, "If Donner whistles the opening of Beethoven's Fifth in six/eight time once more I'll *kill him*!"?
BEAUCHAMP: John who?
MARTELLO: Augustus John.
BEAUCHAMP: No, no, it was Edith Sitwell.
MARTELLO: Rubbish! – you're getting old, Beauchamp.   (77)

This talk of killing is designed to encourage our suspicions, as is Stoppard's emphasis upon the pair's ill temper and the way they magnify small irritations, so that when we move down the time-loop we will be on the look-out for some minor grudge that brought one or the other of the old men to violence.

However, in that journey, we discover instead those ambiguous, deceiving sounds. The initial tape-recording sets off a trail of slaps and thumps that leads to the scene in France where flies buzz in the summer heat and the talk is interrupted by smacks as the young men swat at them. Accordingly, Beauchamp says more than he intends when, just before leaving to buy some fly-spray, he tells Donner "that in this loop of tape there is some truth about how we live" (115). During the final scene, as the two old men continue their mutual recriminations, the listener discovers that there has been no murder. The tape actually captured Donner's attack on a fly that buzzed around the recorder, a sequence which is now repeated, except for the climactic crash through the bannisters, as Beauchamp takes up the hunt:

BEAUCHAMP: That fly has been driving me mad. Where is he?
MARTELLO: Somewhere over there . . .
BEAUCHAMP: Right.

The original loop of TAPE *is hereby reproduced*:
  (a) *Fly droning.*
  (b) *Careful footsteps approach. A board creaks.*
  (c) *The fly settles.*
  (d) BEAUCHAMP *halts.*
  (e) BEAUCHAMP: *'Ah! There you are.'*
  (f) *Two more quick steps and then: Thump!*
BEAUCHAMP: Got him!   (116)

In this way, the deceptive loop of tape does contain the truth about
the way the characters have lived, for the relationship between all
four of them evolved from just such a moment of equivocal evidence,
a misinterpretation that led to fifty years of anguish, just as
Beauchamp's tape will lead to each aged survivor's torture of the
other.

After the Great War, just before she lost her sight completely,
Sophie had attended the trio's first exhibition, "Frontiers in Art",
and had been particularly attracted by the face of one of them, though
she had never learned who was who. However, she had seen a
newspaper photograph in which the three were posed beside their
work, and her man was shown standing by a painting of what looked
like a field of snow behind a low black railing. There had only been
one snow scene, and that was Beauchamp's, but years later Martello
tells Donner how Sophie's description of the picture suggested a
much taller fence and that he had long suspected that the painting
she meant was actually Donner's picture of thick white posts against a
black background (114).

Artist Descending offers its listeners more than an ingenious union
of ideas and comic artifice. Behind the glittering cleverness, Stoppard's depiction of sorrow and misunderstanding injects the play
with an emotion that is all the more moving because of his con-
strained handling of a potentially saccharine plot. The script's contrivance detaches us from the sentimental, yet its patterning also
colours our sympathies as we move from scene to scene along the
time-loop knowing what the characters must come to. And in the
light of Stoppard's preoccupation at this time with his own responsibilities as an artist, the play makes a stirring, if indirect statement
about the connection between artistic discipline and human feeling.
Donner, the most consistently sensitive of the three friends, discovers himself as an artist once he learns that Sophie had perhaps
loved him all along. Invigorated by this feeling, he gives up dabbling
in facile experimentation to engage "in the infinitely more difficult
task of painting what the eye sees" (81) by creating his tribute to
Sophie. This dénouement suggests that sympathy and openness

are essential to the artist, for Donner, despite his years of tawdry enslavement to the trendy, is finally redeemed by his ability to feel, whereas Beauchamp and Martello can never pass beyond cynical detachment, an attitude that always did and always will infect their 'art'. There is a connection here with *Jumpers*, for George, though no artist, ultimately fails because he cannot put his intuitive feelings into practice: *between the emotion and the response falls the shadow.*

Like him, Donner has always been on the periphery of life (and art), though he has the potential to be more than a by-stander. Nicknamed " 'Mouse' because he enters quietly" (93), it was none the less he who was open to the realities of the French walking-tour – "I nearly drowned trying to cross a laughing torrent, the honest locals have stolen most of our money" (105–6) – while the other two indulged themselves in games with coconuts or fantasies "about my next work, a beautiful woman, as described in the Song of Solomon" (109) as the guns exploded around them. Their Exhibition represented a withdrawal into unfeeling mockery by turning the Great War's actual frontier into "a lark" through their pictures "of barbed wire fences and signboards saying 'You are now entering Patagonia' " (95). It was Donner alone who noticed Sophie at the gallery – "I believe we exchanged a look!" (101) – and it was he who felt compelled to remain with her. The other two never progress beyond schoolboy larks, either as individuals or as artists. Their accusations over Donner's dead body devolve into destructive sarcasm and petty insult, and their art has a similar sterility. Martello in fact recognizes his own empty acrobatics but cannot free himself: "no wonder I have achieved nothing with my life! – my brain is on a flying trapeze that outstrips all the possibilities of action. Mental acrobatics, . . . whereas you . . . came to grips with life at least this once, and killed Donner" (78).

In this speech, Stoppard himself comes to grips with those critics who were accusing him of mental acrobatics, and the entire play stands as his eloquent defence. Beauchamp and Martello's arty larks are empty of meaning because neither of them savours or feels curious about life. Donner, on the other hand, had always been susceptible to the world around him. He can never remake the past with Sophie and he *is* to "die ridiculously", but before he does so he comes to terms with his feelings for her through the expression of his art. Though he admits that Martello's suggestion as to Sophie's mistake may have been a lie in revenge for Donner's having damaged his figure of her, the mere possibility that she truly loved him gives meaning to his work. This new sense of commitment also alters

Donner's opinions about art itself and so enfolds the play's debate about art and life in a personal crisis.

That Donner's views before and after Martello's revelation differ so markedly suggests that the human factor in itself forms a dividing line between skilled talent and artistic truth, though whether the artist can have any direct impact on life continues to be the nagging question at the centre of Stoppard's work from this point on. The senseless horror of the Great War had made the form and structure of conventional art seem a fraudulent perversion of what life was really like and had led the three friends to "nonsense art" just as it led Duchamp from Cubism to Dadaist non-sequitur. Yet at their first Exhibition, though Sophie liked "the way you roared with laughter at all your friends" (95), she found their work "frivolous and not very difficult to do" (100), a statement that Martello and Beauchamp are quick to agree with.

Stoppard, an admitted master of the frivolous, does not, however, see frivolity, when it means shapelessness, as any truer a reflection of life's chaos. Championing both sides of the argument with typical conviction, he makes Sophie the spokeswoman for a painstaking naturalism and Martello the advocate of the unexpected. Neither view cancels the other because both point to the artist's imaginative truth. She sees the artist as "celebrating the impulse to paint in general, the imagination to paint something in particular, and the ability to make the painting in question" (100), whereas he feels that the artist cannot teach people to think in one particular way but should "paint an utterly simple shape in order to ambush the mind with something quite unexpected about that shape by hanging it in a frame and forcing you to see it, as it were, for the first time" (101). The essential difference between them lies in the degree of skill it takes to make that imaginative statement, and here Stoppard has Sophie deliver something of a lecture on the fact that art "celebrates a world which includes itself – I mean, part of what there is to celebrate is the capability of the artist" (100).

Art as complex *celebration* or as a *frame* that ambushes the mind points directly to Stoppard's own concern with the 'play' of ideas, though ironically he gives the one to the anti-frivolous Sophie and the other to the anti-formal Martello. Yet though he undercuts Sophie's stance by means of her own naive earnestness and Beauchamp's joking query as to whether she wears appropriately blue stockings, the argument is weighted her way because of Donner's conversion to her viewpoint (in a previous scene) and the lack of something vital in the natures of the other two. Donner has come to see Beauchamp's recordings as "the mechanical expression of a small intellectual idea" (81). He goes on to define the artist as "someone who is gifted in some way which enables him to do something more or less well which can only be done badly or not at all by someone who is not thus gifted" (83), to which Beauchamp, failing to swat a fly, shouts "Missed!" And, to a certain extent, Donner has done so, for, as he continues to explain, "An artistic imagination coupled with skill is talent." Skill defines talent and also submits creativity to certain "standards outside itself" for comparison, but it need not make art. What the play and the reason behind Donner's conversion both imply leads back to Martello's lament. The artist, no matter how imaginative or skilful, must come to grips with life.

Stoppard thus acknowledges that hummingbird flights of fancy would be nothing more than skilled acrobatics unless their whirring flight path traced certain human truths. His dilemma is that of Yeats' "Sailing to Byzantium", where the artist, seeking an objective distance from the "sensual music" of everyday life, finds that creative artifice, in order to be art, must still "sing / To lords and ladies of Byzantium / Of what is past, or passing, or to come". The human centre within the elaborate structure of Stoppard's more serious plays vindicates him on this. But other aspects of the artist's relation to life defy solution. What use is the artist to society; should one talk of 'use' at all? Does the artist's picture of life have any effect on the direction society will take; should one expect it to? As Donner explains to Martello, looking back on their days in Paris after the War, all art, whether rational or their own "anti-art of lost faith . . . was all the same insult to a one-legged soldier and the one-legged, one-armed, one-eyed regiment of the maimed" (89).

In the rest of the play, Stoppard debates these issues in comic vein. Even before the War, Beauchamp could talk breezily about surprise and that "Art should never conform" (104). When he asks Donner to explain why he became an artist, the reply is suitably nonconformist: "I heard there were opportunities to meet naked women." But Beauchamp wants him to say that the artist should not need to justify his place in the community:

. . . he cannot, and should stop boring people with his egocentric need to try. The artist is a lucky dog. That is all there is to say about him. In any community of a thousand souls there will be nine hundred doing the work, ninety doing well, nine doing good, and one lucky dog painting or writing about the other nine hundred and ninety-nine. (105)

Yet, over the years, Donner has felt guilty at being "a lucky dog", and his ultimate experiment sought to justify art to anyone whose main concern is survival: "The answer, like all great insights, was simple: make it edible" (87). Stoppard whirls this non-answer into curlicues of fancy as Martello exclaims that Donner's sugar sculptures "will give cubism a new lease of life" (88) or that his ceramic steaks will "put taste where it belongs".

After his conversion, however, Donner can see that their anti-rational creations freed them from any sort of social accountability, and this no longer worries him. Instead he makes his art accountable only to himself and the dead Sophie. Before Martello's revelation, Donner's hopeless love had meant "that, even when life was at its best there was a small part missing and I knew that I was going to die without ever feeling that my life was complete" (113). But in painting Sophie with the unicorn, he gives himself up to the memory of what she truly was: her appearance, her courageous wit, her taste in pictures. Although Beauchamp thinks that to paint an Academy portrait is as ludicrous and useless as any of their past experiments – "surely you can see that a post-Pop pre-Raphaelite is pure dada brought up to date" (84) – for Donner it brings him close to Sophie, and the last words he hears from Beauchamp suggest that finally through art he has captured her and found his own completion: "Poor Sophie. I think you've got her, Donner" (115).

The implications of *Artist Descending* – that the artist's responsibilities are ultimately to his own sense of truth and to the standards of historic tradition – become the undisguised centre of debate in *Travesties*.[11] In the stage play, Stoppard meets the jibes about his refusal to commit himself to direct political and social statement head-on. Just before the play opened, he had defended his "oblique, distant, generalized" stance by maintaining "that's what art is best at. The objective is the universal perception, isn't it?"[12] Yet in *Jumpers*, George's "respect for absolute values . . . universal truths – *philoso-phy*" made him deaf to Clegthorpe's plea for help, and in *Artist Descending* the friends' proclamations about aesthetic truths made them oblivious to the realities of war. In *Travesties*, Stoppard sheds any lingering unease about his own neutrality by turning Switzerland into a metaphor of artistic detachment: "to be an artist *at all* is like living in Switzerland during a world war. To be an artist *in Zurich, in 1917*, implies a degree of self-absorption that would have glazed over the eyes of Narcissus" (38). Furthermore, the reality which his characters ignore has greater impact on our own lives than either the brave new world of the Rad-Libs or the Edwardian sunset of the Great War. Across the play looms the figure of Lenin, for whom there can be no artistic neutrality: "Literature must become party literature". Instead of shaping society, the artist now becomes the measure of its worth: "The easiest way of knowing whether good has triumphed over evil is to examine the freedom of the artist" (39).

Travesties is such a grab-bag of styles and incidents – Stoppard called it "a pig's breakfast"[13] – that to quote lines out of context risks betraying the many-sidedness of the playwright's continual debate with himself through the opposed voices of his characters. All the more so because the action on stage reflects the prejudiced and rusting memory of its narrator, the aged Henry Carr. In *Artist Descending*, the old men's memories appear equally defective, as when they wrangle over what Edith Sitwell might or might not have said on this or that occasion in the past. But though every episode, as we move back and forth in time, is generated by some remark at the end of the previous sequence, we experience each event as it actually happened and not, as in *Travesties*, through the contorted filter of a guide. Sitting in his apartment in Zurich, Carr remembers himself as the British Consul, instead of the consular functionary he really was, and transforms Bennett, the actual Consul, into his manservant. To complicate things further, Carr's memories of Zurich in 1917 are shaped by the plot and verbal rhythms of Oscar Wilde's *The Importance of Being Earnest* in which he triumphed as – "not Ernest, the other one" – Algernon Moncrieff, a performance he places one year earlier than history allows so that James Joyce, the troupe's business manager, meets both Tristan Tzara, who in reality had nothing to do with the production, and Lenin, who "was the leader of millions by the time [Carr did his] Algernon".

Through Old Carr, Stoppard has brought together three archetypical attitudes to art and the function of the artist, and those views, though somewhat twisted by Carr, do none the less convey aspects of their speakers' actual personalities and, through the play's shaping, add up to a final statement of Stoppard's own position. Furthermore, the debate has a greater immediacy than the one in *Artist Descending* because the political utilitarianism of Lenin and his amanuensis, Cecily, challenges artistic expression in the present day and collides with Stoppard's innate antipathy towards rigid thinking.

Tzara's attitude, like Martello's or Beauchamp's, echoes the War which has made everything meaningless. To proclaim that absurdity, he and his friends at the Cabaret Voltaire recite fragmented poems to fractured jazz music under the banner of Dada, a word that can either stand for childish babble or for a double 'yes' to a life freed from traditional ideas: nowadays, "A man may be an artist by exhibiting his hindquarters. He may be a poet by drawing words out of a hat" (38). Stoppard gives Carr Donner's rebuttal about artistic skill but then pushes the argument further by having Tzara point out that, in making 'Art' mean whatever he wants it to mean, he is only doing what the Establishment does "with words like *patriotism, duty, love, freedom*, king and country" (39). This idea that language can be "conscripted" into the service of various ideologies lies at the heart of Stoppard's work (particularly *Jumpers*) and will be exemplified by Lenin. Yet Carr, and part of Stoppard, cannot accept that. Somehow those words must possess some unadulterated currency; the Dadaists' cynical views "merely demonstrate the freedom of the artist to be ungrateful, hostile, self-centred and talentless, for which freedom I went to war, and a more selfless ideal for a man of my taste it would be difficult to imagine". In a later flurry, Carr displays some envy towards the artist's special freedom which, like a schoolboy's sick-note from Matron, excuses him from physical duties: "you were let off to spend the afternoon messing about in the Art Room. Labour or Art. And you've got a chit for *life*? (*passionately*) Where did you get it?" (46).

But if Carr dismisses the idea of the artist's privileged role as "art's greatest achievement, and it's a fake!" (47), Joyce embodies that specialness. By means of an elaborate piece of staging, Stoppard sets the word-magician against the iconoclast by having Joyce conjure a carnation, coloured flags and finally a rabbit from the hat in which he had deposited the small bits of paper that made Tzara's improvised poem. If the Dadaists are "demolition men to smash centuries of baroque subtlety, to bring down the temple" (62), Joyce's role is to document the destruction of those temples and give them permanence:

What now of the Trojan War if it had been passed over by the artist's touch? Dust. A forgotten expedition prompted by Greek merchants looking for new markets. A minor redistribution of broken pots. But it is we who stand enriched, by a tale of heroes, of a golden apple, a wooden horse, a face that launched a thousand ships – and above all, of Ulysses, the wanderer, the most human, the most complete of all heroes – (62)

The images of Troy resound with the splendour of an artistic heritage that stands as one of mankind's glories and which dramatizes Stoppard's most overt statement about the artist's function. Although he builds Joyce's speech up to an anticlimactic exit – *Ulysses* will add further vitality to the legend but will "*leave the world precisely as it finds it*" (63) – the force of those images proves his point. A work of art has no immediate effect on society but contributes in the long run to a cultural climate, ethical standards against which society measures itself.

Stoppard's interviews at this time raise the same idea with still greater directness. To the suggestion that his plays make no clear (political) statement, he admits his inability to take sides: "Few statements remain unrebutted", because "*I just don't know.*"[14]

However, he goes on to argue that his dialectical stance is just as effective as the direct approach because no play, in the short term, can move mountains in the way a newspaper article can. He instances a story in the *Guardian* about wages in South Africa: "Within 48 hours the wages went up. Now Athol Fugard [the South African playwright] can't do that."[5] What writers like Fugard do is to create a social awareness which would enable the *Guardian* to know that the article on wages was actually worth printing. "Briefly, art . . . is important because it provides the moral matrix, the moral sensibility, from which we make our judgments about the world."

In *Travesties*, Joyce's statement is one of the few that go unrebutted. And, for many in the audience, Lenin's speeches in Act 2 would re-emphasize the importance of the artist as guardian and nurturer of moral sensibility. Stoppard again organizes his stage picture to achieve that emphasis. Lenin and his wife describe their arrangements for their journey on the sealed train which will take them across Europe to St Petersburg. We hear the sounds of the train setting off as Tzara announces its prompt departure and leaves the stage to Carr, who now comes to the decision that the Lenins must be stopped. As he decides, the train noise grows louder and, on Carr's exit, rises to a deafening crescendo to imitate the way its sound still ricochets around the world. A light then focuses on the lone figure of Lenin in the exact pose of a famous photograph which "Stalin had re-touched so as to expunge Kamenev and Trotsky who feature prominently in the original" (84). The stage directions call for the speech to be "delivered from the strongest possible position" so that Lenin, high on his rostrum, will create a dramatic contrast to all that has gone before: "Down with non-partisan literature! Down with literary supermen!" (85).

Denying the artist a privileged role, Lenin proclaims that everything to do with the printed word must come under party control. Then, in a passage that amplifies Tzara's remarks on the use of language, he maintains that the new order will make the artist truly free. Free to write whatever he wishes, although he must recognize that "every voluntary association, including the party, is also free to expel members who use the name of the party to advocate anti-party views". Free because he need no longer depend on the money-market. Free because his words will serve "the millions and tens of millions of working people, the flower of the country, its strength and its future" (86). The image grows all the more chilling when his wife, Nadya, explains from the sidelines that these words come from one of Lenin's actual speeches, or when we hear his own brand of iconoclasm as he shreds artists through his political grinder. From his view, Tolstoy the "sincere protester against social injustice" is also "the jaded hysterical sniveller known as the Russian intellectual".

Reactionary though this portrait will seem to other segments of his audience, Stoppard does present a sympathetic case for Lenin's hatred of 'arty' intellectuals. Fulminating against the Dadaist excesses of Mayakovsky for which the Commissar of Education, who permitted them, "should be flogged for his futurism" (87), Lenin changes his opinion on seeing the hungry but enthusiastic young faces in the communes to whom the poet's works speak. "After this", says Nadya, "Ilyich took a more favourable view of Mayakovsky. He admitted that he was not a competent judge of poetical talent." No other character in *Travesties* exhibits Lenin's self-doubt. Describing his instinctive reaction to Beethoven's 'Appassionata', he may stand condemned from his own mouth and, incidentally, provide a shining example of art's humanizing influence, but he also makes clear that the conditions of Revolution necessitate the sacrifice of such instincts:

... superhuman music. It always makes me feel, perhaps naively, it makes me feel proud of the miracles that human beings can perform. But I can't listen to music often. It affects my nerves, makes me want to say nice stupid things and pat the heads of those people who while living in this vile hell can create such beauty. Nowadays we can't pat heads or we'll get our hands bitten off. We've got to *hit* heads, hit them without mercy, though ideally we're against doing violence to people ... (89)

Stoppard himself has attested to the power of this sequence when performed by actors able to convey their own human ordinariness: "When they walk on the stage you don't really think that man has contradicted himself throughout ... You think he really had a burden to carry ... The equation is different, and even I am seduced by it."[16] Stoppard does not intend to show that position A is better than B, for both Joyce and Lenin's views are simply different attitudes to the same problem: how the artist serves society for the common good. The decision-making comes, as it does in *Jumpers*, when two attitudes, Joyce's egoism and Lenin's self-abnegation, are held up to the light of an ultimate morality; as Stoppard remarks, in describing all his serious work, "At the ideal centre there is a way of behaving towards people which is good and a way which is bad ..."[17] In that light, the politician stands condemned and the artist appears as a bulwark of social morality, even though he does nothing directly. It is this that we are left to ponder after Old Carr's speech that closes Act I in which he imagines arraigning Joyce: "... and I *flung* at him – 'And what did you do in the Great War?' 'I wrote *Ulysses*,' he said. 'What did you do?' Bloody nerve" (65).

Nonetheless, other aspects of *Travesties* belie that humanity. Oddly, the serio-comic debate over the artist's responsibility, which Stoppard cares so much about and presents so forcefully in *Artist Descending*, now has little human feeling behind it. Where *Jumpers* balances frivolity and seriousness on either side of a central pivot, George and Dotty's anguish, in *Travesties* there is no such centre, and the play pulls in opposite directions. Stoppard has noted how the two plays share a similar structure:

You start with a prologue which is slightly strange. Then you have an interminable monologue which is rather funny. Then you have scenes. Then you end up with another monologue. And you have unexpected bits of music and dance, and at the same time people are playing ping-pong with various intellectual arguments.[18]

The big difference, however, lies in his decision to make Old Carr his viewfinder for most of the action. In the theatre this invites confusion. The "strange" prologue in the Zurich Public Library introduces everyone but Carr. It is amusingly disorientating in that hardly a word of English is spoken, though the characters at their separate tables behave much as they might have done in actuality: Tzara takes a large pair of scissors to what he has just written, cuts out each word, pops them into his hat, empties out the pieces and then recites the resulting 'poem'; Joyce dictates to Gwendolen (Carr's sister) fragmented words from what some may recognize as *Ulysses*; the Lenins talk in Russian about the revolution in St Petersburg; Cecily bustles in and out to call "Sssssh!" The sequence ends with one of Joyce's limericks, but when he strolls off, with rakish hat and stick, crooning "If you ever go across the sea to Ireland", his manner seems that of a fantasy figure.

It is only after this change of tone that Carr takes up the narrative to tell of the "James Joyce I Knew". The script allows for the possibility of making the old man an on-stage observer from the outset, and the original production had him strum on a piano as Joyce sang and the Library set disappeared, additions which clearly established the characters as creatures of memory. But no such allowance occurs at the start of Act 2, where Stoppard deliberately breaks the reminiscences to have Cecily lecture the audience on Marxism and the Lenins. The break can be justified by the fact that Carr never met the Lenins; however, since we learn this from Old Cecily only at the end of the play, dramatically the lecture comes as a startling interruption which initiates the uneasy alliance throughout the rest of Act 2 between Carr's fantasies, as shaped by *Earnest*, and the Lenins, as presented through historical memoirs and letters.

But Carr's major effect is to rob the play's ideas of most of their impact. The old man has very little connection with the play's critique about art and the artist, and certainly no emotional investment in it. For him, the plot justifies his own importance amidst a group of 'artsy' charlatans and political nobodies: "And don't forget, *he wasn't Lenin then! I mean who was he!* as it were" (81). What drives him is a fury, which still rankles, at the way Joyce tipped him a few francs after his triumph in *Earnest* and refused to defray the cost of his wardrobe. In real life, Carr and Joyce had gone to court, the one to recover his expenses, the other to sue for threats and libel. In the theatre, the way the old man's feelings travesty the events of 1915–18 proves Wildely amusing but it also creates a barrier between the audience and the play's ideas.

Carr's first "interminable monologue" illustrates that effect. In *Jumpers*, George's efforts to organize his thoughts about God reach an impasse or become derailed in much the same manner as Carr's memories. But we overhear George through the invisible 'fourth wall', sharing a frustration whose full meaning is brought home to us by the play's ensuing action. Old Carr addresses us directly with the self-consciousness of a stand-up comedian. His recollections deliberately parody the titles and style of Edwardian memoirs, though his verbose and punning detachment occasionally breaks down to reveal more than he intends as he brands Joyce "a liar and a hypocrite, a tight-fisted, sponging, fornicating drunk not worth the paper, that's that bit done" (23). The last self-conscious phrase reins in his animosity. We then enter the play proper light-heartedly, diverted by Carr's late-night-review, *Beyond the Fringe* performance, a manner which colours the remainder of Act 1.

When the action begins, Carr's interchange with Bennett recalls Algy's with Lane in *Earnest*, and the verbal short-circuits, emphasized by a quick dimming of the lights, also maintain an air of performance. Each time Bennett interjects the line, "Yes, sir. I have put the newspapers and telegrams on the sideboard, sir", the conversation takes off on a fresh tangent to convey the quirks of Carr's memory and to allow the transmission of information about the War and the Russian Revolution in a style that "breaks its neck"[19] to be funny. Tzara arrives as a stage-Frenchman and Joyce enters as "an Irish nonsense". Together with Gwen, the quartet break into a cross-fire of dialogue which chimes together as a series of overtly clever limericks. Such stylization re-creates the puppet theatre of Old Carr's imagination, but it also weaves a gauze between the audience and what the characters say, confronting us instead with *the way* things are said. Consequently, when these figures deliver their views on art, those ideas seem to spin from the top of their heads. No one within the purlieu of Carr's memory shows any caring. If they lose their tempers, they simply obey the stop-and-start patterns of the narrative, so that when every argument disintegrates into the same childish invective we are again faced with the play's style rather than its content:

CARR: My God, you little Rumanian wog – you bloody dago – you jumped-up phrase-making smart-alecy arty-intellectual Balkan turd!!! Think you know it all! – while we poor dupes think we're fighting for ideals, you've got a profound understanding of what is *really* going on, underneath! – you've got a phrase for it! (40)

Carr and his characters all have "a phrase for it"; their ideas do not plummet down to their inner selves. They have no inner selves. Knowing that an artist, however committed, can never guide his society directly, Stoppard seems to taunt his critics with the dispassionate and apparently uncaring surface of *Travesties*. The gambit is Oscar Wilde's, but Stoppard's nothing-up-my-sleeve artifice in reply to mutterings about his own intellectual wizardry falsifies the essential humanity which propels his argument. This confrontation rises to the play's surface in Act 2, when Cecily, the disciple of Marxism, maintains that art must serve and change society, whereas Carr posits Wilde as the exemplum of the detached artist who feeds man's spirit:

CARR: . . . Wilde was indifferent to politics. He may occasionally have been a little overdressed but he made up for it by being immensely uncommitted.
CECILY: That is my objection to him. The sole duty and justification for art is social criticism. (74)

Carr happens to be quite wrong about Wilde, and though he may act here as Stoppard's dislocating mouthpiece, his opinion and the style of both speakers pander to an image of Oscar-the-dandy that will probably be uppermost in the minds of those who know nothing of Wilde's "The Critic as Artist" or "The Soul of Man under Socialism". Furthermore, Carr's reminiscences, which dance to the tune of *Earnest*'s stylized rotundities, work against Stoppard's defence of art as something which, in Martello's phrase, comes "to grips with life". Wilde's *Earnest*, in defying the late-Victorians' ultra-serious attitude to life, derives much of its energy and conviction from the determination of Algy and Jack to win their respective ladies. *Travesties* explodes out of Carr's unrequited fury over Joyce's high-handed behaviour after his success as Algy. The way this Jack – no, the other one – wins his Jill, despite misunderstandings as to the artistic and philosophic merits of Joyce and Lenin, matters not in the least to the play's central thesis.

In Act 2, Carr goes to the library disguised as Tristan, in a furtive attempt to discover the Lenins' plans. As he listens to Cecily's lecture – "the rich own the poor and the men own the women" (78) – he imagines her as a nightclub stripper. Through his eyes, we watch her librarian's desk light up as she gyrates to "The Stripper" while proclaiming Marx and Lenin. His *"Get 'em off!"* chimes exactly with what we know of the irascible Old Carr, but the image of his young self teeters precariously, and the parallel between *Travesties* and *Earnest* becomes a contrivance. Carr has no real interest in Cecily's charms, *pace* Stoppard's attempted cover-up: "I should like to make it clear that my feelings for Cecily are genuine" (82). Animating both Carrs, young and old, is the business of the trousers, his animosity towards Joyce, and the nine-days'-wonder of his performance as Algy. So *Travesties'* final marriage-go-round only emphasizes the ingenious yet tenuous way Stoppard has engineered his plot, which turns on the accidental exchange of Joyce's and Lenin's work in progress, to accord with *Earnest*'s ultimate revelation about a lost handbag. And though Old Carr's final statement diverts us deliberately and comically from the matter at hand (in an echo of Charlie's confusion in *Dogg's Our Pet*), his speech also reduces the battle between art and politics to a shrug of the shoulders:

I learned three things in Zurich during the war. I wrote them down. Firstly, you're either a revolutionary or you're not, and if you're not you might as well be an artist as anything else. Secondly, if you can't be an artist, you might as well be a revolutionary . . . I forget the third thing.   (98–9)

The failure of *Travesties*, therefore, is not the result of its zany mix of styles, since the library scene immediately establishes and supports that stylistic hodgepodge, nor can it be blamed on the counterpoint between travestied characters like Joyce and Tzara and those like the Lenins who basically appear as their historical selves, although the latter pair do tend to travel (literally and metaphorically) in an enclosed compartment. As his final words indicate, the alliance between the play's farcical action and serious ideas ends in divorce because of Old Carr. Where the play depicts the artist as a type of revolutionary, Carr amusingly sees them as opposites and – more damagingly – shrugs off their whole debate with the 'so what?' attitude that also colours his version of every serious argument between the characters whom he derails in explosions of personal invective.

Had the action been stage-managed by a more translucent narrator, *Travesties* might stand ironically as Stoppard's most Brechtian fable, with its snatches of song and dance, open stage, self-contained episodes, dialectical argument, and undisguised theatricality. But given the subjective quirkiness of Carr, each character's independent point of view is subverted by a narrator whose own attitude is epitomized by his attraction to *The Importance of Being Earnest* as an opportunity for several changes of costume and for whom the Great War (between nations or between himself and Joyce) centres upon the quality of one's trousers. Yet the ideas in *Travesties* cannot be shrugged aside as so much dandified nonsense. It surely does matter that though the artistic revolutionary, unlike his political counterpart, has no immediate effect on society, it is his work which ultimately shapes our ethics because he refuses to submit to the State. For though the artist may appear "irresponsible" when he demands, as Tzara does, "the right to urinate in different colours" (61), given Lenin and the Marxists' sense of social responsibility "multi-coloured micturition is no trick to those boys, they'll have you pissing blood" (83).

It is Carr who says that, but the terror of this remark in no way affects his older self, and so the idea is reduced to a snappy one-liner. This is characteristic of much of *Travesties*. Jokes and puns fly out at us in rapid profusion. Lines like "jewelled escapements and refugees of all kinds" (23) or the description of "a Swiss redlight district, pornographic fretwork shops, vice dens, get a grip on yourself" (24) make inventive and, at each given moment, effective detours into Carr's jackdaw mind. But at other times, the jokes are either so elaborate as to lose their point in the theatre, as when Tzara's pieced-together nonsense poem turns out, if one takes the time to wrestle with it, to make considerable sense in French (for example, "noon avuncular ill day Clara" (18) converts into " 'nous n'avons que l'art', il déclara") or they simply go on too long. The limerick sequence in Act 1 or Gwendoline and Cecily's later "Mr Gallagher and Mr Shean" routine stretch out to the point of self-indulgence, while the prolonged interview between Tzara and Joyce (a parody of the catechism in *Ulysses* and Lady Bracknell's interrogation of Mr Worthing) halts the action in order to deliver undiluted information about Dadaism, a tactic as diversionary as Cecily's much-criticized sermonette on Lenin. In all these cases, the play's style draws our attention away from its content or back to the self-regarding Carr, who like some rusted Lord Malquist, withdraws from chaos with style. But, however entertaining that might be, the old man's egocentric and barren version of history eventually trivializes the central idea that the artist's independent vision and humanity turns fact into spiritual gold.

Chapter 6
Ethics and manners

After *Travesties*, Stoppard changed tack. To write *anything* is a chancy business: a combination of calculated intent, lucky accident, and inspired connections. Stoppard has himself described the way he often starts with an image, like the dead body in *Inspector Hound* or the collapsing human pyramid of *Jumpers*, and then chips away at it until the play's ultimate pattern explains his initial picture.[1] But for a playwright there then comes the problem of conveying that pattern to a person sitting in row F. The near-débâcle of *Rosencrantz* at Edinburgh had shown how vulnerable a script is to actors and director. And though Stoppard could later command the resources of the National Theatre or the Royal Shakespeare Company and, from *Jumpers* on, the directorial skills of Peter Wood, his particular brand of theatrical audacity was not easy to bring off. Daring to break the action of *Travesties* with Cecily's extended lecture on the history of the Russian Revolution and then, as the audience recovered, to discountenance them still further with the prosaic Lenins and the ladies' rhythmical "Mr Gallagher and Mr Shean" sparring match proved too confusing on the stage, so out went most of Cecily's sermonette. Understandably, in an interview just after that première, Stoppard acknowledged the riskiness of such theatrical display: "ideally what I'd like to write now is something that takes place in a whitewashed room with no music and no jumping about, but which is a literary piece – so that the energy can go into the literary side of what I do. I'd like to write a quiet play."[2] Looking back, some two years later, he would admit to the structural faults in *Travesties* but add that the major speeches were still the *o altitudo* of that brand of theatrics: "I don't see much point in trying to do it again, though I probably will, for want of being able to do anything else."[3] The plays that belong to the period between these two comments are neither "quiet" nor safely realist, but they do mark a retreat from the three-ring circus.

Dirty Linen and New-Found-Land,[4] the knickers farce that opened at the Almost Free Theatre in April 1976 and transferred two months later to the Arts, where it ran for years, seems to abandon the comedy of ideas entirely. This "little joke play", an undisguised (and probably liberating) frolic, took shape in response to his promise to write something in honour of Ed Berman's becoming a British citizen. When *Dirty Linen* "went off in a different direction", Stoppard hit upon the idea of *New-Found-Land* to pull things back to the occasion at hand. This concoction, apparently so unlike anything he had done before, bears many characteristic fingerprints. For example, his decision to insert *New-Found-Land* into the silly antics of *Dirty Linen* is, on a minor scale, a typical piece of audacity; if a structural divide cannot be bridged over, then flaunt it. And the isolation of *New-Found-Land*'s two characters from each other and from *Dirty Linen*'s sexual shenanigans exemplifies the way Stoppard's characters passionately maintain a personal vision which occasionally accords, but more usually conflicts with, someone else's. To end the first part of *Dirty Linen*, the members of the Select Committee on parliamentary promiscuity are summoned away by the Division Bell. As one door shuts, another opens; in comes Arthur with a file of papers and shouts back to his colleague, just behind him, that they have at last found an empty room. For a moment two worlds touch when Arthur, clearing away a clutter of newspapers from the table, reacts to a pin-up in one of the tabloids with a wide-eyed "Strewth!" that, by this time, has become a running joke. In all other ways, they seem to belong, as the text maintains, "in another play" (52).

Stoppard accentuates that separateness by making the second civil servant, Bernard, extremely deaf and endearingly senile. As Big Ben crashes out the hour just above their heads, Arthur cringes but Bernard "looks around vaguely" (55). If the one cannot hear, the other will not listen, because he has heard Bernard's story about winning a fiver from Lloyd George *ad infinitum*. To cut across the preceding action with a doddering account of how "father knew Lloyd George" is a cheeky gambit, and the elderly clerk's obsession allows even this part of the play to wander away from the business of Ed Berman's naturalization papers which the two men have met to consider. Yet this apparent break in tone is not bewilderingly tricksy, for an audience will feel immediately familiar with the Lloyd George chestnut and, when it transpires that the statesman was more intimately acquainted with Bernard's *mother*, this story rapidly attaches itself to the sexual innuendo that threads through the entire action. Though daringly unorthodox, the surprising entrance of this pair quickly attunes with the prevailing mood and then becomes a launching-pad for two Stoppardian monologues.

The first one emerges from a ripple of verbal misunderstanding, as Bernard produces the treasured £5 note he won from the then Prime Minister, and Arthur reminds him that they are supposed to advise their own Minister about the naturalization papers. It is soon unclear to which Minister each speaker refers, and when Bernard adds that "he asked me for my views about French, you know" (56), the audience would assume he means Mr French of the Select Committee. But Bernard means the Field Marshal who was replaced by Haig in the First World War, and that thought leads him irrevocably to the famous fiver. For him, the anecdote points to the fact that "Welsh intuition is no match for English cunning" (58): in betting that Big Ben could be seen from the upstairs windows, the Prime Minister had apparently forgotten that "Big Ben is the name of the bell, not the clock." A less self-absorbed listener will perceive that Lloyd George, in pressing the bet, specifically mentions the window of the bedroom in which Bernard's mother "received us gaily, just as though she were in her drawing-room", and will come to his own conclusions on hearing how Bernard, returning home after having his war-wound attended to, meets the Prime Minister coming down the front steps. Offering to return the money, he is told to "keep it, . . . I never spent a better £5".

But no such conclusions arise, since Bernard ends by remarking that the Americans saved Haig (and the Allies) and this prompts Arthur to remember the applicant, who is also American. Stoppard then plays with the biography of the real Ed Berman but, by presenting those details as oddly assorted facts from Arthur's file and by keeping the applicant anonymous, he makes the in-jokes about his friend general enough to amuse any audience and then builds them into an inspired muddle:

BERNARD: . . . A theatrical farmer with buses on the side, doing publishing and community work in a beard . . . are we supposed to tell the Minister that he's just the sort of chap this country needs? Does he say why he wants to be British?
ARTHUR: Yes, because he's American.
BERNARD: Well he's got a point there.   (59)

Finally, one of those comic deflations that Stoppard admires so much in Beckett, as Bernard praises Americans for their modernity, openness, lack of ceremony, generosity, ambition, self-confidence – "Apart from all that I've got nothing against them" – effects a transition to Arthur's rhapsody on "My America!" (60).

This monologue, less inconsequent though otherwise quite similar to those of George Moore and Old Carr, stands as a set piece. It is very much a performance, a moment of unabashed 'showbiz' which makes the stage so attractive to Stoppard. But the theatrics here are more single-minded and one-dimensional. As Arthur warms to his (as opposed to the applicant's) new-found-land, he takes our exclusive attention, since Bernard almost immediately nods off to sleep. No longer the unassuming junior, he embarks on a cliché-packed travelogue set loose by his creator's flair for parody. The speech works by cramming in as many platitudes as possible about America and its landscape. It begins with a grandiose description of the Greyhound of the Deep smashing through the waters of Long Island Sound. The Statue of Liberty glows, to the tears and wonderment of the immigrants who pack the lower decks: "destined, some of them, to become the captains and the kings of industrial empires . . . to put a chicken into every pot, an automobile by every stoop, to organize crime as never before . . . New York! New York! It's a wonderful town!" (60–1). Stereotyped phrases for Wall Street, the Bowery, and The Great White Way tumble out until the Chattanooga train sends us on a circuitous route through New England in the Fall to "Chicago – Chicago! – it's a wonderful town", Kentucky blue grass, hill-billy Tennessee, and on through the Old South to Californian paradise where we stare in Keatsian "wild surmise" at the Pacific. The banalities roll along *con brio*, and Arthur enfolds himself in these American dreams: imagining "a cheerful shoeshine boy with a flashing smile" (62), he sports a pair of stars-and-stripes socks; reaching Galveston, he pulls out a pack of American cigarettes; entering the Wild West, he reveals a tin star on his waistcoat. He is as obsessed with Americana as Bernard was over the fiver, and when the Committee returns for its meeting, he has *become* brash America: "I think you got the wrong room, buster" (65).

Obsession in fact controls all the play's parts, though Stoppard has also invented other smaller links: previously a committee member recalls a train journey he made across America, "but that's another story" (32) – although it isn't, quite – and when *Dirty Linen* resumes, Bernard automatically shows off his fiver, only to have it torn to pieces by the Committee's chairman in mistake for an incriminating note of his own. This misunderstanding creates an instant of surprising poignancy. Otherwise mayhem prevails, though it does not shoot off in all directions, as it tends to do in the longer plays, because everyone on the Select Committee shares the same passion for Maddie Gotobed, their recording secretary, and the same terror of being caught out.

Stoppard's "literary" energies are also unusually circumscribed, and pursue with manic concentration the naughty-postcard aspect of farce. French knickers and Freudian slips turn up all over the place. The action is simple-minded, but the dialogue exploits the twists and traps of language. *Dirty Linen* begins with a less demanding variant of the first library scene in *Travesties*. Cocklebury-Smythe and McTeazle (the MPs and their secretary have crassly provocative names) arrive together at the overspill meeting-room in the Big Ben tower. For several minutes their exchange consists entirely of foreign expressions, like *"C'est la vie"*, *"Ooh la-la!"* and *"faux pas"*. Tired phrases, in whatever language, are to colour every section of the play. When Maddie arrives, so do the *double entendres*, and words skid into pot-holes as each man, without rousing the suspicion of his colleague, tries to persuade Maddie to deny any liaison at the Coq d'Or. Their dialogue is also waylaid by the charms of the lady herself: "why don't you have a quick poke, peek, in the Members' Bra – or the cafeteria, they're probably guzzling coffee and Swedish panties, (MADDIE *has crossed her legs*) Danish . . ." (22). Language becomes abstract and playful, as in *Dogg's Our Pet*, when both MPs reel off alliterative lists of pubs and restaurants, tongue-twisting alibis which Maddie must then repeat as best she can. Puns run the gamut from the clever to the plain awful: "It's a brief case", says the Chairman as he hides away his underwear (43). And by having the Committee investigate (or circumvent) charges in the newspapers about "Moral Standards in Public Life", Stoppard makes fun of parliamentary jargon and the tabloids' cheap suggestiveness. Mr French, recognizing the secretary's pin-up in the *Sun*, reads on:

Maddie Takes It Down!

'Madeleine Gotobed, twenty-one, is a model secretary in Whitehall where she says her ambition is to be Permanent Under Secretary. Meanwhile, titian-haired, green-eyed Maddie loves being taken out, but says the men tend to look down on a figure like hers – whenever they get the chance!' – disgusting – 'Matching bra and suspender belt, Fenwicks £5.35. French knickers, Janet Reger £8.95.' (51)

To underscore the one-track minds of all his characters, Stoppard uses the stage with minimal flamboyance. The set only requires a suggestion of walls, two functional doors, a table and chairs for the members, a blackboard on which to record the way they voted or, as Maddie sees it, to enter the results: "Home win!" One recurring staging device accentuates the style of the popular press. From time to time, one or other of the gentlemen boggles over a pin-up in the scandal rags before him. At his appreciative "Strewth!", though he is too engrossed to notice, Maddie has moved into an especially provoking pose; that teasing picture is then captured by a flash-bulb as she looks straight out at the audience and freezes. Maddie also loses skirt, slip, and blouse to various unintentional hands and calmly takes back knickers from, or returns underpants to, her former conquests. Yet these realities prove less lip-smacking to the Committee than do the photos in their newspapers.

However, although the *farceur* in Stoppard runs free, *Dirty Linen* does contain a modicum of seriousness. His expressed aim was to torpedo the stereotype that Maddie appears to be: "Her whole attitude in the play is one of innocent, eager willingness to please" (24). He wanted to persuade the audience to dismiss her as a mindless redhead and then show her as the only person on stage with common sense.[5] But he plays his hand too soon. Having bedded the people who count on Fleet Street, Maddie knows that "they've got more people writing about football than writing about you and that's in the *cricket* season" (37). So it comes as little surprise when the Committee adopts her point of view in their final report. We have perceived her good sense for some time, even though her secretarial talents are ludicrous, and the destruction of the stereotype is hardly less predictable than the change in Mr French who, as a puritan stickler for rules of all sorts, eventually must – in this type of comedy – join his philandering colleagues. Nevertheless, in allowing Maddie to think, Stoppard injects the farce with ideas about the responsibilities of the press which go back to his early concerns in "The Story" and which will later be developed entirely seriously in *Night and Day*.

Cocklebury-Smythe, who happens to belong to the National Union of Journalists, feels that "newspapers *are* the people in a sense – they are the channel of the government's answerability to the governed" (36). Mrs Ebury sweeps that ideal aside:

And on top of that they're as smug a collection of inaccurate, hypocritical, self-important, bullying, shoddily printed sick-bags as you'd hope to find in a month of Sundays, and dailies, and the weeklies aren't much better.

Withenshaw, the Chairman, had also attacked the journalists' altruism; muck-raking is simply a way to sell more papers in a slow season by "sticking their noses into upper reaches of top drawers looking for hankie panties, etcetera" (30). Yet the Committee accept a journalist's moral right to investigate the private habits of public figures even as they agree with Maddie that newspapers are just as much a commodity as haberdashery. So it is she who, from her own extensive knowledge of the journalists' sex-lives, reminds them that the press is run by the same sort of people as they are and that the private life of politicians is nobody's business but their own. Eventually, Mr French will dress that up in more formal attire, adding the proviso that such behaviour should "not transgress the rights of others or the law of the land" (72), but Maddie's version is the more succinct:

All this fuss! The whole report can go straight in the waste-paper basket. All you need is one paragraph saying that MPs have got just as much right to enjoy themselves in their own way as anyone else, and Fleet Street can take a running jump. (41)

Maddie's down-to-earth style typifies the brash comedy of this joke play, but bobbing about midst the panties and the pin-ups are ideas which Stoppard will come back to less lightheartedly. In paring away the theatrical high jinks, while not yet abandoning their high spirits, he returns to his own past as a journalist and begins to explore, however farcically, the rights of the individual. Actually, those rights were first championed in *Jumpers*, when George protested at the way a totalitarian society could change "the rules", and in *Travesties* the artist stood out as the guardian of spiritual, if not political freedom. What moved those themes to the centre of Stoppard's work was the political realities he experienced while wrestling with his next play, *Every Good Boy Deserves Favour*.[6]

In his introduction to that text, Stoppard has described the fortuitous circumstances that led to his final statement. In 1974, André Previn, the conductor of the London Symphony Orchestra, had invited him to write a play which included an actual orchestra. He "jumped at the chance" but, as his deadline came and went, he had reached an impasse. His first idea had been about a millionaire who could afford an orchestra, but, since the little he knew about music went back to his kindergarten days as a triangle-player, he next thought of "a millionaire triangle-player with his own orchestra" (6). When this "whimsical edifice" began to teeter, he imagined what would happen were the triangle-player to imagine the orchestra – he would no longer have to be a millionaire – and "This is where matters stood when in April 1976 I met Victor Fainberg".

The encounter gave him something to write about instead of a logistical problem to solve. Fainberg had been arrested for demonstrating against the Warsaw Pact's invasion of Czechoslovakia. Judged insane, he was committed to a prison-hospital for five years and then exiled:

For Mr Fainberg freedom was, and is, mainly the freedom to double his efforts on behalf of colleagues left behind. His main concern when I met him was to secure the release of Vladimir Bukovsky, himself a victim of the abuse of psychiatry in the USSR, whose revelations about that abuse had got him sentenced to consecutive terms of prison, labour camp and internal exile amounting to twelve years. (6–7)

Fainberg's stand touched a nerve, since Stoppard had been reading about Russian dissidents for a projected television script, and, once he had drawn the connection between a lunatic triangle-player and a "mad" political prisoner, "in a few weeks the play was finished" (7). He had confronted an unusual courage and, in transmuting it for the stage, was brought forcefully against the problem he had voiced through Donner in *Artist Descending*: "How can one justify art to a man with an empty belly?" – or with a twelve-year prison sentence.

The experience was not quite Saul's on the road to Damascus, but from this time on Stoppard's plays become explicitly political.

Every Good Boy is as economical as the best of the radio plays. It requires little physical action and concentrates on the actors' voices, which, in key moments, derive added impact from Previn's music. However, one effect which could not be achieved on radio depends on the spatial and emotional distance between the three acting areas set amidst an orchestra which is always there before us. As the play begins, Ivanov, the lunatic, and Alexander, the dissident, are seated on their beds as if in a cell; the two other spaces, representing an office and a schoolroom, are in darkness, though Sacha, Alexander's son, is already at his desk and his teacher stands over him. Things start normally enough as the orchestra tune up, but after a time they do so in mime. Once this dislocating silence has been established, Ivanov stands up with his triangle and rod at the ready and the players become still. The silence grows even more disturbing when Ivanov eventually strikes his instrument and the orchestra burst into a mimed performance. All we hear is an intermittent ping from the triangle as Ivanov concentrates on his part. What we see are the busy musicians and, in the cell, "a man watching another man occasionally hitting a triangle" (15). Soon the music begins to be audible, growing louder until the lights come up brightly on the orchestra and we realize that the triangle has its part in a Russian-sounding symphony which now goes at full swing. The strategy is characteristically unsettling, but here Stoppard manœuvres us into a moment of madness to which we react less stoically than does Alexander himself, a scheme he is to develop through the rest of the action.

Since we are bound to bring feelings of outrage to Alexander's situation, Stoppard concentrates our focus on the lunatic Ivanov rather than on the hospital authorities, in order to dramatize both the madness and threat of this place. For Ivanov is a threatening figure despite his air of apparent harmlessness. His barrage of words, as he apologizes to Alexander for the inadequacies of his imagined orchestra, presents an extended version of the way the prison doctor and Sacha's teacher brush aside all argument, and his mad logic parallels their sweet reason, which could at any moment slide into violence. The incipient threat is made the more fearsome by Ivanov's comic mask, and Alexander reacts to him from the outset with a wary calm.

At first, Ivanov's contempt for his own musicians and his insistence that Alexander must be an instrumentalist of some kind appear as an amusing tyranny until, without the slightest change of tone, the interrogator reveals a darker side: "Give me a clue. If I beat you to a pulp would you try to protect your face or your hands? Which would be the more serious – if you couldn't sit down for a week or couldn't stand up? I'm trying to narrow it down, you see" (17). As this sequence develops, Stoppard draws the narrowest of lines between the comedy of Ivanov's whirling obsession (so reminiscent of Old Carr's) and its political subtext, which infects as seemingly farcical a remark as "the Jew's harp has applied for a visa" and which rises to the surface without warning:

– why, I know people who make the orchestra eat in the kitchen, off scraps, the way you'd throw a trombone to a dog, I mean a second violinist, I mean to the lions; I love musicians, I respect them, human beings to a man. Let me put it like this: if I smashed this instrument of yours over your head, would you need a carpenter, a welder, or a brain surgeon? (18)

Having presented the terrors of the hospital–prison in this comic way, Stoppard draws in his other characters with a straight-faced understatement which gains emotional power the more it is seen in parallel to Ivanov's mad volatility. To achieve this, he depends on effects of light and sound during the transitions between the three acting areas and on the patterned structure that connects each episode to the next. For example, the first scene ends as Ivanov offers advice to his cell-mate – "Number three – *practise!*" – and strikes his triangle. That note leads, as the lights fade, to the doh–ray–me sound of a school band, whose performance soon goes awry because of an obtrusive triangle in it. Eventually its hectic notes are all we hear. When they stop, the lights come up on the schoolmistress who, with cool sarcasm, reprimands Sacha for subverting the concert. The connection is tightened by the teacher's deliberate word-play as she decides on Sacha's punishment – "Detention is becoming a family tradition" – and tells him to open a book: "Any book. *Fathers and Sons*, perhaps" (19). Her autocratic style is more placid yet no less blinkered than Ivanov's, and through Sacha we now view dissidence with unchecked pathos.

Like his father, whose name he bears in diminutive form, he does not want to play in an orchestra, though the triangle he resists is both musical and Euclid's "polygon bounded by the fewest possible sides", a definition he must copy out neatly ten times from his geometry book. It may be objected that these connections lead to unfortunate connotations when the teacher tells Sacha that the authorities make his father copy out a million times, "I am a member of an orchestra and we must play together."[7] That the State is like a well-run orchestra is her own vindictive equation but, lest we accept that, the music itself is often so radiant or so in sympathy with Alexander, when it punctuates his long speech about his arrest, that we are surely brought to wonder how orchestrated societies could produce such sound or, since Previn echoes composers like Prokofiev and Shostakovich, how artists create in spite of State directives.

Stoppard dramatizes that same contradiction through the Doctor who, in the third scene, rises from his place amidst the strings section. As he sheds his role as violinist and moves towards his office to assume power, the entire orchestra mock that authority with music which exactly matches his walk and with a *glissando* from the strings as he sits down behind his desk. So it is as prison doctor that he seems most mechanical and, appropriately, his first interview is with Ivanov who has his own mad rigidity. These ideas come directly to the fore some scenes later when Alexander enters the office:

DOCTOR *in his* OFFICE *playing violin solo. Violin cuts out.*
DOCTOR: Come in.
(ALEXANDER *enters the* DOCTOR's *light.*)
DOCTOR: Hello. Sit down please. Do you play a musical instrument?
ALEXANDER: (*Taken aback*) Are you a patient?
DOCTOR: (*Cheerfully*) No, I am a doctor. *You* are a patient. It's a distinction which we try to keep going here, though I'm told it's coming under scrutiny in more advanced circles of psychiatric medicine . . .   (26)

Later still, Sacha visits the prison and mistakes Ivanov for the Doctor at whose desk he sits (33). But the Doctor himself is drawn entirely seriously. The comedy arises out of these misunderstandings and from the clash of views, especially when, having convinced Ivanov that there is no orchestra, he remembers he has a performance of his own and races across to his place amongst the actual musicians.

The new ingredient in Stoppard's blend of serious–play is the restraint with which he presents all the characters except his lunatic triangle-player. This is particularly noticeable in the way he develops Alexander, who voices his suffering in matter-of-fact terms and whose rebellion takes the form of a quiet, stubborn refusal. That firmness appears from the outset in his careful defence against Ivanov, yet his position is made the more delicate by his struggle not to cough and so ruin his violent cell-mate's imagined concert. His pain shows in a similarly indirect fashion at the end of the first school scene, when Sacha cries out against his father's punishment and, from across the stage, Alexander calls the boy's name so that the teacher's self-righteous treatment of the son becomes the father's nightmare. The anguish of that dream comes mainly from the percussive music which cuts into the voices from the darkened stage.

The music is also crucial to the emotion behind Alexander's account of his arrest. A long orchestral prelude turns into another nightmare: an off-key piccolo distorts the melody, which then builds to a strident climax. Bursting out of his dream, Alexander awakes to Ivanov's peculiar ministrations: "Don't worry . . . Any trumpeter comes at me, I'll kick his teeth in. Violins get it under the chin to boot, this boot, and God help anyone who plays a cello" (22). Ironically, the cellos lead sonorously into Alexander's solo, which is prompted by Ivanov (now the concerned psychiatrist) who asks him to "Tell me about yourself – your home, your childhood, your first piano-teacher . . . how did it all begin?" The speech moves with the cellos, which glide mournfully under the words until "I thought this was most peculiar" (23) when the orchestra takes over and allows us pause to consider the detention of writers who have published "mad" books. Timed to this accompaniment, the next words slow to a colourless monody as Alexander describes how C (Vladimir Bukovsky) went back to the mental hospital for protesting against the arrest of A and B. These impersonal letters match the notes of the musical scale and the points in Sacha's geometric figures but, as the litany progresses to Q, R, S, and T, the rising emotion in the music belies the dispassionate prose. In this way, Stoppard eschews all but the blackest comedy and protects Alexander from self-pity by giving him an air of detached astonishment: "You see all the trouble writers cause" – his words echo the teacher's disapproval and so the school band begins again in the background – "They spoil things for ordinary people."

Alexander considered himself to be ordinary, except that he had a friend who was constantly in trouble, until "one day I did something really crazy" (24). At that, the music gives way to the frenzied beat of a snare drum; we move back to the schoolroom, where Sacha is in trouble for damaging school property, the drum he has progressed to from the triangle. In the teacher's eyes, this behaviour confirms the boy's likeness to his father. The lights fade; we are back in the cell, and slow violins accent Alexander's report of his internment in the Arsenal'naya Psychiatric Hospital where, after two years, he began a hunger strike. Back, too, comes the contradistinction between human achievement and social tyranny: "Russia is a civilized country, very good at Swan Lake and space technology, and it is confusing if people starve themselves to death" (24). Stoppard highlights the most monstrous of the prisoner's sufferings by having Sacha innocently remark that his father smells like "Olga when she does her nails" (25) in dialogue made dreamlike by an undertow of sustained, metallic notes from the orchestra. Then complete silence frames Alexander's bland assertion that, since a starving man gives off the odour of nail-polish-remover, the authorities will give in to this inconveniently well-known dissident, although to save face they "need a formula".

His meeting with Victor Fainberg impressed on Stoppard the "single-mindedness, . . . [the] willingness to make a nuisance of himself" (7) which must have moved the commissars to get rid of him. The subdued style of *Every Good Boy* captures that stubborn dignity, and its dénouement ridicules the officials' embarrassment. Having deputed Sacha to persuade his father not to "be rigid", and failed, the Doctor arrives at stalemate, whereupon a succession of crashing cymbals, drums, and swelling organ announces the grandiloquent entry of "Colonel – or rather Doctor – Rozinsky" (27), the *deus ex machina* of the piece. Rozinsky has prepared his escape route by personally choosing Alexander's cell-mate, the eponymous lunatic, Alexander Ivanov, and, as he quells the bewildered protests of the Doctor and the madman, deliberately puts questions to the two patients that he knows they will answer satisfactorily. Ivanov cannot conceive that the Soviets would "put a sane man into a lunatic asylum" (36), and Alexander has no imaginary orchestra. "There's absolutely nothing wrong with these men" (37). So the play rounds to this calculated, smug conclusion, and Sacha, ascending the corridor that runs through the orchestra, calls from that height to the liberated Alexander.

Some months before *Every Good Boy* was first performed at the Festival Hall in July 1977, Vaclav Havel, a playwright Stoppard much admires, was arrested in Prague along with an actor and a journalist for attempting to deliver a petition (Charter 77) that urged the Czech government to allow citizens the rights guaranteed by the Helsinki Agreement, to which Czechoslovakia had been a signatory. Stoppard does not say so, but it must have crossed his mind that, had his own parents not left Czechoslovakia in his childhood, he might himself have been in Havel's situation. All he could do was add his name to those who protested at the Chartists' arrest. At the time, he was still planning his television play about Russia to commemorate Amnesty International's Prisoner of Conscience Year. In connection with that, he accompanied an Amnesty friend on a short visit to the Soviet Union and was brought too close to want "to trick" the experience out as fiction "but not close enough to enable me to write about it from the inside. Instead, the trip to Russia unlocked a play about Czechoslovakia" (9). This allowed a distance from which to write about a political reality and to confront his own origins and fellow-feeling towards Havel and the Chartists.

Given that aesthetic distance, *Professional Foul* turned out to be the most naturalistic play he had so far written. This was not simply due to the realism which television affords. Having seen repression first-hand, he was unable to dress it up as a comic fable (however carefully managed) or as disguised myth (like *Neutral Ground*). Those theatrical instincts were borne out by his "embarrassed" feelings some months later, when Bukovsky came to a rehearsal of *Every Good Boy* and the reality of the man collided against the quite different reality on stage. "For people working on a piece of theatre, terra firma is a self-contained world even while it mimics the real one. That is the necessary condition of making theatre, and it is also our luxury" (8). After the Chartists and the visit to Russia, he could not permit himself that degree of luxury. Instead, *Professional Foul* poses the case of an English intellectual, protected by his own social expectations and code of good manners, who, while at a conference in Prague, comes to see what frail protection they offer and feels compelled to act against injustice. The play is about being wrenched from a self-contained world into another, less comfortable one, as if George Moore, having refused Clegthorpe's cry for help, were suddenly to lose his moral blinkers and take a stand against the Rad-Lib future.

Professor Anderson, the play's central character, is "fastidious". The first scene on the plane to Prague illustrates that manner, in his neat dabs to the mouth with a serviette as he ends his meal, his covert interest in the girlie magazine left lying on the seat beside him, and his squeamishness about "the way the wings keep *wagging*. I try to look away and think of something else but I am drawn back irresistibly" (44–5). He is also rather vague and out of touch with things, much to the disappointment of Bill McKendrick who, in introducing himself as a fellow speaker at the Colloquium, had expected his name and work to provoke some recognition. Those characteristics, his general politeness, his meticulous way with words stand in contrast to McKendrick's rougher style and are meant to place him for us and for his abashed colleague as representative of "a higher civilization alive and well in the older universities" (48). Their conversation also implants certain clues, ironic signposts to what lies ahead, for Anderson knows "there are some rather dubious things happening in Czechoslovakia. Ethically . . . We must not try to pretend otherwise" (46) and admits to "being a tiny bit naughty" towards the Czech government, though he prefers not to elaborate lest he make McKendrick his "co-conspirator . . . Ethically I should give you the opportunity of choosing to be one or not" (47).

However, the following scene provides an incident which hints at something beyond donnish fastidiousness. Waiting for the lift in the lobby of his hotel, Anderson recognizes members of England's soccer team, in Prague for a World Cup qualifier; so expert is he on the game's finer points that next morning he advises the two players about the Czechs' probable strategy. Stoppard still likes to make and then break a stereotype but, as befits the play's naturalistic style, that surprising side of Anderson is crucial to the logic of his later behaviour and though, in summary, he may seem like another of Stoppard's comic philosophers, his manner and talk are made convincingly lifelike.

Through this portrayal of the unexpected quirks of character in a fastidious and moral man, Stoppard invites us to ponder the way "ethics and manners are interestingly related" (54). At the time, Anderson means *good* manners and, as a guest of the government, refuses to breach them by smuggling his ex-student's doctoral thesis out of the country. He expects the same courtesy from the State and finds Hollar's precautions against bugging-devices unbelievably cloak-and-dagger. However, he *is* momentarily lost for words on learning that this first-class student has been reduced to taking labouring jobs and now cleans public lavatories. Like Vaclav Havel, who worked in a brewery after his plays were banned, Pavel Hollar has written things which in the government's view do breach good manners or – in Anderson's rephrasing – "correct behaviour". Nevertheless, Anderson maintains his principle of good manners despite the fact that he may not agree with his hosts on what correct behaviour is.

Such linguistic shading has much to do with the play's title. During the soccer match, one of the English players deliberately obstructs his opponent in order to stop a sure goal. At the same time, Anderson is about to witness another deliberate foul in Hollar's apartment when the police, having spent hours in search of incriminating writings, claim to discover a package of American dollars. Transparent though that is, they need to arrest Hollar as a black-marketeer because "we do not have laws about philosophy. He is an ordinary criminal" (70). Later, after a passing glance at the bad table manners of an American professor, the theme takes on a further irony when a drunkenly boorish McKendrick harangues some of the lads from the English team:

ANDERSON: McKendrick, you are being offensive.
MCKENDRICK: Anderson is one of life's cricketers. Clap, clap. (*He claps in a well-bred sort of way and puts on a well-bred voice.*) Well played, sir. Bad luck, old chap. The comparison with cricket may suggest to you that yob ethics are working class . . . It may be simply that football attracts a certain kind of person, namely yobs – (85–6)

But Anderson's own behaviour is no longer *quite cricket*; "trying to look away" has grown increasingly impossible. After his skirmish with the police, he rewrites his paper for the next day's Colloquium, whereupon the Chairman counters that "discourtesy" with a professional foul of his own. As Anderson heads for goal by asking the delegates to consider a "State ethic which finds itself in conflict with individual rights", fire-bells ring and the philosophers are requested to leave "in an orderly manner" (91). In the final scene, as their departing plane taxis down the runway, Anderson admits to yet another professional foul: he had concealed Hollar's thesis in McKendrick's brief-case since he knew his own luggage would be thoroughly searched. McKendrick is horrified at the risk he has been put to: "It's not quite playing the game is it?" But then, as Anderson wryly points out, "Ethics is a very complicated business. That's why they have these congresses" (93).

The play needs this ironic, tightly-structured scheme in order to support an ethical debate of a more complex kind. The title of Anderson's advertised paper, "Ethical Fictions as Ethical Foundations", could well fit the thesis Hollar himself professes in the hotel bedroom: that each individual, "the human being, not the citizen", has inalienable rights which might not be logically justifiable to certain political theorists – or philosophers, for that matter – but which are essential to each human's idea of himself. From a logical point of view they are fictions, but they are also inventions which, in Hollar's view, express an actual human need: "I observe. I observe my son for example" (55). Though Anderson is not yet ready to accept that, the idea that human truths are self-evident leads back to *Jumpers* and George's assertion that something as "trivial" as the greeting between two long-distance lorry-drivers in the night "seems to affirm some common ground that is not animal". The idea also lies at the heart of Stoppard's own thinking. A 1981 interview elaborates on Hollar's condensed reference to his son:

I'm finding it hard to keep little boys out of my plays – my four sons . . . may or may not be relevant – but something which has preoccupied me for a long time is the desire to simplify questions and take the sophistication out . . . If somebody came out of East Germany through the gate in the wall and wished to communicate the idea that life inside this wall was admirable or indeed platonically good, he'd have a reasonable chance of succeeding in this if he were addressing himself to a sophisticated person. But if you tried to do this to a child, he'd blow it to smithereens. A child would say, "But the wall is there to keep people in, so there must be some reason why people want to get out."[8]

And, incidentally, that topic is also fundamental to Stoppard's insistence that theatrical artifice, even in all its razzmatazz, need not falsify the serious truths that it supports: "Ethical Fictions as Ethical Foundations".

The turning-point of *Professional Foul*, when, to coin a phrase, Anderson does something really crazy, is not the sentimental reaction it might at first appear to be. The erstwhile professor of fastidious ethics does find that his cosy theories about social contracts crumble before the policemen's utilitarian sense of purpose and the evident despair of Mrs Hollar and her son. But that experience is not what changes him, even though the original telecast milked the emotion of his meeting with Sacha and his mother for all it was worth, despite Stoppard's request for "rather a tough little boy" (73). Anderson's own sense of panic on discovering how his secure world can shake on its axis causes him to reconsider Hollar's thesis: conclusions he had once thought "unsafe for me", because they were intellectually precarious, have become dangerous to his person. In his revised paper he takes the plunge, defining "rights as fictions" which ought to be respected as truths:

A small child who cries "that's not fair" when punished for something done by his brother or sister is apparently appealing to an idea of justice which is, for want of a better word, natural. And we must see that natural justice, however illusory, does inspire many people's behaviour much of the time.

(90)

However they were to have been interpreted in his original paper, the ethical fictions of the rewritten version are the frail signs of unarguable truths; as Hollar had told him, "You see, to me the idea of an inherent right is intelligible. I believe that we have such rights, and they are paramount" (55). Such a conclusion was not new to Stoppard: "I can honestly say that I have held Anderson's final view on the subject for years and years." In accord with that, he draws his interviewers' attention to the fact that *Jumpers* also shows a moral philosopher "trying to separate absolute values from local ones and local situations. That description would apply to either play, yet one is a rampant farce and the other is a piece of naturalistic TV drama."[9]

McKendrick's paper for the Colloquium is also important to the play. We do not hear it directly, since Anderson, our view-finder, was "a tiny bit naughty" that afternoon and sneaked away to the soccer match, though he got no farther than the Hollars' flat. But that evening at the dinner table, McKendrick explains his interpretation of the catastrophe theory, an idea which actually derives from contemporary philosophy[10] and which applies nicely to Anderson's volatile feelings after his brush with Czech authority:

MCKENDRICK: There's a point – the catastrophe point – where your progress along one line of behaviour jumps you into the opposite line; the principle reverses itself at the point where a rational man would abandon it.

(78)

For Anderson, about to jettison his Oxbridge safety-net, such a theory reduces man to an automaton, in that moral courage becomes simply a predictable pattern of behaviour. However, Stoppard's own point is to show that a moral man is no pre-programmed robot. Anderson's turnabout *has* an ethical rationale (Hollar's thesis and experiences) and his decision to reverse his earlier concept of correct behaviour finally absolves him from McKendrick's charge that "you end up using a moral principle as your excuse for acting against a moral interest".

The first paper at the Colloquium is delivered by the American Professor Stone. His assertion that "the ambiguity of ordinary language raises special problems for a logical language" (61) provides a context for Stoppard's habitual quirks of style and for most of the play's funny moments. But the paper also points to the way linguistic ambiguities can become the tools of politicians (again see *Jumpers*). Incongruities have coloured the play's first scene, in that Anderson's academic vagary causes a series of misunderstandings. McKendrick, looking down the aircraft to a third colleague, Chetwyn, the one activist amongst them, happens to ask whether Anderson knows Prague. Anderson eyes Chetwyn warily: "Not personally. I know the name" (45). A similarly harmless confusion involves McKendrick, who takes the English soccer players for philosophers and so misunderstands Anderson's explanation of their relative positions in the field: "He's what used to be called left wing. Broadbent's in the centre. He's an opportunist more than anything" (50). At the Colloquium, Stone's over-earnest 'academese' allows Stoppard to move to the fantastical edge of his realist compass. As Stone expands upon his theme, the cameras cut to the translators' booth, where the interpreters miss the idiom of his examples or fall apart completely, thus providing a comic illustration of the semantic confusion Stone's paper is all about (62). The lecture ends in further ambiguity when Anderson rises to make a quick getaway and is understood to be asking a question.

Stoppard makes Anderson concoct a face-saving ad lib on verbal meaning in order to create a parallel with what Hollar had said about moral meaning, and this is signalled by the professor's sly twist of Wittgenstein's most famous dictum into "Whereof we cannot speak, thereof we are by no means silent." For language is not the only way humans communicate nor can it be expected to be logical:

... the important truths are simple and monolithic. The essentials of a given situation speak for themselves, and language is as capable of obscuring the truth as of revealing it.
(63)

These conclusions inform the events which immediately follow in the Hollars' apartment. Though Anderson speaks no Czech, he (and the viewer) can understand the language of fear and of force. Mrs Hollar's anger and distress at the injustice of the police are as self-evident as the fact that a lavatory attendant could not have the capital to launch himself in the money business. Anderson's taxi-driver is able to interpret his request to wait five minutes while he delivers something: he "did all the things people do when they talk to each other without a language" (72). In those fundamental ways the characters communicate more honestly than when they use the same national language, for the police chief, who can speak English, does so to terrorize and confuse. He can suggest that Anderson's only reason for accepting the government's invitation was to attend the soccer match, that Hollar's letter to the Czech President was slanderous, and that naturally he is under surveillance as a well-known black-marketeer. In its own way, too, the whole scene speaks out for the right to speak out.

After finishing the script, Stoppard visited Czechoslovakia for the first time in his adult life and was there able to talk to Vaclav Havel directly. Yet although this literal return to his roots might have looked in 1977 like the culmination of the interior journey he had travelled after *Travesties*, the three plays which belong to that period will not support a theory of The Sudden Politicization of Tom Stoppard. The "politics" of undeniable human truths and inalienable human rights begins with *Jumpers* and continues to define the roles of Joyce and the Lenins in *Travesties*. What *is* new about Stoppard from that point on is the simplicity with which he formulates those ideas dramatically: the undeviating, obsessive line that links *Dirty Linen* and *New-Found-Land*; the tight patterns that surround the madman and the prisoner in *Every Good Boy*, whereby the farce eats like acid into the authorities' bland and pompous reasonableness; the carefully worked cause-and-effect structure that moves Anderson from "correct" to "incorrect" behaviour in *Professional Foul*. What is also new, and why Stoppard appears to become more political, is that each of the plays makes a direct, unambiguous statement. For the time, he abandons his intellectual "leap-frog", or rather his leap-frogging arrives at a distinctive terminus. Here, Tom Stoppard does *know* things which before he had only suggested.

That the next full-length play, *Night and Day*, [11] also happened to be naturalistic seemed to confirm the idea of his "movement from withdrawal to involvement, as some have it ... as if you were covering your cleverness in order to force it to serve a more serious moral purpose".[12] Stoppard's move towards realism blinded his commentators to that play's return to an open-ended debate in which one argument overtops its predecessor, and on to infinity.

Yet arguably, and here we are back to the impenetrabilities of a writer's self-conscious intent, his standpoint in this script is the most alien, the most un-English, the one where his origins show more pointedly than in either of the two previous plays dealing more or less directly with injustice in the Eastern Bloc. The point, and the problem, of *Night and Day* derives from the conviction which drives the play and cuts through its arguments about the press: "People do awful things to each other. But it's worse in places where everybody is kept in the dark. It really is. Information is light. Information, in itself, about anything, is light. That's all you can say, really" (92). To anyone less close to the state of things in a totalitarian society, in other words to the cosy majority of his West End or Broadway audience, an idea like that does not burn on the brain. As an ex-journalist and as someone whom recent events in Czechoslovakia must have filled with a sense of there-but-for-the-grace-of-God, Stoppard embarks on a debate whose pros and cons affect him deeply but which his audience would be apt to regard somewhat coolly. Stoppard seems not to have allowed for that. For him, freedom of information is so vital an issue that he assumes debate in itself will be dramatic enough to provoke an equally passionate interest.

English audiences have always loathed being lectured to in the theatre. This is not to say that they are scared of ideas, but that those ideas must be dramatized with a vivacity that intrigues, surprises, persuades. Shaw knew that, yet, curiously enough, *Night and Day*, the one instance where Stoppard does not lure his audiences' intellect, has frequently been labelled "Shavian". It is true that no other playwright since Shaw has made ideas so exciting as Stoppard does at his playful best. But that playfulness is not much like Shaw's, which is energized by rhetorically heightened dialogue and an appetite for the clash of mighty opposites. Outrageously disruptive of social complacence on both sides of the footlights, that energy, an essentially dramatic one, crackles from the stage and invests the ideas with a dynamic it is hard to capture when reading the printed text. Stoppard at play is more conscious of the stage as a stage, more intellectually bizarre, more Central European. Any such literary affiliation is a matter of temperament, as Stoppard himself stresses when discussing the way he writes. Yet one can, for instance, see something of Kafka in the bewilderment which imprisons Rosencrantz and Guildenstern or of Brecht in the overt theatricality of *Travesties* or of Nabokov in his delight at word-games. Several commentators note

resemblances to the style and themes of Havel's plays, a "kinship"
Stoppard readily admits to:

When I read *The Garden Party* about twelve years ago, I just thought he was
somebody who wrote like I would like to write if I was writing on the same
subject. There are playwrights one admires because one could never do what
they do, and there are those one admires because one could do exactly what
they do and would wish to.[13]

Havel and Stoppard share a way of seizing on a certain situation, a
particular place, a premise which, though quite ordinary in itself, acts
as an oddly arresting frame around the play's ideas and becomes a
metaphor which controls and colours the way we see. The Players of
Hamlet, the plot-line of *Earnest*, the Rad-Libs' victory party, the
orchestra in *Every Good Boy* all work in that manner. In the more
realistic plays, the same can be said of the quiet hospital in *A Separate
Peace* or the congress of philosophers which affects how we view the
collective behaviour of the footballers and the police in *Professional
Foul*. No such metaphor governs the ideas of *Night and Day*, an
absence which has nothing to do with the nature of realism but which
might account for a disappointing flatness.

   Night and Day develops many of *Dirty Linen*'s ideas about journalists and journalism, but does so less successfully. However frivolous
Dirty Linen is, its opening premise – everyone but Mr French, male
and female, has bedded Maddie – makes us see the workings of the
Committee in a peculiar light and enlivens each member's attitude to
the press. For example, Maddie's opinion of a free press has much to
do with her personal relationships on Fleet Street; to put things
crassly, she knows how these men live:

They're not writing it for the people, they're writing it for the writers writing
it on the other papers. "Look what I've got that you haven't got." There don't
have to be any *people* reading it at all so long as there's a few journalists around
to say, "Old Bill got a good one there!" That's what they're doing it for. I
thought you'd have worked that out by now.　　　　　　　　　(42)

In *Night and Day*, Dick Wagner says much the same thing; as a
hard-bitten journalist, he too knows the territory, but that rationale
does not seem as invitingly off-kilter as Maddie's. He thinks as we
might expect him to, and his opinion strikes us with straight-faced
authority:

It's good stuff but it's too much I-was-there. It's somebody who wants to
impress the world and doesn't know that the world isn't impressed by
reporters . . . except other reporters – who can work out that you were there
without having it rammed down their throats.　　　　　　　　　(30)

This directness has little allure. Wagner tells us what to think; Maddie's personality allows us to share her thoughts. As a consequence, *Night and Day* seems to deposit a *report* of a serious and witty debate into the middle of a well-tailored and less earnest psychodrama.

Yet *Night and Day* starts with a typically disarming prelude. It at first seems real but turns out to be a bad dream. The stage is deserted; a gorgeous sky fades rapidly at sunset; suddenly out of the silence and the gathering dark comes the whirr of a helicopter. Soon it hovers directly overhead; its blades shake the trees and form shadows in a spotlight which rakes the stage before the machine moves away. From nowhere, a vehicle swerves onto the dark stage, blinding us with the glare of its lights. All hell breaks loose: a machine-gun clatters, the helicopter roars above, its searchlight catches a figure leaping from the jeep, which speeds away; the figure crouches down in the blackness:

> *Then the spotlight finds him. He stands up into the light with his arms spread out, shouting. The gun is firing bursts. He moves away from the corner. A burst catches him and knocks him over.*
>
> *A late afternoon light reveals* GUTHRIE *stretched out on a long garden chair. Sundown. The steps to the verandah and the room are behind him.*
>
> (15–16)

Such a beginning obviously has an arresting and ultimately disorienting effect, but it does not order our way of looking at journalism other than to remind us that it can sometimes be dangerous. This distinction becomes striking if we think of the similarly deceptive prologue to *Jumpers*, which surrounds the certainty of the logical-positivists in irony just as, in quieter vein, the initial coin-spinning in *Rosencrantz* organizes a relationship between games of chance and fatal play. For all its legerdemain, Guthrie's dream simply organizes the plot. At the end of the first episode, a helicopter swoops low over the garden so that Guthrie is again made to cower. Buzzing the house turns out to be Carson's signal to his servant to collect him in the car from the landing-pad. A third replay, reported to us in Act 2, describes the death of Milne and not of Guthrie himself.

The dream may also help to establish the reality of interior thoughts, but in doing so it points us directly to Stoppard's characterization of Ruth. It is she who arouses most interest, because we are party to thoughts she prefers to hide from those around her. To permit that, Stoppard employs the simple, but none the less provocative and dramatic device of having Ruth Carson voice things that go through her mind at moments of social or emotional embarrassment. Outwardly, she defends herself with a dry mockery which she has adopted over the years so that it has become automatic. However, hers is a performance, even when she thinks she is alone (hence the role's attractiveness to star actresses and their audience). Her first entrance catches that mannered style as she makes to turn off the African rock band on her servant's cassette-player with a melodramatic "Oh, those drums, those damned drums", and so explodes the cliché neurosis of white-heroine-beset-by-pounding-Heart-of-Darkness. Her next remark, on noticing Guthrie lying out in the garden, is just as posed: "Francis, there's a man under that tree" (16).

One might expect to see behind those defences when Ruth gives voice to her inner thoughts, but on that level, too, she continues to act a part, though her mockery tends to be directed towards herself as much as to others. Characteristically, when she learns that Dick Wagner, the journalist whom she had allowed a one-night-stand in London, will soon be at her home in Kambawe, the outer Ruth skips a beat then asks, "Is he a composer?" (17). When the inner Ruth takes over, her first "Help" is followed by a commentary upon her public self, a stance which is just as protective: "Just what you needed, Ruth, and serve you right. Nothing is for free, you always pay, and Guthrie has brought the bill. Silly Woman!" (18). Even this part of her assumes a role while admitting "I don't feel up to being witty today." So Stoppard defuses her second "Help" with the sound of a piano chord which, when repeated after "I need somebody", turns what might have been a moment of genuine panic into the Beatles' song, "Help!" The fact that we never do reach the bed-rock of Ruth's self, despite appearances on stage, makes her an especially fascinating character.

That the "two" Ruths are not unlike each other leads also to the play's most inventive episode, one which deceives us for some minutes as to which Ruth is which. The second Act opens on the darkened room, where an apparently 'interior' Ruth acts out a romantic welcome to Jacob Milne after his dangerous assignment with Guthrie. When Milne appears from the shadows, we quickly revise that picture and, given the play's established conventions, understand this as Milne's actual return and Ruth's acknowledged attraction to him as part of her double dialogue until, that is, he responds to an invitation to kiss her. Now it seems she can tell her thoughts and, though still self-mocking, her guard slips to reveal glimpses of a franker self as when her cheery account of her first marriage fails to cover over all of its unhappiness:

I was almost a tart with my first husband, but he was a rotter in his own way. He was frankly proud of his left-hook . . . Unjustifiably so. You could slip it quite easily and get him with a right-cross. What a way to live. To get *me*, all Geoffrey had to do was clear his throat and hold the door.   (67–8)

The scene ends in what looks like complete surrender. As Milne leaves, Ruth lets her kaftan fall away and, trailing it behind her, follows him naked into the dark. Carson enters and watches 'her' go until Ruth, still elegantly gowned, appears behind him and asks for a cigarette. Everything we had seen and heard since the Act began had been a performance of the interior Ruth's. Milne had not returned; Ruth's new frankness was imaginary and, thanks to a 'double', she had never left the room; Carson had been simply musing into space.

In the words Ruth imagines for Milne on his last exit, "You're really something, Ruth. I don't know what" (69). Stoppard keeps us guessing as to what lies behind her double act. Although the two levels she speaks on make her seem the riven sister of Gladys Jenkins or Dotty Moore, neither of her aspects reveals their kind of despair. The nearest we come to an answer is at the play's end, when she wearily suggests that Wagner should take her to bed: "I want to be hammered out, disjointed, folded up and put away like linen in a drawer" (94). Stoppard enfolds even this in theatricality as Ruth coolly smashes an empty whisky bottle against the mantelpiece and, seeing Wagner at the telex keyboard, croons out "The Lady is a Tramp", as we hear 'his' piano accompaniment at the keyboard. The artifice makes for a neat ending but, because Ruth's motives have continually defied analysis, we are unlikely to feel she acts out of character, despite her having sworn never to go to bed with Wagner a second time.

Ruth's real feelings have little to do with what she says and does. Her performance keeps her afloat, and her life in Kambawe, her marriage to Carson, her brush with Milne, her interior conversations are all part of that act: "I don't share with strangers. All you're saying is, 'Who do you think you are?' Well, I don't have to be anybody" (54). Rare moments do force her to take stock of her behaviour. When she realized that her son had not written home for name tapes for his school uniform because he instinctively knew she was not the sort of mother who would order them, she wept "buckets" on her own in London, and the memory provokes "a sniff, the nearest she gets to a tear" in the whole play (50). Otherwise, she presses on with the show, and if that means a second bout with Wagner, "That's it" (95). Ruth is an extended version of Lady Malquist. Both of them behave irresponsibly in order not to have to stop and look, and the impersonal abandon of the play's last moments exactly captures that.

That we never know precisely what Ruth would see, were she to stop and look, stimulates a curiosity towards her which has but the slenderest connection with the rest of the play; as she herself says jokingly, "I'm in the wrong movie, I think" (51). For though she keeps us entertained, that pleasure has nothing to do with how we are asked to think about journalism. Stoppard tries to bind those two strands together by making Ruth the past victim of scandal-hungry journalists during her divorce proceedings. That she should "despise" them and instantly cover over that feeling with a sophisticated cynicism is to be expected. That she should express this disinterested contempt at some length (the lady doth protest too much) is of more than passing interest, but one which focuses us on *her* rather than on what she says. Her attitude to the popular press, however she tries to mask it, is emotional, and yet the objections she ultimately arrives at are stylistic, "that Lego-set language they have", and moral. So her words put Stoppard's arguments briskly, but their logic works loose from her mood of the moment:

. . . Heartbreak Parrot Woman In Plea for Earl's Brother. Earl's brother. That's the bit. Of all the husbands who ran off with somebody's wife that week, Geoffrey qualified because he had a measly-title and if the right three-hundred people went down on the Royal Yacht he'd be Duke of Bognor. *Has anybody ever bothered to find out whether anybody really cares?* The populace and the popular press. What a grubby symbiosis it is.   (48)

Her separation from the politics of *Night and Day* shows clearly in the climactic scene with President Mageeba. Stoppard uses her flippant asides to lighten the talk about rebel armies, *Globe* interviews, and "uninvited foreigners". Then, somewhat desperately, since Ruth has had less and less to do, he has her break in with a 'thought' about the label on her grandmother's packet of salt to show she "was miles away" (80). Given that detachment and the dangerous electricity of Mageeba's presence, her subsequent attack on Wagner's opinion of press lords, amusingly acted out as a discussion she has had with her son, is not an entirely convincing moment. Later still, her final outburst is motivated only if we allow that her "thing" for Milne was strong enough to provoke it; even then, the emotion and the ideas jostle each other:

As far as I'm concerned, Jake died for the product. He died for the women's page, and the crossword, and the racing results, and the heartbreak beauty queens and somewhere at the end of a long list I suppose he died for the leading article too, but it's never worth *that* —
(*She has started to swipe at* GUTHRIE *with a newspaper and she ends up flinging it at him . . .*)   (91–2)

If Ruth sails away on her own, the debate about the function of the press and the ethics of journalists is not sufficiently dramatized to vie for our attention. Dick Wagner, around whom those arguments gather, has little of her appeal, so the play does not achieve the balance of a *Jumpers*, where two separate worlds both relate to the same central pain and intellectual confusion. Not that philosophers are intrinsically more dramatic than journalists. George Moore (and Professor Anderson, too) is defined *first* as a struggling, thinking human being whose profession is incidental, whereas Wagner (and Guthrie, his photographer) is a journalist first and last. Like Ruth, Wagner acts a role much of the time, for Stoppard was "interested by the way journalists tend to ape their fictitious models. It's a certain way of behaving which derives from 'tough' films."[14] But when Wagner stops performing, he still lives only for his job, and his character admits none of the human question-marks Ruth's does. Consequently, unless we too happen to be journalists, we react dispassionately to a figure who is substantial enough to carry the events of the plot but who makes a cardboard-thin spokesman of ideas. He and Guthrie represent a failure of imagination on Stoppard's part. He can project his own humanity onto his professors and female neurotics but, familiar with the jargon and lifestyle of the press, he takes his journalists for granted, makes no such leap, and so they lack a dimension we too can enter.

This is not the case with Jacob Milne. As innocent abroad, his *persona* had been part of Stoppard's imagination from the very start in Bristol, and later when he wrote the *Scene* articles under the pseudonym William Boot. As Stoppard said, Evelyn Waugh's original "is really a Moon too",[15] and the archetype appears in a host of Stoppard's characters from Mr Moon to Professor Anderson either as a naive failure (a Moon) or as the innocent who succeeds in spite of himself (a Boot). In going back to his own early memories, while writing *Night and Day*, Stoppard naturally returned to that parody of his journalistic experience, "I'm a Moon myself", and to Waugh's novel, *Scoop*, details from which he scatters through the play.

Stoppard once described Waugh's William Boot as "a journalist who brought a kind of innocent incompetence and contempt to what he was doing".[16] Ruth describes Milne as someone with "a way of being gauche which suggests that you've got the edge on people who know the ground and prepare their effects" (68), and when he first stumbles onto the stage he seems to be exactly as Wagner and Guthrie had imagined the amateur reporter who somehow scooped the lot of them with "one of those cameras with a little picture of a cloud and a little picture of the sun and you slide it across according to the weather" (24). Waugh's innocent is actually more of a bungler and his "contempt" is far less conscious. The reclusive author of *Lush Places*, a "bi-weekly half-column devoted to Nature . . . 'Feather-footed through the plashy fen passes the questing vole'",[17] Boot lives in the country with his eccentric aunts and uncles and their equally dotty retainers. Mistaken for John Boot, novelist and writer of "modish works on history and travel", he finds himself reporting a revolution in Africa for *The Beast* and muddles on to glory, all the while protected by an obliviousness to what goes on both in Ishmaelia and back in Fleet Street. Boot is so naive that he believes reporters send their stories by native runners with cleft sticks, supplied by the Army and Navy Stores; in Stoppard's Jeddu, "the hotel doesn't have cleft sticks", let alone a telex (23). And there are other reminders of *Scoop* in the play: lying official-press-officers; dumpy hotels with "journalists hanging out of the windows"; the competition on the wrong trail, "following armoured car patrols into the bush in broken-down taxis" (26). Stoppard's most affectionate nods take the form of two in-jokes. Milne's christian name, Jake, links him to "the fabulous Wenlock Jakes" of *Scoop*, and Wagner quotes one of the novel's catch-phrases, "Up to a point, Lord Copper" (72), which *The Beast*'s foreign editor always uses when he disagrees with his lordly employer. *Scoop* and Boot had been the comic side of Stoppard's journalist fantasies when "I wanted to be Noel Barber on the *Daily Mail* or Sefton Delmer on the *Daily Express* – that kind of big-name, roving reporter."[18] Remembering those days, he projects that young self into Jacob Milne, the reporter from the provinces whose "idea was to get myself in on a good foreign story without too much competition" (32).

Human though Milne is, he is not dominant enough to be the twin centre of *Night and Day*, particularly since he only exists in Ruth's imagination by the second Act. But when he speaks of the ethics and manners of the press, we are apt to listen less passively than to Wagner's Aussie version of the hard-bitten reporter. Milne has a history of moral decision-making behind him. In Grimsby he had refused to join a strike against the *Evening Messenger*. Once the dispute was settled, he was expelled by his Union, which then threatened a further shut-down since Milne had decided to "give them a problem" by not appealing against his expulsion. The management stood by him, but he resigned in order to head off another strike (38–9). Wagner condemns him as "the Grimsby scab", and through their confrontation Stoppard derails the old class conflicts – the *Messenger* is "not a private coal-mine sending somebody's son to Eton" – and introduces what is to be his major point when Milne sneers at the strikers' "pique" over the printers' higher pay-scale as he flicks through the captions in the popular papers:

It's *crap*. And it's written by grown men earning maybe ten thousand a year. If I was a printer, I'd look at some of the stuff I'm given to print, and I'd ask myself what is supposed to be so special about the people who write it . . .

(39)

Although Milne does not make his ultimate point until first meeting Ruth, Stoppard already loads the dice his way. Wagner is so much the jargon-ridden, hard-nosed Union man, the sort who earns Milne's contemptuous reaction: "it was as if their brains had been taken out and replaced by one of those little golf-ball things you get in electric typewriters" (37). Stoppard has confessed to an ambivalence towards Wagner: "I would admire him if he existed. I admire good professionals."[19] Wagner *is* good at what he does, but the play makes it hard to remember that. Less morally alive than Milne, he is not allowed a flicker of self-wonder when he respects a "bloody useless" reporter because "he's bloody good at squeezing the management" and he is made the butt of Ruth's more lacerating attacks. Milne, on the other hand, grows from the comic amateur who misunderstands the professionals' lingo – "A *pigeon?* No, we've got a little beyond that in Fleet Street" (32) – into a debater whose sincerity stands firm against Ruth's wit.

The play argues many sides of the issue, but Milne becomes the major spokesman for Stoppard's own views about a free press: "Milne has my prejudice if you like. Somehow, unconsciously, I wanted him to be known to be speaking the truth."[20] The *Globe* and its competitors represent more than just "a million packets of journalism manufactured every week by businessmen using journalists for their labour" (58). Milne objects to Wagner's assumption that all journalists should unite solidly behind their union; for him, "a free press, free expression – it's the last line of defence for all the other freedoms", and the play itself underlines the relationship between those two freedoms in that Wagner, refusing to work with a scab, also quashes a rival's story and the public's right to know the latest developments in Kambawe. For Milne (and Stoppard) a free press ensures the defeat of all unjust power groups.

Milne dies amidst panicked bursts of crossfire on his way back to the rebels and the latest scoop, but his death comes from his desire for a story as well as from his wish to tell that story. Wagner is even more ambitious and has no scruples about how he gets his story through, yet those reports also proclaim the freedom to know. The ambiguities surrounding those motives and freedoms crystallize in the figure of President Mageeba during the play's second Act.

The President can quote chapter and verse concerning the principles of free expression from his student days at the London School of Economics. As old-school-tie as Milne, as unscrupulous as Wagner, Mageeba exudes "the power to dictate", whereas the newspapers' power to expose is less certain. Time and circumstance weigh heavily: he cannot afford to dabble with ethical theories any more than Lenin could give room to artistic ones. Stoppard mixes the comedy of Ruth's asides, "Compose yourself, Wagner" (75), with Mageeba's dangerous suavity to create the tensest moment of the play, but the longer that tension lasts the more the ideas get in the way. Wagner is again made an ass of when he tries to ingratiate himself with Mageeba, congratulating him on his "determined stand against Russian imperialism in Africa" and allying himself with the President's dislike of press lords: "a newspaper is too important to be merely a rich man's property" (82). But there is really no contest. Mageeba has no need for argument. We await the inevitable and, as the talk goes on, we listen somewhat distractedly to Mageeba's explanation of his circumstances, however cleverly put:

The population cannot yet support a number of competing papers offering a natural balance of opinion . . . You may smile, but does freedom of the press mean freedom to choose its own standards? . . . No, no – freedom with responsibility, that was the elusive formula we pondered all those years ago at the LSE. And that is what I found. From the ashes there arose, by public subscription, a new *Daily Citizen*, responsible and relatively free . . . Do you know what I mean by a relatively free press, Mr Wagner? . . . I mean a free press which is edited by one of my relatives. (84–5)

This debate seems imposed, halting the action until Mageeba finally explodes, smashing his stick down on Wagner's head and ranting about the rebellious Colonel Shimbu: "I'll give him equal space. Six foot long and six foot deep, just like any other traitor and communist jackal" (86). Stoppard feels he must put the case for Mageeba's point of view, but the President does not need to justify his sophisticated brutishness. That power alone gives sufficient urgency to Guthrie's final rallying cry: "Information is light."

Night and Day is both entertaining and thought-provoking, a rare enough combination in the commercial theatre, but it fails to bond those qualities into a satisfying whole. Ruth's enigmatic performances pull us one way and the play's ideas, which do not vitally involve her, are not presented dynamically enough to pull us back. Ruth's two voices move us closer to her than to any other character, Milne included, and the fact that she will never share with strangers makes us want to move still closer. Like all the major characters, she is frequently undermined by the comedy, but that subversive laughter rarely detaches our sympathies, as it does from the others; since it nearly always rises out of her own self-mockery, we laugh *with* her. And Stoppard seems not to have realized that debate about a free press is not dramatic in itself. Animated as he is by that issue, he has not found a way of bringing the majority of his audience wholeheartedly along with him.

Chapter 7

The real thing?

Whatever its problems, *Night and Day* more than held its own in the West End. Responding to Diana Rigg's elegantly cool Ruth or to the mannered frenzy of Maggie Smith, who succeeded to the part in the second year of the run, audiences came away delighting in a sophistication made all the more challenging by those knotty interludes of undisguised talk; as Stoppard puts it, "one's appeal to an audience is less to do with what one is saying than how one is saying it".[1] Yet the critics were more leery. Bernard Levin, for whom, after *Every Good Boy*, "this man could write a comedy about Auschwitz, at which we would sit laughing helplessly until we cried with inextinguishable anger",[2] found the play "deeply disappointing" and, striking nearer the heart of things, suggested that Stoppard "has put his viewpoint before his drama".[3] The favourably inclined praised the way that viewpoint could evolve within the limitations of a well-crafted plot: "even for him it is a signal triumph to have related such remote subjects within the discipline of a nuts and bolts naturalistic play".[4] Mixed or lukewarm reviews and enthusiastic queues at the box office have become something of a norm for the later plays, a phenomenon which is less interesting for what it says about the relative perceptiveness of critics and audiences than for the reaction it provokes in Stoppard himself: "I find that people ... are divided along [*sic*] those who congratulate me on getting past the 'hummingbird' phase and those who say 'What are you doing? It's all naturalistic, with a beginning, a middle, and an end!' But there's no external position where you say, 'I think that in view of what so-and-so's been writing about me I'd better get to grips with something recognisable and do it properly.'"[5] From the very beginning he had "written what appealed to me ... with the assumption that it would appeal to everybody else",[6] but as he grew confident in his own powers as a writer so he became less reluctant to reveal his private self.

All Stoppard's plays come from the core of himself, but at oblique angles. However, as his style gained simplicity, his personality (indirectly ever present in his idiosyncratic way of looking at things and at the words we find to describe them) drives those recurring themes and ideas more directly. *Every Good Boy* and *Professional Foul* relate closely to his work for the Committee Against Psychiatric Abuse, with whom he marched to the Soviet Embassy in 1976, or to his commitment to Amnesty International, and each of those plays makes an explicit statement. Though the intellectual leapfrog resumes in *Night and Day*, Milne, Stoppard's serio-comic portrait of himself when young, proclaims the same moral absolutes. And here Stoppard no longer depends on other writers or on phrases and situations which have passed into popular lore, like "Lloyd George knew my father" or painting the Forth Bridge. Although Waugh's *Scoop* and Idi Amin (as popularly imagined) flicker through the script, neither *motif* becomes a means of distancing the ideas. Instead, those ideas are sustained by a plot which is woven from old dreams[7] and doubts and from the sort of people he met as a journalist, so that he runs the risk of forgetting what "would appeal to everybody else". The emergence of that self was not a specifically political journey, though his moral and social principles were bound to approach the surface of the plays along with the rest of him, for even his adaptations and translations, which obviously contain no immediate statement of his own, reveal a growing self-assurance as he journeyed from the colourless and literal *Tango* (1966) to the free-wheeling verve of *On the Razzle* (1981) and the idiosyncratic counterpoint of *Dalliance* (1986).

Over the years, Stoppard has also made new adaptations of his own earlier ideas, and his personal development in the seventies shows nowhere more clearly than in *Dogg's Hamlet, Cahoot's Macbeth* (1979).[8] This was another of his pieces for Ed Berman, and the play's first Act reworks *Dogg's Our Pet* so as to free it from its original occasion, the inauguration of a theatre. Stoppard had hoped "one day . . . to make full use of that little idea",[9] and he now combines his lesson in Dogg with its articulate opposite, the language of *Hamlet* selected so that it relates all the shifts of Shakespeare's plot in approximately fifteen minutes. That mini-version also had an independent existence. Arranged for seven actors to perform on the top deck of Berman's Fun Art Bus, the script was somehow mislaid for four years until, in 1976, it was presented by Dogg's Troupe on the esplanade outside the National Theatre.[10] During his 1977 visit to Czechoslovakia, Stoppard met Pavel Kohout, a playwright who was forbidden to work in the theatre, and Pavel Landovsky, the actor who had been arrested with Havel. The impetus for combining his two independent scripts came in a letter from Kohout in the following year:

As one of them who cannot live without theatre I was searching for a possibility to do theatre in spite of circumstances. Now I am glad to tell you that in a few days, after eight weeks rehearsals – a Living-Room Theatre is opening, with nothing smaller but Macbeth.

What is L R T? A call-group. Everybody, who wants to have Macbeth at home with two great and forbidden Czech actors, Pavel Landovsky and Vlasta Chramostova, can invite his friends and call us. Five people will come with one suitcase. (8)

Reminded of his own condensed *Hamlet* and the improvised surroundings of Dogg's Troupe, Stoppard dovetailed his scripts into one panel of a diptych whose other half showed his own idea of living-room Shakespeare behind The Wall.

This conjunction represents something more than a move from the abstract word-games of the first panel to the emotionally charged farce of the second or from passionless intellect to passionate involvement. Its major significance lies in the fact that for Stoppard there *is* no divide between those two aspects and that Kohout's letter should have prompted him to connect the linguistic curlicues of Dogg to those of the Czech police. The confusion of words and what they signify had its dark side from *Rosencrantz* on, and Stoppard had always dealt passionately, if objectively, with those undertones. At two years' distance from Prague and *Professional Foul*, which explores the same confusion, he reassumes an antic disposition, but that guise shows no less feeling than unmasked naturalism does, for, as the play grows directly political, its heartless dialogue strikes at both the Czech actuality and its seemingly harmless twin in the first Act.

To effect this mirror-image which dominates his subsequent plays, Stoppard reorganizes *Dogg's Our Pet*. Charlie, once the school caretaker, becomes another of the schoolboys and, having implanted the basics of a new language code through their ball game and an exchange of sandwiches, the boys begin to rehearse a school play though, from their toneless recitation, the words of *Hamlet* appear to be as half-perceived a mystery to them as Dogg's are to us. In the middle of all this, a lorry drives up and Baker, signalling towards the wings, directs the driver in Dogg: "Cauliflower . . . cauliflower . . . hardly . . . onyx hardly" (19). Easy, the odd-man-out linguistically, has come to deliver blocks, slabs, and so forth with which to build a stage for the boys' play. His verbal building-blocks are certainly ours, and yet their construct is Pinteresque, a cross between Davies and Mick of *The Caretaker*; to appreciate that parody we therefore depend on yet another code:

I'll need a bit of a hand, being as I'm on my own, seeing as my mate got struck down in a thunderstorm on the A412 near Rickmansworth – a bizarre accident . . . a bolt from the blue, zig-zagged right on to the perforated snout of his Micky Mouse gas mask. He was delivering five of them at the bacteriological research children's party – entering into the spirit of it – when, shazam! – it was an electrifying moment . . . (20)

After misunderstandings about the platform, the red carpet, and the bouquet for The Lady who now presides at a prize-giving, and having gone through the wall like his earlier counterpart, Easy begins to grapple with Dogg although, as Cahoot remarks later, "You don't learn it, you catch it" (74). This part of the play ends with the boys' synopsis of "Hamlet bedsocks Denmark. Yeti William Shakespeare" (31).

A prologue made up of a fairly coherent jumble of the best-known quotations from *Hamlet* underlines what we have already been shown in the Dogg sequence: that the full meaning and nuance of language depend on a particular frame of reference. Performed on its own, the abridged *Hamlet* would present an ingenious account of the basic plot, an instructive exercise for school audiences and a pre-performance curiosity for adults, but it conveys nothing more. In this new context, the redaction, a welcoming island in a sea of Dogg, turns out to be completely barren. The familiar phrases have been squeezed dry, and this is still more evident in a final encore, which races through the essentials of the story in roughly one minute. The same can be said of the Inspector in *Cahoot's Macbeth*, who fires off volleys of well-worn metaphors which are dead to all feeling.

In reversing the previous action, that second part of the play takes Shakespeare as its basic language, which then disintegrates into Dogg. Unlike the boys' playlet, the living-room version of *Macbeth* admits emotion, mood, and motive: connotations of feeling in addition to the denotations of plot. Within the particular context of an oppressed society, Shakespeare also takes on new meanings. At Lady Macbeth's "I heard the owl scream and the crickets cry", a police-siren is heard nearing the house, and the knocking at the gate turns out to be the Inspector at the apartment door. These correspondences turn farcical when Easy enters and in trying to find someone to receive his consignment of "cake hops . . . almost Leamington Spa" (Dogg for "blocks and that . . . from Leamington") unwittingly appears as the third murderer and then as Banquo's ghost. But the essential message of this living-room performance, as the Inspector very well knows, is defiance, which in turn gives added savour to the downfall of the tyrant Macbeth:

The fact is, when you get a universal and timeless writer like Shakespeare, there's a strong feeling that he could be spitting in the eyes of the beholder when he should be keeping his mind on Verona – hanging around the 'gents'. You know what I mean? Unwittingly, of course. He didn't know he was doing it, at least you couldn't prove he did, . . . (60)

He and his superiors would much prefer that the actors protested their lack of freedom unequivocally. If they continue to claim that they are only speaking as Macbeth or Banquo, the State will put them in an institution just as it would do to people "who say they are Napoleon" (61). Once the actors all catch Dogg, the Inspector panics at what might be another dangerous code, though he cannot prove it. Easy builds a second platform which the Inspector mounts to give fresh significance to words like "Scabs! Stinking slobs – crooks. You're nicked", which The Lady had previously used when congratulating the prize-winners in Dogg. Then he and his two henchmen stand by to receive grey slabs that come flying through the door and which they turn into a wall that, because of the political context, says more than the one the schoolboys built. This wall eloquently blocks up the proscenium and the actors disappear behind it.

The key figure in all this is the Inspector. His arrival at the apartment reflects Easy's at the school in the first part, for both confront a language (Dogg and Shakespeare) which, they come to realize, has some hidden meaning. Easy therefore becomes a reference point in taking the measure of this second intruder. Where the former feels bewildered, the Inspector asserts his own brand of talk, "because if I walk out of this show I take it with me" (56), and these cheery platitudes create an entirely different effect from those of the well-meaning Easy. An air of parody surrounds the Inspector, too, and affects the way we see him; a fiercer version of Inspector Hound (Hound meets Dogg), he has all the smiling brutality of Orton's Inspector Truscott:

The law? I've got the Penal Code tattooed on my whistle, Landovsky, and there's a lot about you in it. Section 98, subversion – anyone acting out of hostility to the state . . . Section 100, incitement – anyone acting out of hostility to the state . . . I could nick you just for acting – and the sentence is double for an organized group, which I can make stick on Robinson Crusoe and his man any day of the week. So don't tell me about the laws. (61)

Beneath those levels of meaning, the Inspector pursues his own imperturbable vision. He speaks in shop-soiled metaphors, pictures which have either no significance for him at all or which, like a Magritte painting, assume deliberately peculiar notations, as in his warning against public performances: "That would be acting without authority – acting without authority! – you'd never believe I make it up as I go along" (56). In a sinister way, the empty space beneath the glib pictures can, in an instant, take on any title or meaning he wishes and, like Dogg, this cynical use of words is catching. 'Macbeth' explains that Cahoot/Banquo growls like a dog because he has become a "non-person" and then begins to talk in the Inspector's own crazy metaphors:

'MACBETH': Your system could do with a few antibodies. If you're afraid to risk the infection of an uncontrolled idea, the first time a new one gets in, it'll run through your system like a rogue bacillus. Remember the last time. (62)

Shunted from one menial job to another, the actors have themselves become surreal portraits which the State labels 'mortuary porter', 'night-watchman', or 'newsvendor'. The Inspector's remarks about the Constitution, which supposedly protects these people, satirizes the system with an exaggeration that equals his and its monstrosity:

The way I see it, life is lived off the record. It's altogether too human for the written word, it happens in pictures . . . metaphors . . . A few years ago you suddenly had it on toast, but when they gave you an inch you overplayed your hand and rocked the boat so they pulled the rug from under you, and now you're in the doghouse . . . I mean, that is pure fact. Metaphorically speaking. It describes what happened to you in a way that anybody can understand. (61)

Understanding what language can do is therefore no mere intellectual exercise, yet Stoppard's critics frequently misunderstand that preoccupation and dismiss him as a clever, but essentially arid stylist. His interviews had shown his sensitivity to the critical industry that surrounds him, but now he was ready to take on those attitudes in the theatre itself. With *The Real Thing* (1982), [11] Stoppard comes nearer than he ever has to baring his breast in public. And what of the heart beneath – or is there one? Not according to those who see him as a glittering wordsmith who puts style before feeling, theatrical trickery before genuine emotion, and who never could write about women. So Stoppard gives them Henry, a playwright in his forties, who thinks words are "sacred", writes and talks with style, is not immune to a theatrical trick or two, and who never could write about women. But in torpedoing that view of himself, as Henry's self-assurance falls apart, Stoppard may still not have exposed his entire and actual self. *The Real Thing* may be his most direct confessional but it is also a hall of mirrors. As usual, honest statement and deceiving appearances go together; neither one cancels the other, and so the play becomes a guessing-game to which there might or might not be a 'real' answer.

In the London production, Peter Wood and his designer hung a painting of Henry on the back wall of his living-room, a portrait which exactly reproduced the characteristically stooped-shouldered stance of Roger Rees so that, when he stood in front of it, there was an actor whose own mannerisms inscribed Henry, who was then reflected in the picture behind him. This sequence of images illustrates the way Stoppard lures us in to *The Real Thing*, which begins with what seems like an actual showdown between an architect and his wife. Their reality is hypnotically persuasive as Max concentrates on his pyramid of playing-cards, which collapses when Charlotte comes through the door. Yet the dialogue also implants the idea of image-within-image and of deception beneath a surface banter:

MAX: Hello, lover.
CHARLOTTE: That's nice. You used to call me lover.
(*She drops the airport bag on his lap and returns towards the suitcase.*)
MAX: Oh, it's you. I thought it was my lover.   (10)

Charlotte has supposedly been to an auction sale in Geneva for Sotheby's – or was it Christie's? Max has found her passport while rifling through her things but begs her pardon for violating her privacy: "I think I just apologized for finding out that you've deceived me" (13). As part of that 'deception', his wife has brought him a Swiss memento, one of those paperweights which make a snowstorm when shaken. In the second episode, which we at first assume to be the continuation of the action, Charlotte appears to have run to her lover, Henry: she emerges from the bedroom wearing his dressing-gown, things are "a mess", and she does not want to see Max. However, we eventually realize that Charlotte is married to Henry and that the first scene was part of his latest play and, later still, that the character Charlotte was playing had really been to Switzerland on a temporary passport but was too affronted to explain away her husband's suspicions.

In betraying one 'reality' after another, Stoppard toys with the very nature of theatrical illusion – as in *Rosencrantz* and *Hound* we are made to wonder how any part of it can be *real* – especially as the second scene's 'real-life' conversation parodies the situation between Eliot and Amanda in Noel Coward's *Private Lives* when Henry tries to recall the insidious little tune played "in some place like Bournemouth or Deauville, and there was an open-air dance floor outside our window . . . and there was this bloody orchestra which kept coming back to the same tune every twenty minutes" (16). This scene, supposedly the real thing between Henry, Charlotte, Max and Annie, his actress wife, sounds more artificial than the previous excerpt from Henry's play. Coward's style continues to flavour their "smart talk" about the Norfolk Broads and the way Henry and Annie act out a normality in front of their respective partners while teetering on the verge of their actual feelings for each other.

These interconnecting pictures dictate the structure of the entire play, so that we continually challenge the reality of one such picture in relation to another. Scene 3 takes place in a living-room, whose layout is somewhat similar to the stage-set Max first appeared in. Now Annie, his 'real' wife, comes through the door to be confronted with the evidence of her own deception with Henry. But there the similarities end, because Max meets this situation with none of his stage-character's wit and polish; his emotions will not let him:

You're filthy.
You filthy cow.
You rotten filthy –
(*He starts to cry, barely audible, immobile.* ANNIE *waits. He recovers his voice.*)
It's not true, is it? (37)

So the scene ends messily as he kicks the radio, from which can be heard his rival's "Desert Island Discs" interview, and flings himself at his wife, who endures his violent embrace with a blank coldness. The alterations establish a difference between life and art, or at least between art as created by Henry in that first betrayal scene which, after the husband's discovery, rolled urbanely on to a gracefully pointed conclusion: the front door closes and, laughing at his wife's ingenuity, the architect pulls the deceiving souvenir from the duty-free airport bag and shakes it.

After Annie has married Henry, there occurs a second variation of this betrayal scene. He, too, has stormed through her things in search of evidence. But when he forces her to admit she has come down on the overnight train from Scotland with her current leading man, he remains articulate, though brusquely and desperately so. Less incoherent than Max's and less debonair than his stage counterpart's, Henry's reaction seems no less probable. Their interconnection reminds us that each of these versions is in fact staged, yet each remains convincing and true at the time.

Other connecting scenes create a similar game of hide-and-seek. Early in the play we hear how Annie had met Private Brodie on a train to London on their way to the same anti-nuclear demonstration. She now serves on the Justice for Brodie Committee after he had been sentenced to six years for burning the memorial wreaths at the Cenotaph and then attacking the two policemen who arrested him, although "they're now both up for perjury on a previous case" (33), so they might have rigged the evidence against him. Eager to keep his name in the public eye, Annie and a TV producer have encouraged Brodie to write a play about his experiences, but when Henry reads the script he finds it one-sided and lifeless. Brodie may have lived through all that, but his version stultifies the real thing:

HENRY: He's got something to say. It happens to be something extremely silly and bigoted. But leaving that aside, there is still the problem that he can't write. He can burn things down, but he can't write.   (50)

Life and art continue to clash in the adjacent Scene 6, which seems to show a televised exchange between Annie and 'Brodie' but quickly turns into an actual train ride where she meets Billy, who is to play opposite her in Glasgow and who is being considered for the Brodie role. Five scenes later, after Annie has told Henry about her 'thing' for Billy, we see the same encounter all over again, but this time, as the lights pull back to reveal the surrounding cameras, she and 'Brodie' *are* performing a script, one which sounds much more probable because Henry has reworked it for Annie's sake.

Finally, the actual Brodie, after his release from prison, watches a tape of that telecast and "liked it better before" Henry went to work on the script. Artistically pruned and shaped though it is, the play did not even effect Brodie's release; according to him, "I'm out because the missiles I was marching against are using up the money they need for a prison to put me in" (82). According to Annie, the 'yob' who sits in her living-room "isn't him", nor was his televised self:

He was helpless, like a three-legged calf, nervous as anything. A boy on the train. Chatting me up. Nice . . . He didn't know anything about a march. He didn't know anything about anything, . . . He tagged on.

In mirroring scene against scene, Stoppard not only aims to point up the odd falsity of 'real' life when compared with art's convincing fable; he also surveys a no-man's-land between the two, where genuine and pictured feeling coalesce. On the train up to Glasgow, Billy, the actor, in trying to attract Annie, soon jettisons his Bill Brodie manner, briefly becomes himself – with side-swipes at the Brodie script – and then takes refuge in his role as Giovanni (Italianate Billy) in the forthcoming production of Ford's *'Tis Pity She's a Whore*. Real feeling intertwines at first with the scripted version: "I' faith, I mean no harm, sister. I'm just scared sick of you. How is 't with ye?" (59). But to push farther, he embroils himself in his Renaissance persona and his actions become increasingly artificial. Annie is reduced to giggles – "you daft idiot" (60) – but he emotes on until the episode ends in melodramatic tatters and more giggles from her. Later we do see a rehearsal which goes strictly according to Ford until he kisses her and Annabella/Annie "returns his kiss in earnest" as she whispers, "Billy" (64). In that way, Stoppard hits at those who complain that his characters' self-conscious role-playing betrays a lack of feeling.

To those same ends, he dangles Henry in front of us as a sort of in-joke version of Stoppard-according-to-his-critics. His play about the architect is called *House of Cards* in response to those who see Stoppard's own elaborate structures as airy nothings. Tynan, for instance, once diagnosed the stasis he perceived in *Travesties* with a phrase borrowed from *Jumpers*: it was "tantamount to constructing a Gothic arch out of junket".[12] With tongue in cheek, Henry rues "the fate of all us artists . . . People saying they preferred the early stuff" (66–7) – a sop to those who liked Stoppard's early hummingbird style. And since friends have characterized him as one for whom "words always precede thoughts. Phrases come first, ideas later",[13] Stoppard makes Henry into someone who is always "going on" and whose way with words allows him to pass "as an ironist in public though a prig in private" (66). Priggish he may seem, but his insistence on the right word in the right place comes from a passion about words in themselves, their use and abuse, so he is apt to correct friends who mix their metaphors or slip on a gerund because what others might consider a trivial error "actually *hurts*" (35). That explanation is not likely to alter their opinion of his unfeeling intellect:

There's something wrong with you.
You've got something missing. You may have all the answers, but having all the answers is not what life's about.

What Henry appears to lack, and what Stoppard's detractors accuse him of lacking, is an ability to commit himself unequivocally to public issues and private emotions.

Regarding public issues, Charlotte maintains that "when Henry comes across a phrase like 'the caring society' he scrunches up the *Guardian* and draws his knees up into his chest" (33). And, like his creator, Henry defends himself with a chiselled wit which could make him sound like an amused dilettante. He cringes from 'the caring society' as a phrase in itself; his reaction is purely aesthetic: "Like the Bauhaus meeting in an Indian restaurant, it's got nothing to do with the food." He goes on to toy with the various motives behind a person's commitment, just as Stoppard likes to argue out loud with himself, so he could be seen to have all the questions rather than "all the answers".

But although Henry continues to put correct language before political slogans, his genuine concern for what words do becomes increasingly apparent. When Annie argues that the importance of Brodie's play, however rough and ready, comes from its having been written in prison by a man whose symbolic protest brought him up against the establishment's savage retribution, Henry sweeps that aside. Politics have nothing to do with his opinion that Brodie is simply "a lout with language" and that words are *the way* to understanding what life is about:

They're innocent, neutral, precise, standing for this, describing that, meaning the other, so if you look after them you can build bridges across incomprehension and chaos . . . They deserve respect. If you get the right ones in the right order, you can nudge the world a little or make a poem which children will speak for you when you're dead. (55)

This appeal to the children of the future verges on joke-vicar earnestness, so Stoppard has Annie read out part of a jerry-built filmscript Henry has been churning out on his typewriter in order to detonate that sententious sentimentality.

But stylish phrases would only get in the way of the images he has to think in when writing for the film producers' money – "alimony doesn't count". Words also tend to flatten out at moments of impassioned argument. Yet true feeling does not necessarily exclude eloquence. In the play's most memorable sequence, just before the outburst about words as bridges, Henry talks with stylish intensity about the way style itself can strike to the centre of things. That intensity gives a peculiar energy to the elegant simplicity of his demonstration. Seizing a cricket bat, so that Annie thinks he might hit her with it in his excitement, Henry hits her with words. The bat, a mundane object in itself, has been put together so that it "is sprung, like a dance floor" (53). If the combination works, the ball will fly; if not, it "will travel about ten feet and you will drop the bat and dance about shouting 'Ouch!' with your hands stuck into your armpits". Henry tries "to write cricket bats", whereas Brodie's script goes "ooh, ouch!" The analogy is provocatively snobbish and would drive someone like McKendrick (of *Professional Foul*) into a fury. It is also as passionate as it is logical. Through Henry, Stoppard pads up at the crease to defend elegance against those who confuse it with Malquistian phrase-making.

As for the sloganeering of the partisan writer, "it's like being run over very slowly by a travelling freak show" (54). The stylist, in his seeming detachment, knows that words like "politics, justice, patriotism" are abstract entities which ought not to be twisted from angle to angle as one can move a concrete thing like a coffee mug. Justice is justice, and trying to call it something else, "as though there were something there to change . . . will finally make you violent". To know that, and to approach words "with humility", will not alter the way things are, but "you may perhaps alter people's perceptions so that they behave a little differently at that axis of behaviour where we locate politics or justice". The arguments go back to the beginnings of Stoppard's career, but Henry voices them with an animus that is quite foreign to Stoppard the interviewee who, fifteen years before, was "not impressed by art *because* it's political, . . . if you are angered or disgusted by a particular injustice or immorality, and you want to do something about it, *now, at once*, then you can hardly do worse than write a play about it".[14] However, he immediately adds the caveat that without plays, bad and good, "the injustice will *never* be eradicated".

Similarly, in this play's next scene, he undercuts Henry's thesis about abstract entities when Annie tries to show Billy how he misuses a phrase like 'the class system': "There's nothing really *there* – it's just the way you see it. Your perception" (58). Yet although Billy laughs away her smugness – "I prefer Brodie. He sounds like rubbish, but you know he's right. You sound all right, but you know it's rubbish" (59) – Henry's ardent polemic is only slightly diminished by this defeat of a half-hearted imitator. And the play's shaping also vindicates Henry's impatience with slogans when Annie finally admits that the 'real' Brodie was an innocent mooncalf who "would have followed me into the Ku Klux Klan" (82). He was her "recruit", so she felt in honour bound to champion him while persuading herself that he was indeed a martyr to the cause. As Henry remarks, "That one I would have known how to write" (84), for early on in the play, with an eye to his own desire for Annie, he had sneered at the motivations of 'the caring society':

One of us is probably kicking his father, a policeman. Another is worried that his image is getting a bit too right-of-centre. Another is in love with a committee member and wishes to gain her approbation . . .   (34)

Brodie's bedazzlement with Annie, the former television star, had led to the Cenotaph, and her sense of obligation led to the Justice for Brodie Committee. In Henry's overblown summation, "Public postures have the configuration of private derangement."

Stoppard's 'public posture' in *The Real Thing* is the paradigm of his long-held feelings about detachment and politics which, while never exactly private, now emerge boldly into direct light. What seems entirely new is the play's special picture of 'private derangement' which, unlike George and Dotty's or Ruth's or Glad's, appears to project Stoppard's own. Henry, the intellectual word-spinner, whose emotions are so well guarded, collapses when Annie embarks on an affair with Billy. Though he struggles to retain a modicum of poise, whereas Max goes to pieces in a similar circumstance, the play's penultimate scene shows that the battle to reason himself into "digni-fied cuckoldry" is a losing one. Alone in the house, after Annie leaves to meet Billy, he dissolves into a cry of deranged anguish: "Oh, please, please, please, please, *don't*" (80).

Seduced by the resemblances between Henry and his creator, and forgetting the inarticulate cries in many of the plays, commentators pounced on the fact that "the Tin Man had a heart after all".[15] Resisting such an autobiographical interpretation, what one sees is a more direct but, once again, familiar conflict between reason and feeling and the latter's ultimate victory: Ros and Guil's mounting panic, George's final plea for help and his self-accusing dream, Alexander's refusal to be reasonable, Anderson's *volte face*, Ruth's what-the-hell reprise with Wagner are all part of that pattern. What *is* new is that those emotions are essentially sexual and lead Stoppard into territory he had previously shied away from, except in the cartoon-like *Dirty Linen*, because the vocabulary of love, like political catch-phrases, tends towards platitude. The central issue of *The Real Thing* is not the dissolution of the self-assured Henry into a fool of love; that is simply another of Stoppard's arch games with those who say "You've got something missing", a non-issue because, as Henry himself says, he will either continue to endure whatever Annie does to him or he will quite suddenly stop: his love will "go on or it will flip into its opposite" (79). Instead, Stoppard uses that story to explore whether a playwright *can* write interestingly and truthfully about love.

Henry can certainly write about it amusingly. When his architect character confronts his wife with her passport, he bombards her with witty and wordy salvoes:

I notice that you never went to Amsterdam when you went to Amsterdam. I must say I take my hat off to you, coming home with Rembrandt place mats for your mother. It's those little touches that lift adultery out of the moral arena and make it a matter of style.   (13)

His very wordiness may hold some truth as an instinctive way of covering over his pain, but though his jokes do turn bitter, the scene ends artfully and shows Henry's concern for his theatre audience. The actors are also concerned with the effect they make; Max, for instance, was pleased that someone came round after the perform-ance to say how moving the reconciliation scene was. But Charlotte's annoyance at the nightly "groan" she gets when the audience "find out . . . she hasn't got a lover at all . . . And they lose interest in me totally" (20) adds spice to her critique of Henry's version of love:

You don't really think that if Henry caught me out with a lover, he'd sit around being witty about place mats? Like hell he would. He'd come apart like pick-a-sticks. His sentence structure would go to pot, closely followed by his sphincter. You know that, don't you, Henry? Henry? No answer. Are you there, Henry? Say something witty. (22)

Yet when we arrive at the real thing between Henry and Annie, once their partners are out of the room, their feelings may be true, but their dialogue goes round in repeated banalities: I love you – I love you – I love you (26–7).

Stoppard makes this point directly in Scene 4, when Henry reads out from *Miss Julie* to help Annie learn the script. The Strindberg lines overlap with their own conversation about how Henry made love when she was "totally zonked" after a sleeping-pill. Compared with that, *Miss Julie* sounds matter-of-fact, but both sets of dialogue depend on a context of feeling which may not come explicitly through the words themselves. Annie explains Strindberg's effectiveness: "You'll have to learn to do sub-text. Mine is supposed to be steaming with lust, but there is nothing rude on the page" (41). But Henry has said that "I don't know how to write love . . . it just comes out embarrassing. It's either childish or it's rude . . . Perhaps I should write it completely artificial. Blank verse. Poetic imagery" (40).

Stoppard's train scene does have snatches of blank verse when Billy, chatting Annie up, breaks into Ford's Carolinian imagery and rips open his shirt to expose "A heart in which is writ the truth I speak" (60). But that, too, depends on a context; baring one's "affliction" on British Rail's upholstery is hardly conducive to 'the truth', so the scene ends in giggles. That same "Music . . . In the ear" sounds more magical at a rehearsal, although it is a simple kiss rather than words which leads Annie to respond as herself to the actor not the brother (64). Love escapes words:

HENRY: I don't know. Loving and being loved is unliterary. It's happiness expressed in banality and lust. It makes me nervous to see three-quarters of a page and no *writing* on it. I mean, I *talk* better than this.
(41)

The divide between Stoppard and his *persona* is tauntingly thin here, as if he were admitting that, because of the "unliterary" nature of love in bloom, he has nowhere to go, save for excursions into Strindberg and Ford, without sounding "childish or rude". Accordingly, to be interesting, the play has to concentrate on the shifts in Henry's feelings. This is again prepared for early on when Annie remarks upon the "gallons of ink and miles of typewriter ribbon expended on the misery of the unrequited lover; not a word about the utter tedium of the unrequiting" (39).

Two crucial episodes in the second Act delineate Henry's fall from assurance to the raw pain of unrequited love. Charlotte, his ex-wife, congratulates him on his sang-froid, although it used to distress her when they were married. Henry takes love for granted, yet Charlotte explains "there are no commitments, only bargains. And they have to be made again every day" (62). Henry can afford to take love easy, to be glib or acid about it, Charlotte says, because he thinks "it sets like a concrete platform, and it'll take any strain". But when the strains come and Annie insists on her freedom to love Billy, Henry feels as if he had "been careless, left a door open somewhere while preoccupied" (78), and unaccustomed doubt invades him unawares. He tries to behave generously, covering up for her to directors when she is delayed by Billy. Although she tells him that her affair is "quite separate . . . You're not replaceable. I *love* you", he does not dare to tell her to stop because that would be pathetic and "unattractive". Even to question her would feel "a little vulgar". Trying to stay reasonable, he can find no part of himself which does not include her. Love knows no reason:

There was a tribe, wasn't there, which worshipped Charlie Chaplin. It worked just as well as any other theology, apparently. They loved Charlie Chaplin. I love you. (79)

So Henry becomes will-less and his story comes to a dead end. Words cannot describe his feelings. He must either worship Annie or "flip", although in the mean time he instinctively tries to find "equilibrium", to shift his weight in order to attain some sort of happiness.

If love is difficult to capture in words, playwrights can write interestingly if not always truthfully about the process of love. Henry's daughter, Debbie, thinks that his *House of Cards* "wasn't about anything, except did she have it off or didn't she? What a crisis. Infidelity among the architect class. Again" (67). But though *The Real Thing* seems to offer a similar plot – will she stop having it off or won't she? – what Stoppard actually writes about and holds up for investigation is the nature of sexual fidelity. Debbie, for instance, simply wants to be happy, "like a warm puppy" (66). And if Henry complains about her T-shirt philosophy, she is content to take her boy friend, Ben, as she finds him. Sometimes she follows him to the fairgrounds he works at, and sometimes she stays at "the squat" they occupy. Tearing down the mystery with which the middle classes enshroud love and sex, she maintains that "most people think *not* having it off is *fidelity*", as exemplified by the hypocrisy of the man from the Council, who spent a lascivious hour or so at the squat discussing his wife's sexual preferences, "but at the last moment he panicked, denied himself, went away. Faithful, you see?" (67). For such people, "all relationships hinge in the middle. Sex or no sex", and she recalls her own obsession at school when every subject except biology gave off the wicked aura of forbidden sex. But when she goes on to describe her idea of love, words fail her, too, and she falls back on T-shirt slogans: "That's what free love is free of – propaganda" (68).

For Henry, relationships hinge on "a sort of knowledge. Personal, final, uncompromised. Knowing, being known. I revere that. Having that is being rich" (69). But his faith in that shared bond makes him deaf to what Charlotte says about commitment being an on-going bargain. His reverence for this private knowledge between two people makes him more than a trifle smug. In the first weeks of his life with Annie, that confidence annoys her and convinces her he does not "care enough to care" that actors she works with often make passes at her (44). But, being in love, Henry revels in "the insularity of passion" which unites the two of them securely amidst a world of anonymous others (45). He describes that same assured possession several years later:

Knowledge is . . . the undealt card, and while it's held, it makes you free and easy and nice to know, and when it's gone, everything is pain. Every single thing. Every object that meets the eye, a pencil, a tangerine, a travel poster . . . Pain. (69)

The irony of this lies not only in the fact that Henry begins to experience this loss in the very next scene but that his foreknowledge of pain and the words he finds to describe it offer no defence when it actually strikes him down. Once again, words fail to convey what love is like. Stoppard leads us along these various paths to show how we never can arrive at the real thing, the experience itself. Try to capture it, and it turns out to be a childish imitation or it falls to pieces in your hands, as it does in Henry's.

Yet playwrights continue to write about love, tying it down with words and shaping it to the two-hour traffic on the stage. And that creates the major problem in *The Real Thing*. Love is untidy, irrational, undefinable yet, in saying that quite brilliantly, Stoppard has ordered, rationalized, and defined certain limits through the structure of the play itself. He gets trapped in Catch 22: a lover's behaviour is inexplicable, but by moulding that idea into a sequential, realist plot he invites questions about his lovers' motivations. This is not too damaging as regards Henry, around whom idea and story fit together in a dramatically satisfying way. When Annie's affair with Billy forces him to deal "the undealt card", he comes toppling down like his own *House of Cards*, which he describes as a play "about self-knowledge through pain" (67). Henry's pain teaches him that nothing he can say or do will bring order to his feelings: he must either sit the situation out, shifting his weight as best he may, or his feelings will suddenly alter.

However, idea and form jostle each other uncomfortably where Annie is concerned. As part of an argument about what love 'really' is, her arbitrary behaviour helps build the case for love's unreason. But when her illogic is embodied in a likable, flesh-and-blood character on stage, we are apt to ask how she can behave that way if she really loves Henry or, still more damagingly, how Henry could put up with such cruel behaviour. The notion that love has nothing to do with her feeling for Billy and that Henry cannot do other than bear *because* he loves has less force in the theatre than does the bewildering power of the staged action. As a consequence, the ideas Annie voices are often memorable but she makes less sense as a person, and a large part of our reaction to *The Real Thing* resembles Debbie's to *House of Cards*: when *will* she stop having it off?

Not that Annie exists merely to further the argument or the plot; in fact, had she been more of a functionary the play might have achieved a more satisfying totality. She is not one of Henry's female characters who exist to serve "drinks and feeds". Annie belongs with Stoppard's other feminine enigmas even though she at first appears so frank and open, and this contradiction makes her difficult to come to terms with. When she arrives at Henry and Charlotte's with her offering of vegetables for crudités, her directness – "Quick one on the carpet then" (27) – does seem a crude contrast to the prevailing "smart talk" but it also establishes our sympathy with her forthright energy, especially when she exposes Henry's procrastination for what it is: "you want to give it time . . . to go wrong, change, spoil. Then you'll know it wasn't the real thing . . . you love me but you don't want it to get around" (27–8). She is equally honest with and about Max: "he wants to punish me with his pain, but I can't come up with the proper guilt . . . It's so *tiring* and so *uninteresting*" (39).

Since we are not party to that extended anguish, we are unlikely to see it from his viewpoint. But when the same thing happens to Henry, Annie appears to want to have her cake and eat it too, loving Henry but being unable to resist Billy. Partly the problem is that we see Henry's pain and very little of Billy's counter-attractions, and partly that Annie can hardly be excused as passion's slave. Her motives are in fact extremely dubious, since only by continuing her affair can she prove to herself it was more than a one-night stand: "But I didn't start it casually, and I can't stop it casually" (79). Her obligation to her relationship with Billy is very like her loyalty to Bill Brodie, a self-deceiving justification for what she would otherwise have to admit were mistakes. Meanwhile Henry pays, and her gratitude and sympathy for him seem cruel, not to say insensitive: "so I'm grateful and I say thank you. I need you. Please don't let it wear away what you feel for me. It won't, will it?" The final scene resolves both those relationships when she slams a bowl of dip into the 'real' Brodie's face and refuses to answer what she thinks to be a phone-call from Billy. But our own ambiguous feelings towards Annie can not be tidied away so neatly. If this is the real thing between herself and Henry, there appear to be rocky times ahead.

For all its craftily angled mirrors and its originality as a play about the inadequacy of plays about love, *The Real Thing* runs into trouble in the last two scenes because they insist on motives, demand an awkward change of sympathy, and invite cosy smiles at the final curtain which are not quite earned. The difficulties are those of focus. Stoppard has always presented women as imponderable, and Annie is no less so than Gladys, Lady Malquist, Dotty, and Ruth, or her nearest counterpart, the unnamed woman in "Reunion". But these other women puzzle us from the outset, a view that one or other of the men around them usually shares: Moon's view of Lady Malquist is our view, and we perceive Dotty first as George sees her and then more sympathetically with the glamorous pathos which someone like Inspector Bones gives her. Annie, however, appears first as an open book, and Henry patronizes her because she is so knowable; then, in those last scenes she seems suddenly to be someone else and, while this points the irony of Henry's trust in his knowledge of her, it causes us a dislocating jolt, though Henry soldiers on with her to a supposedly happy ending. The other women in the play remain for us as Henry sees them, even if we listen harder to their views on love and loyalty than he does: Charlotte's exasperated sarcasm sparks against his priggish self-confidence and makes her a more interesting figure than Debbie, a fairly standard teenage drop-out except that she talks cleverly, with whom Henry can be wise, loving, and irritated.

Conversely, when Brodie arrives in the final scene, the fact that he behaves exactly as the 'yob' that Henry had thought him to be makes him an inadequate opponent in the debate about writing and politics. Other than provoking the play's last visual surprise, the bowl of dip, there is no necessity for him to appear at all: Annie's confession about the boy he once was could have arisen equally well out of Henry's telescript, which in its way is just as much a caricature.

Whatever the problems of those concluding episodes, *The Real Thing* stands as a major achievement. Stoppard continues to play games with stage illusion but the tricks have a subtlety which matches the reticence of his post-*Travesties* style. At the same time, he faces his critics with a new directness, taunting them with Henry's elegance, which seems so smug but which is transparently the expression of a deeply felt attitude to life. Although that attitude is the consummation of nearly everything Stoppard stands for, Henry presents a chimerical version of his creator's public self and behind that lies a vulnerability, a rawness which Stoppard had not felt able to expose – and mock – since "Reunion", that early short story read by the few:

For better or worse, that's it – the love play! I've been aware of the process that's lasted 25 years, of shedding inhibitions about self-revelation. I wouldn't have dreamed of writing about it 10 years ago, but as you get older, you think, who cares?[16]

At first glance there are no self-revelations in the radio script he was working on at the same time. *The Dog It Was That Died* (1982)[17] seems like a return to an earlier style, particularly to the studied zaniness of *Lord Malquist*. But the play also offers a comic cartoon of a search for 'the real thing', just as *Artist Descending* and *Dirty Linen* were "dry runs" for *Travesties* and *Night and Day*. Rupert Purvis has worked as a double-agent for so many years that he no longer remembers what his original loyalties were, and neither the Russians nor the British who have knowingly used him in that double game are able to enlighten him:

They set me going between them like one of those canisters in a department store, and they disappeared leaving me to go back and forth, back and forth, a canister between us and you, or us and them.   (32)

The real thing Purvis eventually clings to is his affinity with the English character, an eccentric individualism which accounts for the play's style and madcap assortment of characters and to which Stoppard pays fond tribute. *The Dog* turns out to be a personal thank-you card (of the funny sort) to his adopted country.

That Englishness emerges at once as Purvis walks through the night city singing World War I goodbye songs while his inner voice rehearses the letter of farewell he has just posted to Blair, his superior in Q6. About to jump off Chelsea Bridge, he can still chortle over a pun or two, "I'm getting out but before I take the plunge" (11), or revel in the comfort of the national idiom: "your good lady", "pulling the wool over your eyes", "brouhaha", "splendid girl", "quiet as the grave and black as your hat" (11–12). Stoppard again plays with a cliché to which there still clings a mite of truth: British phlegm, a crossword-puzzle delight in word-play and idiosyncratic turns of phrase, a fascination with the weather even at times of crisis, as Purvis climbs the parapet and notes a "nice breeze anyway". The funniest twist of the cliché occurs at the end of the scene "with the sound of a quite large dog in sudden and short-lived pain" (13): in his plunge towards the Thames, Purvis has landed on a passing barge and broken the back of the Englishman's best friend. And the letter itself which contains wild references to opium dens, marital infidelity, a belly dancer at Buckingham Palace, and some "savoury business" between Purvis, his vicar, and the choir, "especially Hoskins, third from the end with the eyelashes", seems utterly mad, although the well-trained nose of Hogbin, the man from Q9, sniffs "something funny" about it: "And that's what it was – it's all true" (40). Stoppard's gambit resembles the openings of *Lord Malquist* and *After Magritte* where a seemingly implausible collection of characters or images or, as in Purvis' letter, events, instigates an action designed to explain how 'normal' their combination was. Such an opening works particularly well here because of its overt eccentricity, the keynote of the play's Englishness.

The letter also serves to introduce the idea of appearances which so confuses Purvis, and Stoppard turns cold-war espionage into a fun-fair game in The House of Mirrors. We never hear the Russian side of things directly, but the British approach "the game" as they do all sports (except soccer!) with a mixture of earnest involvement and gentlemanly disdain, a blend which varies according to one's social class. Hogbin has much to learn about sang-froid. Arriving "on the dot" in St James's Park for an assignation with Blair, he insists on the password, which his colleague can only vaguely recall, so he refuses to recognize a man he knows perfectly well. Caught in the middle of this mad game, Purvis has stumbled from one side to the other in search of some sign which would tell him what he is playing for, what he *really* believes in, so he tries saying Communist slogans out loud; sometimes they sound convincing and sometimes not.

One ideology is the other's mirror-image, and beyond them the rules of the game have grown into a riddling maze over the years:

CHIEF: ... This is where it gets tricky ... because if they kept drawing these wrong conclusions while the other thing kept happening ... they would realize that we had got to Purvis after all ... So to keep Purvis in the game we would have to *not* do some of the things which Purvis told them we *would* be doing, ... (44)

Lurching from one illusion to the next, having told his Russian contact what he was told by his British contact and then telling the British contact that he had told the Russian contact what he was told by his British contact, Purvis has "a bit of a *crise*" at finding himself "like one of those Russian dolls – how appropriate! . . . which fit into one another as they get smaller" (34). Only in the rest-home for similarly afflicted agents does he discover the final doll, the inner part of himself "which isn't hollow", his essential Englishness.

The play's centre point, both mathematically and thematically, is the scene at Clifftops. This "funny farm", as Hogbin puts it, represents the lunacy of the secret service writ large. Having gone there to visit Purvis, Blair encounters a bluff figure on a motor-mower whom he takes to be a patient but who soon introduces himself as the head man: "I prefer the term keeper, just as I prefer the term loony. Let's call things by their proper name, eh?" (25). But a minute or two later it becomes evident from the way the old boy blusters on about "the Arlons [who] have been gentlefolk in Middlesex for five generations" (26) that he is indeed one of the inmates. In the process, Stoppard thrusts a comic shaft into the romantic image of "the firm" by means of Commodore Arlon's rambling story of a quarrel over cards at the Naval and Military club, which ends with talk of a manly shoot-out: "if you want to do a chap a favour the next time you find yourself in Pall Mall, I'd like you to take out your service revolver and go straight up to Greenslade and — ". Another false mirage then looms up in the person of 'Matron' whose manner seems convincing until she pulls Blair into a coat cupboard to demand her next mission: "I'm match fit and ready to go – parachute, midget submarine, you name it. The last show wasn't my fault, the maps were out of date" (27). After two such *contretemps*, Blair not surprisingly asks his rescuer, Dr Seddon, for some identification, and though the doctor's story about his code-making in Q10 may sound mad to the listener, the tangled ingenuity of "consonantal transposition" is the sort of complex nonsense Blair lives by. However, when the doctor invites him up to the belfry to see his bats, Blair makes a hasty getaway, only to learn from Purvis that the man really was Dr Seddon, "up in the bell tower collecting guano for the rose-beds" (29). As Seddon has explained, "My time with the firm was excellent preparation for Clifftops" (28).

The rest-home also presents "the English character, a curious bloom which at Clifftops merely appears in its overblown form" (41–2), and there Purvis realizes that everyone he worked with, *except* his Russian contact, had a minor form of the same madness. He finds this "reassuring". Recollecting his British contact who wore "hunting pink to the office" and grumbled that the butter dripped when he ate asparagus after breaking his neck, he knows that he never could have lied to him: "The man was so much himself that one would have been betraying him instead of the system" (42). So all the play's characters are gorgeously themselves and endearingly loony: Blair with his clock collection and his private Folly; Mrs Blair with her donkey sanctuary and first aid in the drawing-room for "poor Empy"; the Chief with his bubble-pipe; the vicar with his love for cheeses. Their personal eccentricities add up to a comic-cuts assemblage of what are popularly thought of as the nation's foibles. Strange hobbies, a passion for animals, the tang of the sea and of Empire go together with a desire to look the other way when a chap has a *crise* or a wife has a tryst in Eaton Square. Vague and unflappable, the gentlemen of "the firm" are amateurs, in the finest sense, who will always muddle through.

Stoppard has always had a fondness for eccentrics, and much has been written about his own English guise, "*plus anglais que les anglais*": his "costly-casual dandyism",[18] his love of cricket, his Home-Counties lifestyle. Colleagues have even suggested its connection with his unwillingness to take sides: "He's basically a displaced person. Therefore, he doesn't want to stick his neck out. He feels grateful to Britain, because he sees himself as a guest here, and that makes it hard for him to criticize Britain."[19] Partly he is laughing at that lurid picture of himself when he laughs at these mad dogs of Englishmen (the play's title comes from Goldsmith's "Elegy on the Death of a Mad Dog"). The whole play turns on this fellow-feeling for the English; no malice waits to pounce from behind the farce. Instead, individualism is revealed as England's saving grace, more powerful than any "system". Consequently his eccentrics are all well-meaning: "the firm" has been completely defanged; the Blairs' marriage ambles along despite Pamela's liaison with the Chief; a general regard for the right of other people to live their own lives prevails.

Talking about his travels abroad, Stoppard once said, "I was very, very pleased to get back to England, and I still am, and I feel at home here in a way which I couldn't feel anywhere else."[20] Respect for the individual has much to do with that feeling of home and underpins his trust in the country's public institutions:

> . . . there is a way of behaving towards people which is good and a way which is bad . . . and alongside that different theories about attaining the common good – in other words, [the political parties] each have different economic theories each designed literally to achieve the maximum general good for everybody . . . merely a disagreement about tactic . . . All I know is that I want to live in a country where that dispute can take place, and not where it's forbidden.[21]

In *The Dog*, Stoppard delivers a paean to the way Englishness absorbs differing styles, modes, and systems into itself. As Blair sits on his park bench he looks out at London:

The view north from St James's Park is utterly astonishing, I always think. Domes and cupolas, strange pinnacles and spires. A distant prospect of St Petersburg, one imagines . . . Where does it all go when one is in the middle of it, standing in Trafalgar Square with Englishness on every side? Monumental Albion, giving credit where credit is due to some sketchbook of a Grand Tour, but all as English as a 49 bus. (13)

Stoppard's attitude to England includes the implication that things might have been otherwise. In *The Dog* everyone except the Russian contact man radiates an enviable insularity to which even the demented Purvis can cling, and this distinction haunts Stoppard. In his preface to *Every Good Boy* he remarks that "although British society is not free of abuses, we are not used to meeting courage because conditions do not demand it" (7), by which he means the social conditions men like Victor Fainberg had to face up to rather than the personal trials which require courage from all of us. Such a contrast must have been much on his mind while writing the radio play, since he had also begun work on a television film about the Solidarity movement in Poland.

Owing to a Byzantine power-struggle between the British and American production companies, not unlike the tangle between Solidarity and Polish authority, *Squaring the Circle*[22] was not broadcast on television until May 1984 and not without suffering compromises which amply vindicate Stoppard's chariness towards film-making: "There's a lot of technicians, and a lot of money, and little time, and a lot of muscle, and a lot of people over the title and, you know, the position of the writer in films is notorious, i.e., supine."[23] The biggest change involved the narrator, whom Stoppard had conceived as the author himself; he became an American commentator, so that "what was supposed to have been a kind of personal dramatized essay turned into a kind of play about an unexplained American in Poland" (14). Naturally this led to a confusion which, along with Stoppard's deliberate refusal to slant the events in one particular way or to interpret the character of the main protagonists, resulted in the play's relative failure. Yet the script is a remarkable one, an artistic if not a popular triumph, a sort of blueprint of the writer Stoppard has become since his epiphany in the waters off Capri.

Here, for instance, is the writer whose fascination with the power of fiction to impress its simpler and therefore clearer version of reality upon the imagination regulates his approach to any topic. Faced with thousands of facts about Polish history, ancient and modern, with documents and tapes, Stoppard responds first to the magnetism of documentary drama, which imposes itself on the viewer as the real thing but which cannot, however well researched, hope to present history as it actually happened. So he invents the narrator and, some time later, the Witness, a common man in various hats, in order to break the hypnotic power of the televised pictures and to establish the story as a personal and (thanks to the Witness) fallible view. The narrator talks to us on camera and as a disembodied voice, continually reminding us that what we see is one man's reconstruction, a Western one at that.

The first image of fraternal greeting between two ageing men on a bench, their topcoats and hats, their suits and laced shoes, and particularly their jargon – "inevitable triumph of Marxist-Leninism", "revisionist element", "allies in the proletariat's struggle" (27) – deliberately plays to our preconceptions about how such a meeting between Communist leaders would be. The narrator then steps into the frame – "Everything is true except the words and the pictures" – to subvert anything a writer can tell us. So the image changes to bright umbrellas, technicolour drinks, Hawaiian shirts, sun-glasses, as Brezhnev harangues the First Secretary of Poland's Politburo in gangster style: "What the hell is going on with you guys? Who's running the country? You or the engine drivers?" (28). In juxtaposing one image upon another, as in *The Real Thing*, Stoppard projects onto the screen the theatricality he has always felt most comfortable with and which he had not been able to capture for any length of time in his previous telescripts. Here the meeting by the Black Sea becomes part of an ironic thread which binds the script together, for Brezhnev meets succeeding First Secretaries every August and their third encounter ends the play with wry casualness. "So, how's tricks?" asks Brezhnev of Jaruzelski, whose trickery has just destroyed the workers' solidarity, and then the Russian leader (dead by the time of the television broadcast) replies to a like enquiry, "To tell you the truth, I haven't been feeling too well", as they stroll off harmoniously down the beach (96).

That framing device affects our view despite the narrator's scepticism towards 'truth' so, as he fits events into this circular frame, the Witness keeps bobbing up with alternative perspectives or with sardonic comments about the way writers select or mould facts for artistic effect. One of the most inventive uses of this convention occurs when the Politburo congratulate each other on having split the leadership of the Free Unions. The jubilant picture suddenly freezes and is then torn in two like paper to reveal the narrator writing away at a café table. As the latter crumples up his efforts and throws them away, the Witness, here an *habitué* of the café, advises him to "Try the other one" (72). Whereupon the cameras roll again for a revised version of the Politburo sequence only to freeze and tear once more. Back in the café, the Witness hints that the writer still has things wrong, and a final version shows the Politburo's alarm at the way Party unity has been split by the workers. As regards the artistic shaping of facts, the narrator introduces Lech Walesa's children to sing a play-song about one of their father's intellectual friends who has just left the house in a rage. The Witness cuts in – "a cheap trick" – and asks why he did not pull out all the emotional stops by giving the kids a dog: "it's a little late to be scrupulous about detail" (84). Another replay then returns the intellectual to the point where he rose to leave, and this time he does so in conciliatory fashion.

Such exchanges between the two commentators and between one or another travestied version of events distance us from pictured history. This estrangement has become a standard device on the modern stage, less so on television, and in itself provides a way of cutting through, and giving order to, a mass of unwieldy fact; the controlling narrator and the interplay between the aristocratic and the military version of things in the musical, *Evita*, are cases in point. But Stoppard's method again reveals his characteristic temperament. The narrator in *Evita* selects and organizes events into an acid commentary upon the oh-so-innocent heroine's rise to power and sainthood, unlike the Brechtian teller-of-the-tale who posits one decision or attitude against the next and encourages us to judge between them, though the shape of the whole narrative affects that choice. Stoppard's commentator offers a slant while confessing his fallibility and presents events or attitudes as opposing fictions rather than truths so that we cannot choose one above the other. The debate is much more open-ended, a variant of his talking the issues out loud. It infuriates those who believe one *must* take sides over Solidarity in no uncertain terms, and it bored many television viewers, who wanted a decisive verdict on events in Poland or a clearly drawn clash of character and motive.

And since he provides few solids to hold on to, no call to arms, no revelations about the 'real' Walesa or Jaruzelski, no actual 'characters' at all, the play can seem cold and inhuman. For the one hard fact Stoppard sees is as impersonal and inevitable as the *Titanic* and the Iceberg, and his story unfolds with a mathematical precision:

> . . . an attempt was made in Poland to put together two ideas which wouldn't fit, the idea of freedom as it is understood in the West, and the idea of socialism as it is understood in the Soviet empire. The attempt failed because it was impossible, in the same sense as it is impossible in geometry to turn a

circle into a square with the same area – not because no one has found out how to do it, but because there is no way in which it can be done. What happened in Poland was that a number of people tried for sixteen months to change the shape of the system without changing the area covered by the original shape. They failed. (29)

Yet from the loaded wording of speeches like this there can be no doubt as to Stoppard's opinion of "the system", and had he been on screen (instead of the American *persona*) these words would have been undisputably his and more like an "essay", a try at gathering his thoughts about what happened in Poland. Instead, a journalist's cool stance works against the playful way the script tries out one idea and then another and so it threatens the bond of Stoppard's serious–play. For, over the years, the 'serious' has become more directly personal while the 'play' no longer "breaks its neck to be funny", and the script as originally conceived unites the two with the daring and tact of his mature style.

It takes daring to be funny about the crushing of Solidarity and the suppression of a nation, especially to audiences who expect serious subjects to have straight faces and forget that one of the ways to discomfit a devil is to laugh at him. The comedy works because Stoppard quickly breaks the illusion of actuality and then aims "the quirky bits" at the techniques of documentary television or at the leaders of the regime whom we sometimes laugh with (in the grim style of *Cahoot*'s Inspector) but more usually laugh at. We do so because the narrator and the Witness keep us distanced from the story's emotional impact, and if some of the jokes against the leaders are broad, they have the effect of political cartoons in cutting pomposity down to size or in making an obvious madness even more so.

Stoppard acknowledges that lampoon style at the beginning of Part 3 when the caption "Courtesy of Prague Radio" comes up under a picture of Walesa writing intense notes at the grille of a confessional; the Party line declares that his instructions to destroy socialism come "straight from the Pope" (68). Play as a metaphor pokes fun at both the documentary and the Party. Stoppard himself is no stranger to the games motif, nor are writers of documentary dramas, since politics and gamesmanship go so readily together. "Why is it always *chess*?" asks the Witness as he ponders his next move on the board before him and his opponent informs us that the Central Committee did not think the time was ripe "to attack on the left" (57). By admitting "ugh, well, you know, it symbolizes", the writer exposes the tricks of his trade and the Witness ruins things by moving his knight improperly, but, in seeming to undermine the symbol, Stoppard neatly prepares us for the way Jaruzelski will make his own sort of move with the army. Stoppard manipulates a card game in the same way, betraying the symbol through the writer and the Witness – "Don't tell me, let me guess. Cards on the table . . . Writers" (88) – and then immediately using it to shape a conference between State, Church, and Unions.

Most of the explicit jokes hit at the politicians' hypocrisy and gangster tactics. First Secretary Gierek goes on television to confess "mistakes in economic policy"; the solid-looking bookcase behind his desk turns out to be a deceptive piece of studio scenery and, during his speech, the camera shows us an exchange between two electricians on a gantry above him: "I think I've seen this before . . . Typical bloody August . . . nothing but repeats" (38). The gangster jokes are also exposed as "a metaphor", nevertheless they recur throughout the script to emphasize the leaders' greed and treachery to each other and to the workers. Enlarging these gangster types to farcical proportions, Stoppard ensures that we see his monsters as cardboard shams. Like an image from an old movie, First Secretary Kania, smothered in his barber's shaving lather, inveighs against "people who think that the Party boss can run the operation like a Chicago gangster" (64) and lists off a string of disasters ("Al Capone wouldn't have lasted out the week") as if he were in some sort of farce. But the social circumstances make it a bitter one.

The "quirky bits" provide Stoppard with a way of saying what he thinks about the regime, because simply to blast them as gangsters, cheats, shams and liars would have sounded as banal as love did to Henry. But the quirkiness also provides him with a way of threading together a vast amount of factual material, as it did in *Jumpers* and *Travesties*. One of the wonders of this script is the economy with which he moves from scene to scene, using his comedy and the vocabulary of film with a sense of design that has grown more subtle and supple since the days of *Neutral Ground*. To convey the unyielding circle around the reformists' zeal, a large conference table interspersed with flags gives a quick sketch of a Warsaw Pact meeting which we come in on as the East German minister concludes his fulminations against the Polish government's weak reaction to "an attack on socialism, an attack on everyone here" (66). A pause adjusts the rhythm of the scene and, out of that, Brezhnev, seated across from the Polish delegation, explains "in a fairly friendly manner" that Russia once had its own free trade union – "He is in a lunatic asylum now, poor fellow" – and that if the Polish Party "cannot defend itself . . . it must be defended". The picture instantly dissolves to a group of high-ranking officers in greatcoats who casually watch their armies' off-screen manœuvres. Marshal Kulikov turns to Jaruzelski and adds the punchline to this cartoon: "Well, I don't know what all this is doing to the Poles but it's scaring the hell out of the Americans" (67).

The laconic rhythms, pictures, and words add to the narrative's inevitability. General Jaruzelski, in particular, plays a waiting game through the first three-quarters of the script. But "when the time comes", the camera shows a number of "crisp separate close ups on a man putting on military uniform" ending with a "pair of tinted glasses worn by Jaruzelski" (81). The scene changes to the First Secretary's office where a flunky arranges files on the empty desk; the General walks in, takes possession and, pleased with what he sees, flicks at his uniform: "You don't think the effect is . . . a bit South American?"

Theatrical illusionist, serious gamester, fence-sitter, master tactician, cold formalist: the old labels could all be applied to the Stoppard of *Squaring the Circle* without accounting for their changing combination from scene to scene and without getting him quite right. That they describe the *way* he writes rather than *what* he writes points up the unarguable fact that it is the style of each play that hits us first. But to stop there is to ignore the man who makes the stylish strokes with each well-made cricket bat. Behind his dash, finesse, and complexity, Stoppard's values are small-'c' conservative and surprisingly simple. Endlessly curious about seeming and being, the way people misunderstand each other, the words that entrap or betray them, and humbled by those confusions, Stoppard distrusts slogans yet loves to pick at clichés. He is essentially benevolent, though wary of sentiment, and his truths are self-evident and inviolate: individuals have a right to be happy and free, and to mistreat people or to persuade them that happiness and freedom are other than they *know* them to be is wrong.[24]

His attitude to Solidarity comes from that centre of himself. For all its quirkiness, the script contains remarkably little word-play, particularly in those scenes which involve the freedom fighters. There his restrained, almost neutral tone shows him shying away from these men as individuals, for were he to listen too closely he would find them as jargon-ruled as their masters. What interests him is not their politics – methods are disputable – but their determination to be free and the way their efforts collapse before an unscrupulous, brute power and a confusion amongst themselves. So their particular demands are incidental to their battle for a human right. George Moore, young Sacha, Professor Anderson stand behind the words of the Witness:

181

Theories don't guarantee social justice, social justice tells you if a theory is any good. Right and wrong are not complicated – when a child cries, "That's not fair!" the child can be believed. (84)

Those in power "lie . . . cheat . . . kick and bite and scratch before they give an inch" (92), and the shipyard workers also fall apart because they play politics against experts, envy the personality cult around Walesa, disagree about methods, lose sight of their basic ideal. In one scene, Walesa sits atop the Soviet war memorial in Warsaw trying to scrub off the painted graffiti just as he vainly tries to erase the scrawl from his revolution's monumental idea.

Stoppard's radical values have always confused the political radicals and, like his own Walesa, he sometimes used to "feel a sort of shame. How brave it sounds, to be a radical" (92). Stoppard has not become more political. Ros and Guil, like the Polish workers and the intellectuals, also wanted to be free but found themselves encircled by an unyielding system and could not say "no" to Elsinore's game. However, Stoppard's humanism has become more insistent as he has seen how systems "kick and bite and scratch". And throughout his career words have been his vital mainstay because by using them with style he can say "That's not fair!" more disruptively than any child can. So it *matters* to write, and write well.

KURON: The written word – I believe in it. When this tower of Babel collapses upon itself you'll need to be reminded what the noise was all about. (83)

After words

... The particle world is the dream world of the intelligence officer. An electron can be here or there at the same moment. . . . It defeats surveillance because when you know what it's doing you can't be certain where it is, and when you know where it is you can't be certain what it's doing: Heisenberg's uncertainty principle; . . .[1]

Despite its apparent solidity, each particle of Stoppard's latest play "can be here or there at the same moment". What starts as a spy story becomes, as you look at it, a metaphor that illustrates the tricksy dream world of spies and counter-spies, "sleepers" and "joes"; look longer, and *Hapgood* depicts the unpredictabilities in every human being. The naturalistic dialogue also has its quantum leaps when words, like many of the characters who speak them, become twins, puns, "double agents". As Clive James noticed, years ago, "the appropriate analogies to Stoppard's vision lie just as much in modern physics as in modern philosophy".[2]

In its elegant ingenuity, *Hapgood* is like a 'thought experiment' designed to probe the randomness behind our perceived realities. The first scene, for example, introduces us subversively to Heisenberg's uncertainty principle.[3] Once the houselights go down, a street map projected onto three hexagonal panels above the empty stage allows us to plot the route of a Russian agent whose Peugeot (red lights on the map) moves through the London streets and stops at a municipal swimming-bath. The set now assembles in semi-darkness; disembodied voices over a two-way radio note, with some alarm, that the agent in question is "not Georgi". They cannot place him, but his route remains predictable as he enters the lobby, nods to the man shaving at a sink (down right), and crosses to one of four changing-cubicles (stage left). What follows next is a playful ballet – choreographed to a whistled tune and jaunty drum beats – in which, as per Heisenberg, we cannot track the actors' movements and positions simultaneously, as they exchange briefcases amongst the four cubicles.

For instance, the actor who plays the Russian must also appear as his twin brother, a trick done with doors and fur hats rather than mirrors. Coming from the pool, he re-enters his cubicle: his wet hair identifies him, and we know his position. But we cannot trace his movements when (presumably) he exits through the back of that cubicle, appears again from the lobby dressed, as his "brother" had been, in a blue tracksuit and fur hat, crosses the stage to another cubicle, leaves through the back of that, and emerges from the first cubicle as the wet-haired twin who, carrying the fur hat, now leaves the building, "in two places at once".

Throughout the rest of the play, the characters' behaviour obscures their actual 'position' at a given moment in the spy plot. By the beginning of Act Two, we know that those Russians with their attention-getting hats were "stooges" and that the double-agent Elizabeth Hapgood must track down is her own assistant, Ridley, and *his* twin brother.[4] However, we cannot be sure of Joseph Kerner's exact place in all this. A nuclear scientist planted in the West by the Russians, he had long ago been "turned" by Hapgood. Blair, the chief of British Intelligence, and Wates, from the CIA, suspect him of passing genuine secrets along with the misinformation he gives his KGB control. Hapgood, who has a son by Kerner, needs to believe that Joseph is still her "joe". Yet, in the first scene of Act Two, the behaviour of the characters deceives us into mistaking the situation they invent to trap Ridley. As in quantum physics, "the act of observing determines the reality".

Again the staging has much to do with this. From the very beginning we share Ridley's focus, since the music that starts the Act does not fade with the lights but becomes what he hears through the headphones of his transistor as he sits waiting with Hapgood (opposite him) and Blair (at Hapgood's desk) for Kerner's arrival. Since Blair spends some time meticulously adjusting the empty chair beside the desk, it would appear that Kerner is to undergo some sort of interrogation. That assessment seems justified when Kerner enters and, perversely ignoring Blair's invitation to "sit here, won't you?", moves the chair downstage. Blair's amusing chat, as he presents the damning evidence against Kerner, also seems random, unplanned, particularly when words slither:

> KERNER: May I ask a question?
> BLAIR: Yes, do.
> KERNER: Why are you sitting in Mrs Hapgood's chair?
> BLAIR: That is a very fair question. The answer is that Mrs Hapgood isn't here. Mr Ridley isn't here either. They are on paid leave, which is why they can't be with us this evening, and which is why this is a friendly interview. (53)

Observing that, we are lured into the reality of the 'scam': to protect his son, Kerner intended to pass his research to the KGB but, because that delivery went awry at the Baths, little Joe has been kidnapped and Hapgood, ever one to "break the rules", needs

Ridley's help to deliver the material in exchange for the boy. Only at the end of the scene, once Ridley has gone, does that reality dissolve as we watch Hapgood talking on the phone to Joe (perfectly safe at school) while Blair and Kerner drink a toast to their successful trap.

Stoppard's ambush here is reminiscent of the lurch into Ruth's fantasy that begins Act Two of *Night and Day*. However, as befits the particle world of *Hapgood*, the traps keep coming in this play for, like his own Alexander Ivanov, Stoppard does "something really crazy" by taunting his audience with the possibility that Hapgood herself has an identical twin. In the printed text, all "Celia's" lines are given unequivocally to Hapgood, but on stage the effect of this double-act grows increasingly disturbing. When Ridley first meets "Celia", she is so obviously an arty cliché that, having been tricked once, we are unlikely to be taken in again, particularly since Ridley can only contact Hapgood on his radio when her comic persona is out of the room. Yet, ironically, once "Celia" arrives at Half Moon Street in the sort of efficient suit that looks like Hapgood, the more unnerving she becomes: her behaviour, as she bluffs her way through the office routine for her secretary, Mr Maggs, makes her 'real' identity difficult to place. This is especially true when she reacts as Celia might to the unexpected blow Ridley deals her so that she will answer the "kidnapper's" phone-call in tears or, at II.5, when she allows Ridley to make love to her. Of course, to *be* Hapgood and carry off the scam, she must have nerves of steel, yet her actions seem so *unlike* Hapgood's (who would never let "her bodice up past [her] brain", 1.5) that she remains a teasing enigma until the final showdown at the Baths.

This restless unpredictability makes unusual demands of the audience, and Stoppard carefully prepares for that in Act One. The ballet with the briefcases is a comparatively subdued opening gambit: it neither disorientates (as the first moments of *Jumpers* or *Night and Day* do) nor deceives (as scene one of *The Real Thing* does). It presents a comic version of the spy game which verges on the surreal when the Russians enter in those hats or when Wates (by the sink) flips his soap at the feet of each departing figure (to effect a Geiger reading on his 'wrist-watch' as the soap is handed back) or when Hapgood emerges, spry and dry beneath an umbrella, from the men's shower. The scene does not, as yet, require us to connect its farcical dance to the careless amorality of international espionage, though it does open the way to that as the set dissolves around Blair and ("here or there at the same moment") reassembles for his meeting with Kerner at Regent's Park Zoo. That episode then demonstrates the play's controlling metaphor with a Brechtian economy.

The undisguised scene-change and the simplicity of the stylized units which represent the zoo establish this sequence as a theatrical set-piece. The dialogue, rather than the action, now dances, but with none of the first scene's frenzy, as Blair toys coolly with the jargon of the spy world and Kerner takes a foreigner's delight in all the idioms of language:

> BLAIR: You're blown, Joseph.
> KERNER: I love it. She blew it and I'm blown: well, I'll be blowed. Nobody teaches that, you know . . .
> BLAIR: Well . . . you're blowed, Joseph. Your career is over.
> KERNER: Except as a scientist, you mean.
> BLAIR: Yes, that's what I mean.
> KERNER: My career as a joe.
> BLAIR: Or as a sleeper. Just an observation. The meet at the pool came unstuck this morning. We have to consider you blown as our joe. The Russians must consider you blown as their sleeper. Either way your career is over. *Which* way, is perhaps an academic question. (9–10)

This artifice allows for the transition from jocular duet to rhetorical aria when Kerner moves behind a panel of vertical bars, down right, to illustrate his thesis: "a double agent is not like a giraffe. A double agent is more like a trick of the light" (10). Apart from Kerner's gestures, as he uses the cage and its shadow to explain how light can be both particles and waves, the action comes to a standstill, and the ideas are directed out at the audience with clarity and deliberation as Kerner instructs Blair in layman's terms and halting English. Yet the lecture is enlivened by the way he plays with Blair's incomprehension and need for certainties:

> KERNER: . . . The act of observing determines the reality.
> BLAIR: How?
> KERNER: Nobody knows. Einstein didn't know. I don't know. There is no explanation in classical physics. Somehow light is particle and wave. The experimenter makes the choice. You get what you interrogate for. And you want to know if I'm a wave or a particle. I meet my Russian friend Georgi, and we exchange material. When the experiment is over, you have a result: I am a British joe with a Russian source. But they also have a result: because I have given Georgi enough information to keep him credible as a KGB control who is running me as a sleeper – *which is what he thinks he is*. (12)

The set-change which instantly moved Blair from baths to zoo suggests another duality in that it transposes one idea of his character over another. Emerging from the shadows of the changing-room and unperturbed by Wates's drawn revolver, he was brusque, professional, in control. At the zoo, however, he seems charming, detached, pragmatic. Like the two giraffes on stage behind him, whose necks appear to tower from the same body, he is two figures in one. And, as the scene progresses, Kerner also has two aspects. Excited by the mystery of scientific theory, he seems peculiarly untouched by the actual risk and moral dilemmas of the spy game.

Those anomalies are confronted directly in the scene that follows. The picture again dissolves, and Blair stands downstage of a school-building suspended in cutout at the rear. Hapgood hurtles in crab-wise, the lone supporter of her son's Junior Colts B team: neat, efficient "Mother" from Half Moon Street has become endearing, scatty Mum at the touchline. These two figures also overlap: Hapgood never uses "bad language" in either role, talks about her male subordinates and her son's masters with the same cosy patronage, and treats the matter of Joe's missing key with intellectual aplomb. Nevertheless, Hapgood would like to keep them separate; "when the sugar hits the fan", she can then lose "Mother" and be Mum. But even as she insists on that separation, her words jump back and forth between the two images to show how impossible it is to draw a boundary line:

> HAPGOOD: Kerner's all right – I run him and he's just doing what I tell him.
> BLAIR: Wates made the same point. Don't take it personally.
> HAPGOOD: Why should I? It isn't personal. (*The referee's whistle – the conversion of the try*) Eighteen. Come on, St Christopher's! Let's get one back! This is personal, all fifteen of them and the referee, who's incidentally a sweetheart, he takes Divinity and says if Joe passes Common Entrance it'll make the loaves and fishes look like a card trick. Everything else is technical. You're personal sometimes; but not this minute which is all right, so what can I tell you? – it isn't Kerner. (17)

With logical precision, Stoppard leads us through each layer of his theme to its human centre, and the rest of Act One deploys the uncertainties of espionage, quantum physics, and individual personality until they interlock at the conclusion of the Act in the play's crucial equation. It is that unchartable boundary – between KGB and MI6, microscopic and macroscopic, one role and another – which is *Hapgood*'s deepest mystery. The properties of the subatomic world can only be described after they have been measured, but since the observer and his measuring instruments are also made up of atoms, where do the unpredictabilities of the particle world become the tangible and connected "realities" of everyday experience?[5] As Kerner explains to Hapgood, at the most extended moment of rest and connection between the two of them,

> [Einstein] believed in the same God as Newton, causality, nothing without a reason, but now one thing led to another until causality was

dead. Quantum mechanics made everything finally random, things can go this way or that way, the mathematics deny certainty, they reveal only probability and chance, and Einstein couldn't believe in a God who threw dice. . . . There is a straight ladder from the atom to the grain of sand, and the only real mystery in physics is the missing rung. Below it, particle physics; above it, classical physics; but in between, metaphysics. All the mystery in life turns out to be this same mystery, the join between things which are distinct and yet continuous, . . . (49–50)

In his elusive Act Two, Stoppard himself plays dice, having prepared us to stay in the game. The way he deconstructs his characters is also calculated. He explains they can have no discernible centre, but the more he involves us in their lives, the more we feel the need to find that "missing rung". But we can never know them, nor can they know each other, because the boundary between intellect and feeling is "distinct yet continuous".

Niels Bohr lived in a house with a horseshoe on the wall. When people cried, for God's sake, Niels, surely *you* don't believe a horseshoe brings you luck!, he said, no, of course not, but I'm told it works even if you don't believe it. (70)

Just such emotionalism pulls Ridley into the others' con-game. The "sister thing" works because he is "potty" about Hapgood and feels he can solve the riddling happenstance of her character in the seeming predictability of Celia Newton. Waiting in a cheap hotel (II.5) for the second "meet" at the baths, Hapgood taunts him with those Newtonian certainties. His intellect tells him that his situation "smells like a dead mackerel" (82). He knows that Elizabeth's job is to lie and, given their past relationship, should know he is "not her type". Yet her attraction makes him want to "get her kid back for her but it's only personal. If she's set me up I'll kill her". Were he to "open the box" (that may or may not contain Kerner's computer-disc), he could take Hapgood's measure, but as she challenges him to do that, she offers him Celia Newton, his (and her) illusion:

RIDLEY: (*Grabbing her*) *Who the hell are you?*
HAPGOOD: I'm your dreamgirl, Ernie – Hapgood without the brains or the taste.
(*She is without resistance, and he takes, without the niceties . . .*) (83)

Ridley reaches the missing rung again at the swimming-bath. He has always been "carrying a torch for her or a gun" (82), and if the one cannot explain who Hapgood is, the other might. But she eludes him there, too: "RIDLEY *has got as far as taking his gun out when* HAPGOOD *shoots him*" (85).

Hapgood's own emotion makes Kerner unknowable. She wants to

marry him, in a half-hearted way: although she no longer needs him as a joe now his cover has been blown, she still *needs* him as Joseph, father of Joe. Kerner shies away from that. His feelings betrayed him once; now his "personal" life revolves round quantum theory. Because she had loved him, Hapgood cannot understand how he felt used – "If love was like that it would not even be healthy" (50) – and she too feels betrayed when he talks of returning to Russia. Detached from that, we see more, but not completely. Kerner *is* fond of his son, and his unwillingness to meet him may suggest how much. He keeps the boy's photograph in the lining of his wallet and sends him presents. But, in the final scene, he could "go this way or that way". Having said an affectionate goodbye to Hapgood, he is drawn back by his son's rugger game and stands, staring out at it, in a moment's curiosity or a lifetime's affection. Sensing him behind her, Hapgood's own reaction, as she "comes alive" on the touchline, might be radiant joy or a brave attempt to hide despair. The tableau is as volatile as Kerner's atom:

> I cannot stand the pictures of atoms they put in schoolbooks, like a little solar system: Bohr's atom. Forget it. You can't make a picture of what Bohr proposed, an electron does not go round like a planet, it is like a moth which was there a moment ago, it gains or loses a quantum of energy and it jumps, . . . (49)

These kaleidoscopic characters, like the disintegrating realities of the plot, dramatize *Hapgood*'s scientific conceits in such a way that the audience *experiences* that chimerical world. Hapgood herself remains as puzzling to us as she is to Ridley. Two things seem certain about her: she adores her son and values middle-class niceties, even though "they happen to be shared by a fair number of people you wouldn't want to be seen dead with, they always were" (23). Yet those certainties evaporate when her lethal efficiency as "Mother" calls them into question. The story of the kidnap unfolds so convincingly and her panic seems so genuine (as she discovers Joe has been picked up from school by a driver who said she had sent him) that the very reality of her anguish undercuts her maternal image when it turns out to have been a charade. Suddenly she is not the Mum we felt she was. Nor is she the conventional lady we took her for when she uses her body as bait to hook Ridley. We ought, of course, to have known that all along; but, as we watch her, our emotions subvert that knowledge (and *vice versa*) until we cannot be sure whether the "little anarchist" inside her (63) is the Mum who lets her son call her on the Downing Street red-line or the Mother who involves him in her dirty games. Like all of us, she can probably be understood both ways, as Kerner says:

So it is with us all, we're not so one-or-the-other. The one who puts on the clothes in the morning is the working majority, but at night – perhaps in the moment before unconsciousness – we meet our sleeper – the priest is visited by the doubter, the Marxist sees the civilising force of the bourgeoisie, the captain of industry admits the justice of common ownership. (72)

Hapgood denies the either/or which any audience seeks to pinpoint. Its disappearing certainties of character and plot prove more bewildering than the ideas, drawn lucidly from espionage and physics, that they imitate. It offers little to hold on to, defying us to empathize or trust our senses. Exquisitely dovetailed, intricate, elusive, each episode recreates the particle world's frustrating mystery. As an intellectual puzzle, the play succeeds completely. However, its restless energy also raises a number of social issues which bob to the surface then disappear again. While it captures the abstract duplicity of quantum theory, *Hapgood* lets go of the political dualities it uncovers and, in consequence, does not connect, passionately and disruptively, with the concrete world.

Yet the play invites such an engagement. By the beginning of Act Two, the implications behind the caper at the baths come to the fore when Ridley, caught in the kidnap story, urges Blair to give Kerner's computer-disc to the Russians: "There's nothing on that disc except physics and it will stay physics till little Hapgood is a merchant banker" (59). Even after ten years, the military application of Kerner's research would be insignificant: "It's a joke. I'd trade it for my cat if I had a cat" (60). An exchange would not betray the actual secrets of Half Moon Street, the names of agents or of covermen in the Moscow Embassy: "a kid like that, he should be in bed anyway, we can all get some sleep" (59). Although Blair acts out a part in the scam by refusing to give up the disc, a second interview at the zoo with Kerner reveals his motives. He will use any means to defend his "values", and Kerner agrees, despite his own "estrangement", that "The West is morally superior". Through democratic elections "the system contains the possibility of its own reversal. . . . Highly theoretical, of course" (73). Those values, which presume honesty and trust, seem still more theoretical when, a moment later, Blair insists on knowing Kerner's true loyalties in order to protect "one of my people". Kerner is wryly amused: "One of your *people?* Oh, Paul. *You* would betray her before I would". Given the intimacies Blair encourages, Hapgood might be surprised that the man who wears her scarf should speak of her impersonally, but she does trust him *as* "a friend" whose views she shares no matter how someone like Ridley perverts them into "a racket which identifies the national interest with the interests of the officer class" (82).

These ironies knit together at the point where Hapgood enters the changing-room to deliver the disc-box. Blair had warned it would "be tricky doing the swap without a boy to swap" but agreed "to do the best we can" (63). When Joe does unexpectedly appear, Hapgood keeps her head. Mission accomplished, and alone with Blair, her anger rises: "You lied to me . . . I'll never forgive you for that, never ever" (86). Then, subsiding into "misery", she is gallant enough to acknowledge her own involvement in the nasty business: "I'm not blaming you about Joe. The truth is I enjoyed it and now I've stopped" (87). Blair has betrayed Hapgood's trust and, looked at another way, done what he can to minimize the risk she takes. Their relationship ends in typical ambivalence as Blair defends the system with his "them or us" and Hapgood, seeing the farce that both sides play, resorts at last to "bad language":

> BLAIR: (*With asperity*) Why am I supposed to feel sorry for Joe? There's worse things. I'd feel a damn sight sorrier for anyone who didn't know there was an either-or and we can't afford to lose. One has to pick oneself up and carry on. It's them or us, isn't it?
> HAPGOOD: Who? Us and the KGB? The opposition! We're just keeping each other in business, we should send each other Christmas cards – oh, f-f-fuck it, Paul!

Oddly, these two speeches, which seem like point and counterpoint, evade each other. Hapgood's both/and, to Blair's either/or, debunks espionage as a futile and unending merry-go-round; it does not attack the methods Blair uses to ensure the system he and she believe in. And so the fact that this affable charmer and the unpleasant Ridley are both driven by the same ruthlessness is allowed to slip away. The final scene completes the process in that Hapgood retreats, as is her wont when troubles come, to her son's playing-field and the "manners maketh man stuff". Blair's manners, too, are old-school-tie.

In *The Dog It Was That Died*, another Blair runs a section of Q6 with serene detachment, and the farcical action never reveals the underside of his well-bred eccentricity. Yet Purvis, shuttled back and forth in the spy game till he can hardly remember which values he believes in, clings to Englishness in suicidal despair. Espionage is a blacker joke in *Hapgood*, but Stoppard does not allow Elizabeth to confront that darkness and thereby reassess her values or defend them knowingly. No chasm yawns for her. Disheartened by the fact that she "must have been buying nothing but lies and chickenfeed since Joe was in his pram" (87), she opts "out of it" and turns instead to her son and his school's conservative standards: a relatively painless escape. Like her, we glimpse the randomness behind those standards without fully experiencing what that implies. The political and moral dualities of Stoppard's theme slide away beneath the last scene's gentle, but inadequate pathos. In consequence, *Hapgood* rocks our minds and senses but, in all its wondrous symmetry, leaves life much as we thought it was.

Notes

1 A free man

1 Tom Stoppard, "The Definite Maybe", *The Author* LXXVIII (Spring 1967), p. 19.
2 Tom Stoppard, "Ambushes for the Audience: Towards a High Comedy of Ideas", *Theatre Quarterly* IV (May–July 1974), p. 4.
3 *Ibid.*
4 Kenneth Tynan, *Show People* (New York: Simon and Schuster, 1979), pp. 72–3.
5 Stoppard, "Ambushes", p. 4.
6 Robert Bolt, *Flowering Cherry* (London: Heinemann, 1959).
7 Tom Stoppard, *Enter A Free Man* (New York: Grove Press, 1972), p. 9. All further references to this edition appear in parentheses.
8 Ronald Hayman, *Tom Stoppard*, 2nd edn (London: Heinemann, 1978), p. 6.
9 Compare Hancock's similar unsinkability after being barred from 'The Poetry Society' (Dec. 1959): "I'll go down to the coffee-house – there's bound to be another movement started up since yesterday. I'll start one of me own! . . . A breakaway group! We'll be anti-everything! The new intellectual movement to shake the world!" Quoted in Roger Wilmut, *Tony Hancock 'Artiste'* (London: Eyre Methuen, 1978), p. 80.
10 Compare the climactic scene between Willy and Biff Loman in Act 2 of Arthur Miller's *Death of a Salesman*:

> BIFF (*Crying, broken*): Will you let me go, for Christ's sake? Will you take that phony dream and burn it before something happens . . .
> WILLY (*After a long pause, astonished, elevated*): Isn't that remarkable? Biff – he likes me! . . . Oh, Biff! . . . That boy – that boy is going to be magnificent!

11 This speech is particularly Milleresque and derives from the appeal of Linda (Willy's *wife*) to her two boys in Act 1: "He's not to be allowed to fall into his grave like an old dog. Attention, attention must be finally paid to such a person."
12 Stoppard, "Ambushes", p. 5.
13 Milton Shulman, "The Limelight Is Too Strong for these Dreams", *Evening Standard* (London), 29 March 1968, p. 4.
14 Stoppard, "Ambushes", p. 4.
15 In Hayman, *Tom Stoppard*, pp. 28–31.
16 *Ibid.*, p. 7.
17 Tom Stoppard, *The Dog It Was That Died and Other Plays* (London: Faber and Faber, 1983), p. 7. All page references in parentheses are to this edition.
18 Hayman, *Tom Stoppard*, pp. 75–6.
19 In *The Dog It Was That Died and Other Plays*, pp. 59–67.

20 Hayman, *Tom Stoppard*, p. 144.
21 In *Albert's Bridge and Other Plays* (New York: Grove Press, 1977), pp. 43–69. All page references are to this edition.
22 Hayman, *Tom Stoppard*, p. 2.
23 In *The Dog It Was That Died and Other Plays*, pp. 165–83.
24 *Ibid.*, p. 7.
25 *Ibid.*, pp. 109–64.
26 The synopsis is in Tynan, *Show People*, pp. 67–9.
27 *Ibid.*, p. 69.

2 Now you see him

1 Tynan, *Show People*, p. 64.
2 Compare Ernest Hemingway's "Cat in the Rain" for a sentence which mimics the ebb and flow of the ocean: "The sea broke in a long line in the rain and slipped back down the beach to come up and break again in a long line in the rain." *In Our Time* (New York: Scribner's, 1925).
3 Stoppard, "Ambushes", p. 4.
4 Stoppard acknowledges these influences in "Footnote to the Bard", *Observer* (London), 9 April 1967, p. 23.
5 Janet Watts, "Tom Stoppard", *Guardian* (London), 21 March 1973, p. 12.
6 Tom Stoppard, *Lord Malquist and Mr Moon* (London: Faber and Faber, 1974). All page numbers refer to this edition.
7 Stoppard, "Ambushes", p. 17.
8 Hayman, *Tom Stoppard*, pp. 143–4.
9 Tynan, *Show People*, p. 61.
10 To the critic, Robert Cushman. Quoted in Tynan, *Show People*, p. 67.
11 In a recorded conversation (1976) with Anthony Smith, *British Council Study Aids*, Stoppard talks about writing out his early neuroses: "And I worried about things like that. . . . And occasionally, something would go spectacularly wrong, and I was curiously reassured when New York had a total blackout. I found great solace in that, because it just worried me that that many lights kept going on when they were needed." In accompanying booklet, unnumbered, p. 14.
12 Compare Stoppard in "Ambushes", pp. 6–7: ". . . there is very often *no* single, clear statement in my plays. What there is, is a series of conflicting statements made by conflicting characters, and they tend to play a sort of infinite leap-frog."
13 Hayman, *Tom Stoppard*, p. 2.
14 "Stoppard's prose is immensely pleased with anything it can come up with." William Pritchard, "Fiction Chronicle", *Hudson Review* XXI (Summer), p. 366.
15 481 copies, according to Tynan, *Show People*, p. 54.
16 Hayman, *Tom Stoppard*, p. 12.
17 Ronald Bryden, "Theatre: Wyndy Excitement", *Observer* (London), 28 August 1966, p. 15.
18 Hayman, *Tom Stoppard*, p. 12.
19 Tynan, *Show People*, pp. 69–70.

20 Stoppard, "Ambushes", p. 6.
21 Tom Stoppard, *Rosencrantz and Guildenstern Are Dead* (London: Faber and Faber, 1968), pp. 57–8. All page numbers refer to this edition.

3 Victims of perspective

1 Tom Stoppard, *The Real Inspector Hound* (London: Faber and Faber, 1968). All page numbers refer to this edition.
2 Stoppard, "Ambushes", p. 8.
3 *Ibid.*
4 *Ibid.*, p. 7.
5 *Ibid.*, p. 8.
6 *Ibid.*
7 *Ibid.*, pp. 16–17. In the National Theatre's 1985 revival, directed by Stoppard himself, the two critics were seated stage right in the front row of a 'theatre' which went back into the wings so that they faced the actors and the audience diagonally. Since the actors faced out through that side proscenium, much of their business was done on the same diagonal, with their backs to the actual auditorium. After Simon and Hound had finished their short stint as critics, a gauze was drawn across, blacking out the space beyond the false proscenium, and the redundant pair simply disappeared from the proceedings. Since *Hound* was performed with Sheridan's *The Critic*, its satire on critics seemed much more prominent than the whodunnit pastiche. In addition, Stoppard and his cast created a delicious parody of 'coarse acting' which helped to extricate the pseudo-*Mousetrap* from its comic cul-de-sac.
8 Agatha Christie, *The Mousetrap* (London: Samuel French, 1954), p. 2. *Hound* parodies the plot as well as the gaucheries of *The Mousetrap*. In the Christie play, the policeman turns out to be the murderer. Puckeridge tries to force Moon, as the second Inspector Hound, into that role while himself assuming the part of Christie's Major, who is finally revealed as the actual policeman. What then became of the "real" Major Muldoon? Had Puckeridge bribed him to leave the cast – or worse? The plot thickens!
9 Stoppard, "Ambushes", p. 8.
10 Tom Stoppard, *After Magritte* (London: Faber and Faber, 1971). All page numbers refer to this edition.
11 Quoted by Suzi Gablik, *Magritte* (Greenwich, Connecticut: New York Graphic Society, 1970), p. 12.
12 The painting is illustrated in Gablik, *Magritte*, p. 49.
13 Ludwig Wittgenstein, *The Blue and Brown Books*. Quoted in Gablik, *Magritte*, p. 96.
14 In *The Dog It Was That Died and Other Plays*, pp. 69–88.
15 In *Albert's Bridge and Other Plays*, pp. 7–41.
16 *Ibid.*, pp. 117–39.
17 Stoppard, "Ambushes", pp. 3–4.
18 John Gale, *Clean Young Englishman* (London: Hodder and Stoughton, 1965), pp. 36–58. Gale had interviewed Stoppard for the London

Observer: "Writing's my 43rd Priority, Says Tom Stoppard", 17 December 1967, p. 4. For the BBC broadcast, Gale became Dale, though Stoppard tells me that John Gale was "more than happy to have his name used". That change meant the disappearance of one minor clue to the identity of Groucho, whose parents sent him honey from Mexico (p. 123). Gale's Honey, like Crawford's Crackers, is a well-known brand name.

4 Trapped in language

1 Quoted in Tynan, *Show People*, p. 90.
2 Ludwig Wittgenstein, *Culture and Value*, trans. Peter Winch (Chicago: University Press, 1980), p. 50e.
3 Hayman, *Tom Stoppard*, p. 8.
4 In *The Dog It Was That Died and Other Plays*, pp. 89–108.
5 Jean-Paul Sartre, *Nausea*, trans. Lloyd Alexander (London: Hamish Hamilton, 1962).
6 These parallels are discussed in Jim Hunter, *Tom Stoppard's Plays* (London: Faber and Faber, 1982), pp. 156–8.
7 Ludwig Wittgenstein, *Tractatus Logico-Philosophicus* (London: Routledge and Kegan Paul, 1922), propositions 5.61 and 6.41.
8 Hayman, *Tom Stoppard*, p. 7.
9 Tom Stoppard, *Jumpers* (London: Faber and Faber, 1972), p. 17. All page numbers refer to this revised edition.
10 Quoted in Hayman, *Tom Stoppard*, p. 86, Tynan, *Show People*, p. 45, and Stoppard, "Ambushes", p. 17.
11 In some ways *Jumpers* offers a burlesque of *Macbeth*. Stoppard will return to the play in which "Confusion now hath made its masterpiece" in *Dogg's Hamlet, Cahoot's Macbeth*. The 1976 revival at the National included a few lines from Archie at the party which let the audience know who the murdered jumper was and so clarified Dotty's quotation from the murder of Duncan. This addition was retained in the 1985 revival at the Aldwych Theatre (as was a sequence which showed George making his phone-call of complaint about the goings-on at his flat; to remain anonymous, he claimed to be Mr Wittgenstein).
12 The "friend" was apparently Professor G. E. M. Anscombe, who recalls this meeting in her *An Introduction to Wittgenstein's Tractatus* (London: Hutchinson, 1959), p. 151.
13 " 'Duncan,' I said, 'Duncan' " parodies a favourite vocative of Bertrand Russell's to the actual G. E. Moore: " ' 'Moore,' I said, 'do you *always* speak the truth?' " *The Autobiography of Bertrand Russell*, I (Boston: Little, Brown, 1967), p. 90. He also thought Moore and Wittgenstein shared a "kind of purity" of genius and character. *Op. cit.*, II, p. 99.
14 For the background to logical positivism, see Tim Brassell, "Jumpers: A Happy Marriage?", *Gambit* X (1981), pp. 42–59.
15 Wittgenstein, *Tractatus*, proposition 7.
16 Quoted in Brassell, "Jumpers", pp. 47–8.
17 *Ibid.*, p. 48.
18 Wittgenstein, *Culture and Value*, p. 85e.

19 These variants occur in the play's first pre-performance edition (1972). Astronaut Scott did fly in, dressed in his space-suit, during the 1985 production. Lord Greystoke, another flying witness, was also summoned since, in the African jungle, he retained his altruism as the wild Tarzan. These additions and the zany pace of the coda necessitated a major – and drastic – cut at the point where Clegthorpe begs George to help him. That cry and George's refusal were omitted in order to maintain the action's frenzy.

5 What did *you* do, Dada?

1 Reviews of *Jumpers* reflect these opinions. Harold Clurman, "Theatre", *Nation* CCXVII (13 August 1973), p. 124 criticizes its "facile, chirping 'pessimism'" as a "pose". John Barber, "Comedy as Erudite as It Is Dotty", *Daily Telegraph* (London), 3 February 1972, p. 11 thinks the play "lacks the firm underpinning of a sober and powerful myth" and calls it "flimsy". Richard Watts, "Theatre: Tom Stoppard's Enigma", *New York Post*, 3 August 1972, p. 22 calls it "an enigma of infuriating deviousness". Stoppard himself admitted that his refusal to make clear statements "gets up a few people's noses", "Ambushes", p. 13.
2 Stoppard, "Ambushes", p. 14.
3 Tom Stoppard to David Gollob and David Roper, "Trad Tom Pops In", *Gambit* X (1981), pp. 10–11.
4 Stoppard, "Ambushes", p. 12.
5 *Ibid.*
6 Hayman, *Tom Stoppard*, p. 142.
7 Tom Stoppard, "Dogg's Our Pet", *Ten of the Best: British Short Plays* (London: Inter-Action Inprint, 1979), pp. 79–94. All page numbers refer to this edition.
8 Ed Berman, "How Long Is An Ephemeron?" introduction to *Ten of the Best*, x–xi.
9 Stoppard, *Ibid.*, p. 80.
10 In *Albert's Bridge and Other Plays*, pp. 71–116.
11 Tom Stoppard, *Travesties* (New York: Grove Press, 1975). All page numbers refer to this edition.
12 Stoppard, "Ambushes", p. 14.
13 Hayman, *Tom Stoppard*, p. 12.
14 Stoppard, "Ambushes", p. 13.
15 *Ibid.*, p. 14.
16 Hayman, *Tom Stoppard*, p. 11.
17 "Trad Tom", p. 16.
18 Hayman, *Tom Stoppard*, p. 12.
19 Stoppard, "Ambushes", p. 16.

6 Ethics and manners

1 Hayman, *Tom Stoppard*, p. 4.
2 *Ibid.*, p. 12.
3 *Ibid.*, p. 138.

4 Tom Stoppard, *Dirty Linen and New-Found-Land* (London: Faber and Faber, 1976), p. 75. All page numbers refer to this edition.
5 Hayman, *Tom Stoppard*, pp. 143–4.
6 Tom Stoppard, *Every Good Boy Deserves Favor and Professional Foul* (New York: Grove Press, 1978). Quotation from both plays is taken from this edition.
7 The play's title, whose initials E G B D F constitute a mnemonic for the notes in the treble clef, links music to geometry in that notes and diagrams can be labelled E G B, etc. In its unabbreviated form, it points to the way the authorities in the play suggest that if Alexander is "good" he will "deserve favour" from the State, and that if Sacha is "a good boy" he will (punningly) "deserve a father" back from 'hospital'.
8 "Trad Tom", pp. 16–17.
9 *Ibid.*, pp. 7–9.
10 Evelyn Cobley, "Catastrophe Theory in Tom Stoppard's *Professional Foul*", *Contemporary Literature* xxv (Spring 1984), pp. 53–65.
11 Tom Stoppard, *Night and Day*, 2nd edn (London: Faber and Faber, 1979). All page numbers refer to this edition.
12 "Trad Tom", p. 6.
13 *Ibid.*, p. 9.
14 *Ibid.*, p. 6.
15 Tynan, *Show People*, p. 67.
16 Stoppard, "Ambushes", p. 17.
17 Evelyn Waugh, *Scoop* (London: Chapman and Hall, 1948), pp. 14–15.
18 Stoppard, "Ambushes", p. 4.
19 "Trad Tom", p. 15.
20 *Ibid.*

7 The real thing?

1 "Trad Tom", p. 11.
2 Bernard Levin, "Theatre: Stoppard's Political Asylum", *Sunday Times* (London), 3 July 1977, p. 37.
3 Bernard Levin, "Theatre: Tom Stoppard's African Journey", *Sunday Times* (London), 12 November 1978, p. 37.
4 Irving Wardle, "*Night and Day:* Phoenix", *The Times* (London), 9 November 1978, p. 11.
5 "Trad Tom", p. 11.
6 Hayman, *Tom Stoppard*, p. 5.
7 "My ambition then . . . was to be lying on the floor of an African airport while machine-gun bullets zoomed over my typewriter", "Footnote to the Bard", p. 23.
8 Tom Stoppard, *Dogg's Hamlet, Cahoot's Macbeth* (London: Faber and Faber, 1980). All page numbers refer to this edition.
9 Hayman, *Tom Stoppard*, p. 6.
10 Ed Berman, *Ten of the Best*, x.
11 Tom Stoppard, *The Real Thing* (London: Faber and Faber, 1982). All page numbers refer to this edition.
12 Tynan, *Show People*, p. 110.

13 Derek Marlowe, quoted in Tynan, p. 113.
14 Stoppard, "Ambushes", p. 14.
15 John Russell Taylor, "From *Rosencrantz* to *The Real Thing*", *Plays and Players* (October 1984), p. 13.
16 Mel Gussow, "Plays On Words", *Toronto Globe and Mail*, 7 January 1984, p. EI.
17 *The Dog It Was That Died and Other Plays*, pp. 9–45.
18 Tynan, *Show People*, pp. 46–7.
19 James Saunders, quoted in Tynan, *Show People*, p. 71.
20 Anthony Smith's taped interview: booklet, p. 15.
21 "Trad Tom", pp. 16–17.
22 Tom Stoppard, *Squaring the Circle* (London: Faber and Faber, 1984). All page numbers refer to this edition.
23 Anthony Smith, p. 20.
24 These strands of Stoppard's personality and thought are again interwoven in his adaptation of Vaclav Havel's *Largo Desolato*, first performed at Bristol, 1986. The play concerns a man who struggles to maintain his own identity since his writings displease the State authorities yet entrance his public.

After words

1 Tom Stoppard, *Hapgood* (London: Faber and Faber, 1988), p. 48. All page numbers in parentheses refer to this edition. Details of sets and staging, sketched out lightly in the printed text, reflect those of the first production at the Aldwych Theatre (8 March 1988) designed by Carl Toms and directed by Peter Wood.
2 Clive James, "Count Zero Splits the Infinite", *Encounter* (London), Nov. 1975, p. 71.
3 Heisenberg's principle (1927) "concerns attempts to measure the position and motion of a quantum object simultaneously . . . The very act of trying to pin down an electron to a specific place introduces an uncontrollable and indeterminate disturbance to its motion, and vice versa", P. G. W. Davies and J. R. Brown, eds., *The Ghost in the Atom* (Cambridge University Press, 1986), p. 6.
4 The Ridley twins are not shown together until an "inter-scene" between II.2 and II.3 in the printed version. Early in the Aldwych run, Stoppard inserted that fleeting encounter in between 1.3 and 1.4, just after Hapgood has deduced the key to Ridley from the grid of past events. Though we cannot know it at the time, we first 'see' both Ridleys in the opening sequence; but his two characters look like one, while the Russian looks like two. Another quantum jump.
5 The mystery has been nicely illustrated by Schrödinger's cat paradox (1935). A cat, closed up in a steel chamber with a Geiger device that *could* release a toxic acid, is (by the rules of quantum mechanics) both dead and alive until the box is opened to discover the result. "The paradox becomes more acute if the cat is replaced by a person, . . . If the experimenter opens the box to discover that the subject is still alive, . . . obviously the friend will reply that he remained 100% alive at all times. Yet this flies in the face of

quantum mechanics, which insists that the friend is in a state of live-dead superposition before the contents of the box were inspected", *The Ghost in the Atom*, pp. 28–31. Hapgood, at the hotel, obeys those quantum rules: she is both Betty and Celia, since Ridley does not open the disc-box, but, as he says earlier, "I'd trade it for my cat if I had a cat."